Patterns For Thinking
Patterns For Transfer

A Cooperative Team Approach for Critical and Creative Thinking in the Classroom

By

Robin Fogarty
and
James Bellanca

ACKNOWLEDGMENTS

Grateful acknowledgment is made to the following authors and agents for their permission to reprint copyrighted materials:

Roger and David Johnson for use of Circles of Learning and Cooperative Groups, from *Circles of Learning*, © 1986.

Sidney J. Parnes for adaptation of Creative Problem-Solving Model, © 1976.

Prentice-Hall, Inc. for "Inductive/Deductive Reasoning Strategies," by Eggen/Kauchak/Harder, in *Strategies For Teachers: Information Processing Models in the Classroom*, © 1979.

Saturday Review for "The Dinner Party," by Mona Gardner, © January 31, 1942.

Warner Books, Inc. for *A Whack On The Side Of The Head* by Roger von Oech, Ph.D., © 1983.

PATTERNS FOR THINKING: PATTERNS FOR TRANSFER
Second Edition, second printing

Published by IRI/Skylight Publishing, Inc.
200 E. Wood Street, Suite 274, Palatine, Illinois 60067
800-348-4474, 708-991-6300
FAX 708-991-6420

Book Design: Michael A. Melasi, Bruce Leckie
Type Composition: Donna Ramirez
Proofreading: Kathleen M. O'Malley

ISBN 0-932935-43-5

441C-11-93

Table Of Contents

Section 1 OVERVIEW

Section 2 AWARENESS

Section 3 CLIMATE

The lines of the wind-blown sand on the dunes
of the snow as it falls in beautiful drifts
the lines of the clouds
in the sky above
and the water that washes upon the sands
forever and ever, these lines repeat
always and always
each one is unique...

Dry leaves rise in a gust
tiny birds in little flocks
gulls soar
insects swarm
seeds whirl and sail
millions of times the formation repeats
each time
each thing
unto itself is unique...

All the stars on a clear still night
all the leaves on a single tree
the many ideas that one may have
Over and over
the basic concept repeats
Yet each star
each leaf
each idea
each one is unique...

Gwen Frostic
Wing-Borne 1967

SECTION 1

OVERVIEW

It must be remembered that the purpose of education is not to fill the minds of students with facts ... it is to teach them to think, if that is possible, and always to think for themselves.

—Robert Hutchins

A Look at the Training —An Overview

A 12-Step Training Model

1. Introductory Material
2. A Definition of Thinking Skills
3. A Survey of Elements To Promote Thinking
4. Overview of Research
5. Setting the Climate
6. Teaching the Explicit Skill
7. Promoting Metacognitive Processing
8. Structuring Team Interaction
9. Guided Practice
10. Transfer and Application of Skills
11. Professional Coaching Networks
12. Designing Lessons for Application to Curriculum

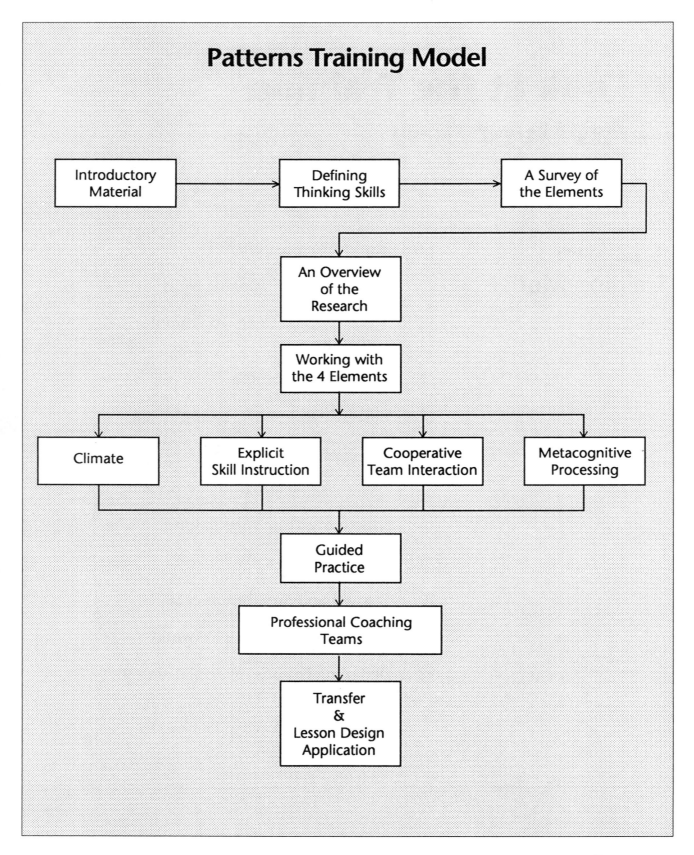

Patterns Training Model

Introductory Material → Defining Thinking Skills → A Survey of the Elements

↓

An Overview of the Research

↓

Working with the 4 Elements

↓

Climate | Explicit Skill Instruction | Cooperative Team Interaction | Metacognitive Processing

↓

Guided Practice

↓

Professional Coaching Teams

↓

Transfer & Lesson Design Application

The Four Elements

Climate (Teaching FOR Thinking)	**Explicit Skill** (Teaching OF Thinking)
Setting a safe climate for thinking by modeling risk taking and acceptance.	Teaching the thinking skill explicitly to students and bridging skill application into relevant situations.
Structured Interaction (Teaching WITH Thinking)	**Metacognitive Processing** (Teaching ABOUT Thinking)
Getting kids to process the information together and interact with the material in experiential activities.	Getting kids to think about their thinking and deliberately bring their patterns for thinking to a conscious level.

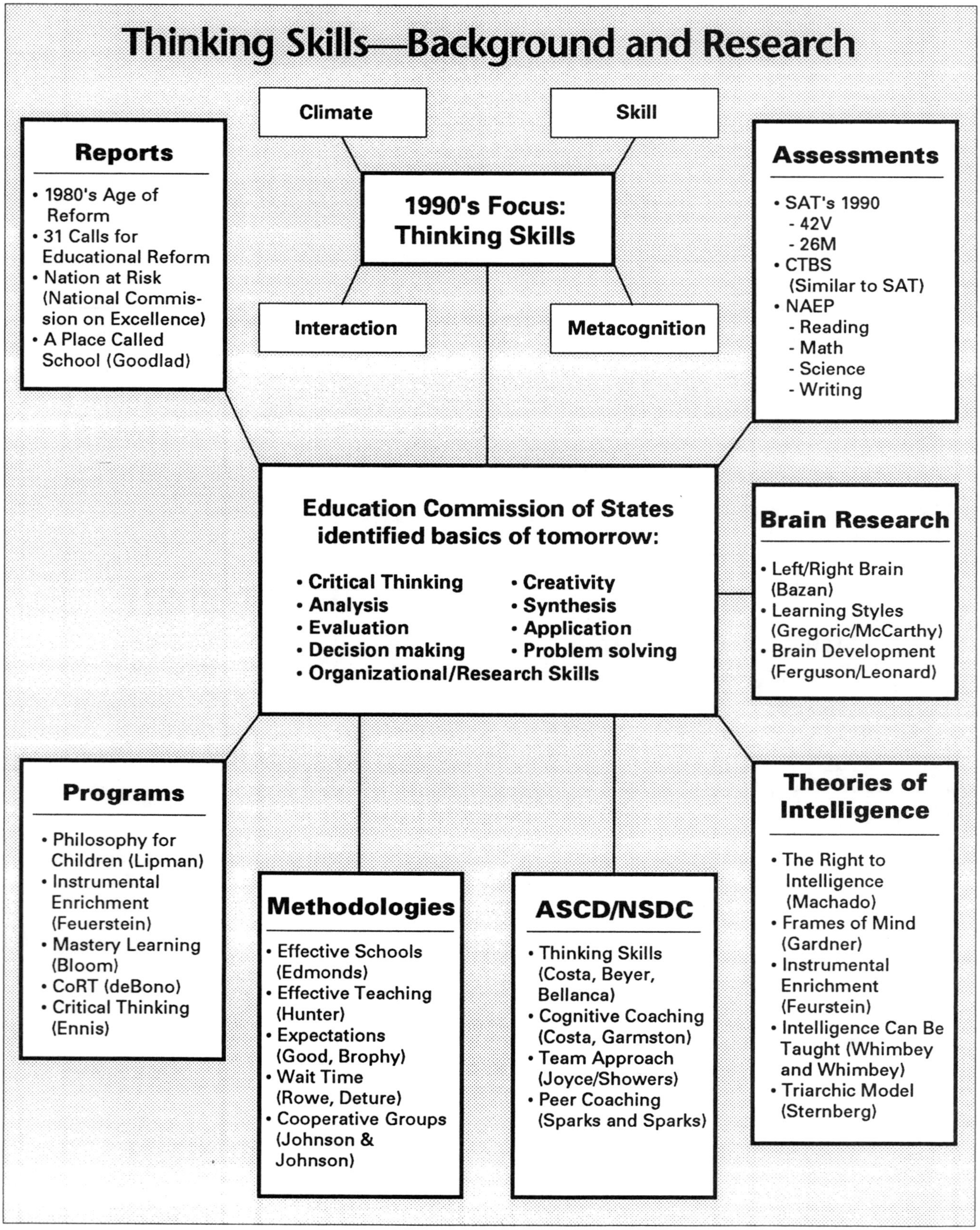

Thinking Skills—Background and Research

Climate

Skill

1990's Focus: Thinking Skills

Interaction

Metacognition

Reports

- 1980's Age of Reform
- 31 Calls for Educational Reform
- Nation at Risk (National Commission on Excellence)
- A Place Called School (Goodlad)

Assessments

- SAT's 1990
  - 42V
  - 26M
- CTBS (Similar to SAT)
- NAEP
  - Reading
  - Math
  - Science
  - Writing

Education Commission of States identified basics of tomorrow:

- **Critical Thinking**
- **Creativity**
- **Analysis**
- **Synthesis**
- **Evaluation**
- **Application**
- **Decision making**
- **Problem solving**
- **Organizational/Research Skills**

Brain Research

- Left/Right Brain (Bazan)
- Learning Styles (Gregoric/McCarthy)
- Brain Development (Ferguson/Leonard)

Programs

- Philosophy for Children (Lipman)
- Instrumental Enrichment (Feuerstein)
- Mastery Learning (Bloom)
- CoRT (deBono)
- Critical Thinking (Ennis)

Methodologies

- Effective Schools (Edmonds)
- Effective Teaching (Hunter)
- Expectations (Good, Brophy)
- Wait Time (Rowe, Deture)
- Cooperative Groups (Johnson & Johnson)

ASCD/NSDC

- Thinking Skills (Costa, Beyer, Bellanca)
- Cognitive Coaching (Costa, Garmston)
- Team Approach (Joyce/Showers)
- Peer Coaching (Sparks and Sparks)

Theories of Intelligence

- The Right to Intelligence (Machado)
- Frames of Mind (Gardner)
- Instrumental Enrichment (Feurstein)
- Intelligence Can Be Taught (Whimbey and Whimbey)
- Triarchic Model (Sternberg)

Critical and Creative Thinking

An important distinction is made in *Patterns For Thinking—Patterns For Transfer.* This comprehensive (K-12) thinking skills curriculum specifically cites both creative synthesis and critical analysis as patterns for thinking. Both are essential ingredients in productive problem solving and mindful decision making. The creative aspect visualizes, forecasts and generates ideas. The critical mind analyzes, compares and chooses. Judgment keeps imagination on track, but imagination enlightens judgment.

The overriding goal of the *Patterns For Thinking* training is to help teachers promote thinking in the classroom. By deliberately focusing attention on both the critical and creative nature of thinking, students are encouraged to dream and imagine new visions as well as critique present choices.

The thinking classroom shifts the emphasis from a content/product orientation to a problem-solving process approach. We live in a time of information overload, with radical discoveries uprooting traditionally accepted theories. One university professor laments to his students at the close of his course, that fifty percent of the information taught in medical school will be obsolete before they graduate. He goes on to add that his biggest dilemma is the fact that he can't even tell them which half it will be.

In short, both creative and critical thinking are vital skills for our young people if they are to become productive problem solvers and mindful decision makers as they shape their world.

Two years in preparation, the *Patterns For Thinking* curriculum synthesizes the best practices which promote thinking by all children into practical classroom lessons. It integrates the principles of motivation, reinforcement, and transfer of the research-based practices of effective instruction (e.g. wait time, higher order questioning, guided practice, cooperative groups) and the thinking skills practices of explicit instruction, structured interaction, and metacognition. Instruction is explicit, with modeling, practice, feedback, and transfer integrated within the training design. In addition, follow-up Networks are established during the training.

Teachers will leave the workshop ready to use the explicit lessons in their own classrooms. Principals will leave with the beginnings of a thinking curriculum for adaptation in their schools.

Patterns for Thinking

To prepare youngsters for the possibilities and probabilities of a future we cannot even imagine, the wisest course seems to be one that triggers the critical and creative patterns for thinking. By causing kids to THINK! QUESTION! DOUBT! WONDER! EXPLORE! ANALYZE! DEBATE! ADVOCATE! HYPOTHESIZE! IDEALIZE! and CREATE!, we provide fertile ground for them to think about their thinking and to learn about their learning. There are many answers, and even more questions to the situations life presents. Our young people need experience in examining situations, exchanging ideas, and generating alternatives in preparation for the many unknowns of their tomorrows.

Creative Thinking

Divergent, generative, productive thinking at a synthesis level.

A young child intrinsically accepts challenge - any challenge! He senses that to reach beyond is to grow and to know. And he doesn't want to miss a single thing. He'll risk all to take that step beyond. What happens to that bold and daring child adventurer between crib and college? Why does the lure of challenge subside? When does the risk become too great? How does courage, the champion of the creative process, become trapped in the web of self-doubt? And what part do we play in this apparent tragedy of human endeavor?

CREATIVITY: One study shows that "creativity scores invariably drop about 90% between the ages of five and seven: by age forty an individual is only 2% as creative as at age five" (Ferguson, 1973). And yet, according to Sagan, "Ten to 100 billion neurons interacting with a thousand each at one time implies that the brain is capable of processing from ten to 100 trillion bits of information in a lifetime" (Sagan, 1977). Leonard observes: "A brain composed of such numbers of neurons obviously can never be 'filled up.' Perhaps the more it knows, the more it can know and create. Perhaps, in fact, we can now propose an incredible hypothesis: The ultimate creative capacity of the brain may be, for all practical purposes, infinite" (Leonard in Ferguson, 1973). But of what consequence is this, if we are no longer willing to venture forth with our instincts and ideas? Are we willing to take up the challenge and resolve to see it through?

THE CHILD'S PART

THE CHILD'S CHALLENGE: AN INVITATION TO PERSIST! RESIST! ENLIST! WELCOME CHALLENGE! ACCEPT RISK!

PERSIST IN YOUR CURIOSITY

Observe! Perceive patterns! Seek structure! Recognize relationships! Construct connections! Be a child!

ENLIST ADVOCATES

Form a network of thinkers and creators! Exchange ideas! Encourage! Study the lives of creative people! Emulate!

INSIST ON INQUIRY

Question assumptions! Ask why! Ask why not! Ask how! Estimate! Guess! Hypothesize! Try! Try!

RESIST DISCOURAGEMENT

Look at things in new ways! See the world differently! Investigate! Incubate! Improvise! Invent! Originate!

WELCOME THE WONDER OF CHALLENGE... ACCEPT RISK WITH CHILDLIKE VISION... CREATE...

Consciously, constructively, consistently, continually.

The Teacher's Part

The need is real! As stated in Silberman's *Crisis in the Classroom,* "Students need to learn far more than the basic skills. Children who have just started school may be in the labor force in the year 2030.... To be practical, an education should prepare man for work that does not yet exist and whose nature cannot even be imagined. This can be done only by teaching children how to learn and by giving them the kind of intellectual discipline that will enable them to apply man's accumulated wisdom to new problems." Roger Lewin similarly warns, "Too often we give children answers to remember, rather than problems to solve."

To develop the intellectual discipline to which Silberman refers, requires teaching the processes of abstract and logical reasoning, which are the prerequisites for functional, creative problem solving. Webster defines reasoning as "the ability to think, infer, form judgments, reach conclusions, analyze, discuss, support, justify and apply." The emphasis in developing reasoning skills focuses on the why and how, instead of on the who, what, when, and where.

Children are born with an intrinsic curiosity to learn and tremendous creative capacities that enhance that basic learning. They intuitively ask for the reasons why. They naturally experiment to seek answers to the how. By providing them with experiential background in the reasoning processes, kids will continue that quest for discovery of the whys and hows. We can add new dimensions to their repertoire of possibilities.

Introducing children to reasoning from the onset, as an underlying current in our educational programs, leads to familiarity. The reasoning processes become natural and ever-present thought patterns that children feel comfortable and confident using. Only at this stage does true application, synthesis and evaluation of data occur. This, then, must be our challenge!

OUR CHALLENGE, as educators is...TO CHALLENGE: consciously, constructively, consistently, continually, and creatively.

TO CHALLENGE CONSCIOUSLY—
with an acute awareness of the special needs from the onset.

TO CHALLENGE CONSTRUCTIVELY—
with an accepting, approving atmosphere that fosters curiosity.

TO CHALLENGE CONSISTENTLY—
with all available avenues of advocates, advisors, and aides as resources.

TO CHALLENGE CONTINUALLY—
with an accountable action agenda that ensures ongoing development of the individual's pursuit of the unknown.

TO CHALLENGE CREATIVELY—
with an open-ended approach of actively assessing available alternatives that motivate and inspire.

Robert E. Hutchins practically impels us toward these objectives by DARING us to "...unsettle the minds of the young and inflame their intellect."

Patterns For Thinking elaborates on teacher-tested, tried and true ideas that range in scope from primary to high school levels and encompass all basic curriculum areas. The highlighted lessons present extensive possibilities for adaptation in part or whole for classrooms.

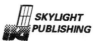

The focus is on higher level thinking processes and questioning strategies. "In teaching," Ashley Montague advises, "it is the method not the content that is the message...the drawing out, not the pumping in." Become an EXPERT CHALLENGER:

- ✦ **EXHIBIT** genuine enthusiasm and create the same feeling in the kids.
- ✦ **EXCITE** with ideas and embrace the experimentation of kids.
- ✦ **EXAMINE** ideas with inquiry methods and evoke further inquiry in children.
- ✦ **EXTRACT** the uniqueness of each situation, each moment, each child.
- ✦ **EXHAUST** them with inspiration!
- ✦ **EXCEL** and demand excellence in children.
- ✦ **EXALT** in the joyful "aahs" of children as they discover the world in which they live.
- ✦ **EXHALE** and pause momentarily and push on toward beckoning horizons.

The intellectual capabilities that impel one toward inquiry and the psychological capacities that permit the luxury of risk taking are essential to the development of optimal creative potentials. To challenge assumption and question what most people take as the truth requires the courage to take risks. We as teachers and parents can assist the child in his quest. In fact, "the teacher must establish an environment which promotes and allows for active inquiry" (Rowe, 1973). We should "provide students with many opportunities not only to develop intellectual independence, but also to learn how to formulate questions" (Eisner, 1983). An open environment is created and a questioning posture is assumed most effectively through intentional implementation of the instructional strategies of inquiry. In other words, the good teacher helps the learner see relationships that are both new and interesting, valuable, satisfying, relevant, and/or harmonious. He thus provides a setting for many, many "aha" feelings.

"What would happen if, from the earliest days of formal teaching, the teacher or parent, after presenting a new bit of information, would inevitably ask next, 'How might you use this bit of information? What new ways might you connect this with something else you know?' I would predict that by this one deceptively simple tactic, we might launch the next generation into a completely new level of mental power" (Parnes, 1975). We must constantly ask the listener to make those personal connections, to take that next step and link new information with other elements of unique experience within himself so that, as he feeds his mental computer, he will always be generating relationships beyond those provided.

By "...learning how to learn—how to generate new and harmonious relationships—(one) can do this all of (one's) life in all new circumstances (one) encounters. (One) learns to cope with whatever life brings (one), using (one's) own resources" (Parnes, 1975). To help a child learn how to learn, we must recognize that inquiry and risk taking go hand in hand. To question, to doubt...and to air those questions and doubts in public takes tremendous belief in one's self. And is it not this very belief that we call courage? Isn't that the idea we as parents and educators strive to achieve? To develop inquiring minds and courageous thinkers, begin the lifelong journey into inquiry and experience the magnificent "ahas" of risky thinking.

Eight Ways To Foster Creativity

1. **Encourage inventiveness**
2. **Reward fresh insights**
3. **Reinforce initiative**
4. **Praise experimentation**
5. **Listen actively**
6. **Tolerate failure**
7. **Encourage cooperative efforts**
8. **Provide "time to create"**

Critical Thinking

Among the "higher level" thinking skills, analysis and evaluation are the most commonly used in classrooms, although students may never know it. As a consequence, half the value of critical thinking is lost. How often, for instance, does a math teacher ask students to retrace the thinking processes they used to solve a complex problem? When does a science teacher point out that her questions on the scientific process were designed to give a patterned way to think about scientific application of those skills to new tasks? When does a teacher ask for a critique on an article for bias?

Usually, the answers to these questions are strongly negative. Teachers themselves are usually not formally trained in thinking skills, so they cannot easily teach the skills of thinking to their students. Instead, they repeat the same errors they were taught, in this case, to use critical skills without knowing it and without benefiting from them.

To promote analytical and evaluative thinking in the classroom, there are several guidelines that become important to review:

(1) We enhance student skill development when we make explicit that the skill development is an objective. Most students play the never-ending guessing game of trying to figure out what the teacher wants. For the most part, they have learned that the teacher wants students to listen passively. In this context, it is no wonder that students, when asked to analyze, sink

deeper into silence. "Tell us, don't ask us." To counter this habit, the effective teacher will use all the basic tools to give clear explicit directions, focus attention, and expect clear thinking from all.

(2) We enhance student skill development when we look to feedback methods that encourage students to take risks in how they respond. Wait time, silence after a response, body language, clarifying and extending questions create a stress-free environment in which the exploration of ideas is valued. In short, "Can I, the teacher, shut up after I've started the minds bubbling with ideas?"

(3) We enhance student skill development when we take the time to develop the skills. Time-on-task research tells us how basic skills are enhanced as we allow more time for a skill. Likewise, if we value analytical thinking we will not only allot the time, but we will instruct so there is a high mental engagement and successful task completion.

The first cry we face in teacher training programs is "When will I have the time?" That is a real and major concern that goes back to the school board and administration. Currently, most districts have too much legislated, mandated, packed and pushed into the curriculum. Like rabbits, teachers run from one idea to another. Coverage, speed and quantity are the values acted upon. "Quality sounds nice, but it's impractical." The results? More students can parrot answers and fewer, according to the National Assessment, can solve problems, analyze situations, or think critically.

(4) We enhance student development when we provide concrete experiences that lead to abstract thought. The microbiologist Restak has found strong support for Piaget theories of cognitive development, not the least of which tells us that new information is processed on the right side of the brain and conceptualized on the left. Most often, this pattern is violated in the classroom. We begin with language (abstract concepts) and then proceed to analyze without sufficient concrete experience. Another way to say this in the language of the logician: learning is inductive, not deductive.

Watch the small child. He sees a small flying bug. His big sister says, "fly." He sees another. His mother says, "fly." He sees a third flying insect. "Fly," he says. From the experience comes a label. Later, in a book, he sees another fly. "Fly," and so it goes.

Later as adults, we follow the same sequence. You go to a beach. The water is dirty. You don't swim, but many others do. Later, a rash breaks out on those who swam. The doctor isolates the dirty water as the common cause. The next time you go to the beach, the water is dirty again. You elect not to swim. You used your past experience to make a cause-effect relationship between the water and the rash.

In the classroom, this principle, concrete to abstract, is often used to an advantage. Cuisenaire rods are an excellent example; so are such programs as the Bay Area Writing Project, SCIS and drama in the classroom. More often, the process is reversed and instruction begins with abstractions. Some students make the quick jump; others are muddled.

Five Ways to Foster Critical Thinking:

1. State an objective which emphasizes specific thinking skills.

2. Begin activities with structured group experiences and proceed to the analysis, evaluation and application of what was learned.

3. Facilitate analysis and evaluation; do not do the thinking for the students. Provide the strategies, the 'patterns for thinking' that lead students into the process.

4. Use your time well.

5. Practice your essential questioning skills to communicate your valuing of student thinking (i.e.: compare/contrast, classify, rank, judge, decide, critique, make an analogy).

Six Explicit Thinking Skills

Creative Thinking Skills:	Acronym
1. Brainstorming	THINK
2. Predicting	BET
3. Visualizing	IMAGE

Critical Thinking Skills:	Acronym
1. Attributing	TRAITS
2. Classifying	CLUE
3. Prioritizing	RANK

"The principal goal of education is to create men who are capable of doing new things, not simply of repeating what other generations have done—men who are creative, inventive, and discoverers. The second goal of education is to form minds which can be critical, can verify, and not accept everything they are offered."

—Jean Piaget

Professional Coaching Networks

Self-directed Coaching Groups

Many groups have as their purpose the learning of specific materials or procedures by their members. Group learning occurs in all sorts of educational ways—from preschool programs to postgraduate seminars, from athletic teams to special conferences and workshops. A discussion group is a group whose purpose is mastering a particular subject.

Productive groups require the conscious development of an effective group. They must know how to build an effective group. An emphasis in any group has to be upon developing the necessary skills and climate for a productive discussion to be held.

A prerequisite for a group discussion, therefore, is the development of a clear understanding of the group's goals, the criteria against which the performance of the group is to be evaluated, the behaviors needed to ensure an effective learning group, the expectations of the coordinator, and what is expected of the group members.

1. **Definitions of terms and concepts.** To take up a subject, a group must have a shared understanding of the language that will be used.

2. **Establish discussion goals.** Identify major themes to be discussed. At the start, the goals or objectives of the learning sessions need to be clear and the criteria used to determine goal accomplishment need to be specified.

3. **Allocation of time.** Time should be allocated or set aside for each of the remaining steps, and a timekeeper should be appointed to see to it that the allocations are observed. The themes should be ranked according to their priority, with the important themes given more time than the less important themes. Often a discussion group will spend so much time on minor topics that the major themes never get reviewed.

4. **Discussion of the major themes and subtopics.** The discussion of each theme and subtopic now begins within the time limit specified in the previous step. Members contribute their information, analyses, opinions, ideas, feelings and reactions. Controversy is encouraged to increase the involvement, excitement, and fun of the members, and to arrive at creative synthesis of the material to be learned. Every group member should be able to say what the major themes are and what the group has concluded. Quoted sources supporting or questioning the validity of the conclusions made should be presented. Questions should be framed to help group members test the usefulness of specific conclusions.

5. **Integration of the material.** The purpose of this step is to guard against learning that is fragmentary and isolated from other knowledge. It may be that there is little

with which to integrate the new information, but usually this step increases in importance as the group has more and more sessions. Relating the material to previous topics; discussing material; adding one's ideas about the meaning or usefulness of new material in understanding other ideas or concepts; stating how the new material contradicts, substantiates, or amplifies some previously-developed point; summarizing into compact statements the points others have made; reviewing puzzling aspects of the material being discussed—all these are useful procedures in this step.

6. **Application of the material.** Group members should try to identify the implications of the material for their own lives, the work they do, and their relationships with other people. The personal delivery of the material being learned should be clear. Group members may wish to share an experience that emphasizes the point being discussed; they should look carefully to see if the learning can be applied in the here-and-now situation. They should also state how the learning might be applied in a future situation in which many or all of the group members might find themselves. As much as possible, discussion topics should be applied to the life situations of the group members.

7. **Evaluation of the quality of discussion.** Here group members should take a critical look at their performance as a group and as individual members. They should try to solve problems that hamper the learning within the discussion group.

Characteristics of Professional Learning Networks

To evaluate how it is functioning, a learning group must have some notion of how it should operate, some standard of performance, and some ground rules for productive discourse. The following criteria may be helpful (Hill, 1962; Johnson, 1970).

1. The group climate should be warm, accepting and non-threatening. This kind of climate is of particular importance because it is invariably necessary for members to expose their ignorance, take risks with their ideas, and engage in controversy with other group members. Good discussions are possible only if members are protected by a warm, understanding group climate.

2. Learning should be approached as a cooperative enterprise. The only way in which a group can function is for a high level of cooperation to prevail among group members. Members should help each other develop an understanding of the material being presented. They must feel free to ask for help from one another without social stigma, and be willing to offer it whenever it is needed. Rewards for group participation must be given on the basis of cooperative behaviors, which promote the learning of all members. Competitive behavior, one-upmanship, status seeking and ridicule are all unhelpful in a discussion group. All controversy should be approached as a fun activity that results in solutions to mutual problems and a more creative synthesis of the material to be learned.

3. Learning should be accepted as the primary purpose of the group. The material must be adequately and efficiently covered, and members must learn it. The whole point of having a discussion is to promote the learning of the members, and if such learning is not taking place, the group cannot be considered productive.

4. Every member should participate in the discussion. A group in which only a few members take part is obviously not a productive discussion group. Members will not all participate to the same degree; even so, all should take part some of the time. If a member does not participate, he may not be getting anything from the group; more importantly, he is not contributing anything to the group. When silent members are asked about their lack of participation they typically respond that although they are not talking they are getting a lot out of the group discussion. The question they are avoiding, however, is what are they contributing? A group discussion is successful only if all members contribute.

5. Leadership functions should be distributed. Responsibility for making the group operate productively should not be deleted or usurped by one or a few members. If all members are going to learn, they must all participate, interact, and perform leadership functions.

6. Group sessions and the learning tasks should be enjoyable. Group sessions are meant to be lively and pleasant experiences. If no one is having fun, something is wrong. One of the major functions of controversy is often to spark more involvement and enjoyment in a discussion.

7. Evaluation should be accepted as an integral part of the group operation. A productive network is one that accepts the fact that there will be process problems, and is willing to evaluate the group's progress from time to time. Through evaluation, group members learn what is required to improve the group's function, and they gain a better understanding of how and when to contribute to its needs. Group skills, therefore, are improved through evaluation.

8. Members should attend regularly and come prepared. A productive group discussion is one in which members are present and prepared to discuss the material; only then can the resources they have to offer be used fully. Absenteeism, moreover, often demoralizes other members.

Required Member Behaviors

Although a self-directed professional network will have rotating leadership roles, any member should feel free to behave in any way that will increase the productivity of a discussion group. Some suggested behaviors are:

1. Initiating and contributing ideas and information.

2. Giving and asking for information, ideas, opinions and feelings.

3. Clarifying, synthesizing and giving examples.

4. Periodically summarizing what has taken place and the major points discussed.

5. Encouraging and supporting participation by all members.

6. Evaluating the effectiveness of the group and diagnosing difficulties in group functioning.
7. Observing process.
8. Giving direction to the discussion.
9. Energizing the discussion.
10. Helping the sending skills of the members.
11. Helping the receiving skills of the members.
12. Being an active listener.
13. Testing whether decisions have been made and what the procedure has been when making those decisions.
14. Moderating controversies by disagreeing with others on an intellectual level—without personal rejection—and helping other members disagree in the same manner.
15. Beginning, ending and being on time during training.

Rotating Leadership

For every discussion group there is usually a designated leader or coordinator. The responsibilities of such a person are hard to define specifically because the coordinator needs to promote discussion without controlling or dominating it; he needs to help in a process where a group of people learn from their discussion and interaction with one another. Some of the coordinator's responsibilities are to introduce the discussion session: to be task-oriented, keeping the group moving so that it does not get side-tracked or bogged down; to restate and call attention to the main ideas of the discussion so that learning is focused; to promote a climate of acceptance, openness, warmth, and support to facilitate learning; and to know when to provide a sense of closure.

In a self-directed professional network, all group members are responsible for behaving in ways that help one another learn. It helps to rotate specific leadership or coordinator responsibility. What are the responsibilities in this role? The first is the instructional behavior of resource expert. The second behavior is that of process observer. As such, the coordinator must not only diagnose present functioning of the group, but intervene in the group in ways that improve its effectiveness.

Finally, a coordinator needs to be concerned with how the meeting is ended. A few minutes before the group discussion is scheduled to close, or when it appears that the group has exhausted the subject, the session can be concluded with a summarization of the significant points by a member or by the coordinator. This summary should be brief, but it should not be a last-minute statement given to the tune of moving chairs and scuffling feet. The summary is helpful and vital because it leaves the group with a sense of achievement, it clarifies group thinking, and it tests the conclusions of the summarizer against those of other group members. After the summary, the group should evaluate how it has functioned as a group. Finally, the coordinator may express his appreciation to the group. If the group is to meet again, he may wish to explain where and when. And if a final report is required, it should be done before the fine points of the discussion are forgotten.

To facilitate a self-directed coaching network, a high degree of commitment and skill is required of all members. All must be prepared to rotate the key leadership responsibilities which are divided among the group members.

(1) The *task leader* knows the cooperative goal, keeps other members on task, and guides the structure and content.

(2) The *recorder* uses the newsprint.

(3) The *materials manager* sees that the room is ready, refreshments are provided, equipment is available, etc.

(4) The *process observer* notes how the process worked and provides feedback on behavior in the group.

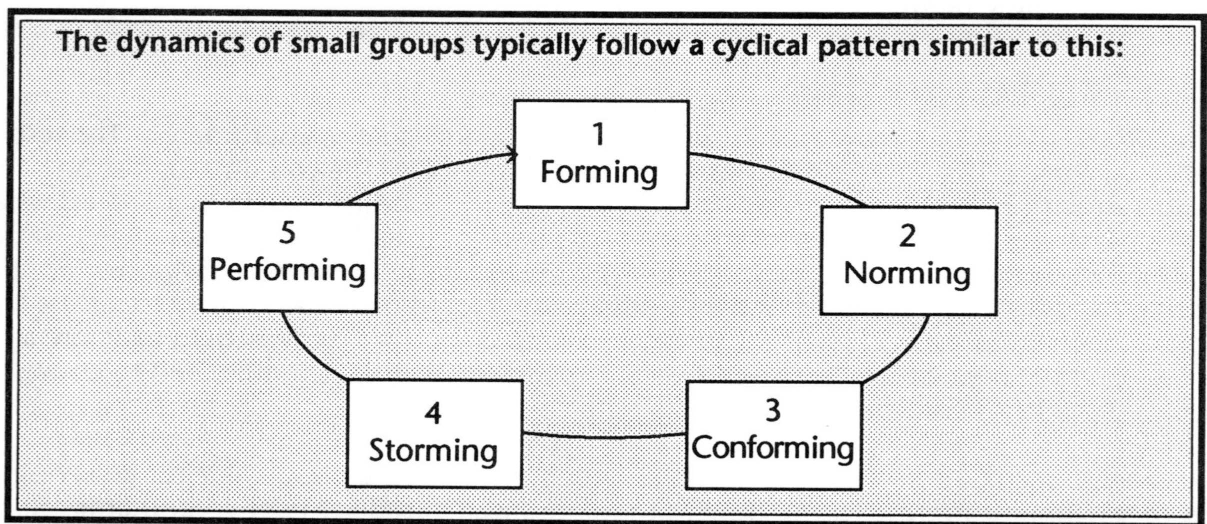

1) **FORMING:** Interpersonal acceptance and the formation of trust is the focus of members' concerns.

2) **NORMING:** Concern shifts from personal to group; norms develop in relation to how the group will function.

3) **CONFORMING:** Members try to please and be accepted by group.

4) **STORMING:** Decision making is somewhat hampered at this stage as individuals establish their roles within the structure of the group goals.

5) **PERFORMING:** Achievement of goals is accomplished as the group develops comfortable and flexible task structures.

6) **RE-FORMING:** The cycle begins again with each change in membership and/or realignment of the goals.

It is interesting to note these stages as part of the group evaluation process in determining the effectiveness of the group periodically. Just the awareness that developing groups usually experience these various steps is often encouragement enough to persevere through the 'storming' stage. Since observation of the group process is an integral part of the whole structure, tracking the group with these insights might prove helpful.

A Professional Discussion

Use the satire, "Low Learning in the Land of Log" as a catalyst for discussion at an initial professional coaching network session. The ensuing dialogue may clarify philosophical view-points and provide opportunity for colleagues to share feelings about the art and craft of the teaching of thinking.

Low Learning in the Land of Log

Once upon a time in the Land of Log, King Og summoned his Minister of Education, Sir Bog.
"Sir Bog, why am I hearing so many complaints about the schools?"
"I don't know, your highness. What are the complaints?"
"Here, read this list. In the past week alone I've had 34 complaints," huffed the unhappy king.

LOG EDUCATION COMPLAINT DEPARTMENT

4 School is too interesting.
2 My child has to think too much.
4 My brilliant son has to work with idiot kids.
5 My child has to share with other children.
2 The teacher lectures are too short.
5 My child has to explain her answers in math.
3 The science teacher makes my child do experiments.
2 My child has to read literature.
7 My child has to write about themes and ideas.

"My goodness, your highness. That's a terrible list," said Sir Bog.
"What do you intend to do?" asked King Og.
"Well, off the top of my head, I have some immediate cures. I will issue an order to every teacher and command them to follow the Ten Commandments of Teaching you issued at your coronation."

OG'S TEN COMMANDMENTS OF TEACHING

1. Teachers shall not allow any child to share any materials, ideas or work.
2. Teachers shall not use any materials except purple ditto sheets, black line masters and textbooks with more pictures than words.
3. Teachers shall not ask any question that causes a child to think.
4. Teachers will not allow any child to read textbooks at or above the child's grade level.
5. Teachers shall not vary activities, materials or methods.
6. Teachers shall not allow students to help each other.
7. Teachers shall not honor any special learning styles, especially the visual style.
8. Teachers shall not ask any child to explain an answer.
9. Teachers shall not allow any child to go through the week with out at least three pullout classes.
10. Teachers shall do nothing to motivate student interest in learning.

"Those are very wise commandments, your majesty," Sir Bog added.

"To be sure," said the King. "And I know these complaints probably came from my enemies. I know our teachers are well skilled in the low road model."

"As usual you are correct, your majesty. I recently saw the master checklist. Over 90 percent of our teachers are faithful to your royal seven-step lesson design. Moreover, the royal publisher is printing a record number of ditto sheets, black line masters and fill-in-the-blank workbooks. Our new programmed learning worksheets are a best seller."

"That is reassuring to this royal crown."

"Even more, only three principals reported seeing any of that cooperative learning fad. The offending teachers were sentenced to remediation classes."

"Good, good," smiled King Og. "What about these rumors of critical thinking and problem-solving lessons?"

"Don't worry, your majesty. The teachers who caused the complaints have been punished severely."

"You have done well, Sir Bog. I know of no other Minister of Education who could more readily put into practice what our royal researchers helped us understand. It won't be long now, I am certain, before we have ensured every student will have been brought down to the minimal competency level."

"True, your majesty, true. With the curriculum broken into as many minute parts as possible, with the texts and workbooks to ensure our students will have the best memories, and with your removal of any unsanctioned thought from the curriculum, your dream is on the verge of completion."

"Now go forth, Sir Bog," commanded King Og, "and clean up these last complaints. Once and for all, see that our commandments are carried out." ■

Planning for Thinking

The Elements For Effective Planning

A network planning session was designed to introduce the element of effective planning. We gathered at the intermediate service center.

"It would help me, Don, if you would show us a planning model. I know there are different approaches to planning, but I need a framework," said a committee member.

"That's a fair request," I replied, "as long as we agree that the model is more a process than a product, pieces for you to select and to arrange, not a step by step recipe, I think I can help. First, let me list the ten important elements that help in the planning process."

1. Clarifying your mission
2. Selecting your objective
3. Designing your framework
4. Determining your decision-making process
5. Selecting your curriculum
6. Assessing staff needs
7. Designing staff development
8. Considering coaching and peer support
9. Supervising and helping in transfer
10. Evaluating the results

"For each of these elements you will want to decide (a) its relevance to your district, (b) its importance to your plan, and (c) its components. As I raise the questions, give a +(plus) for a strong positive answer, ? (question mark) for unsure, and -(minus) for a negative answer.

1. The Mission Statement

a.	You know what it is that you want to accomplish regarding thinking skills.	+	?	-
b.	You know why this is important.	+	?	-
c.	Is the mission supported by central office, middle management, the union, leadership and the staff?	+	?	-
d.	Are goals and objectives clear to all?	+	?	-
e.	Is there a school-based steering committee to monitor and adjust the district program?	+	?	-
f.	Is everyone clear on the budget details?	+	?	-

2. School-based Objectives

a. Has the school staff personalized the mission to the needs of its students? + ? -
b. Are all clear on the training and development priorities? + ? -
c. Are all aware of the program and its implications for school improvement? + ? -

3. The Framework

a. How well developed is the conceptual construction on which your program will rest? + ? -
b. To what degree does the program honor the critical attributes of an effective thinking skills program, the conditions that promote thinking by all—explicit skills, structured interaction, and metacognitive processing? + ? -
c. Is it related to cognitive research? + ? -

4. Decision-Making Process

a. Does the process honor critical thinking and creative problem solving? + ? -
b. Does the process value the contribution of those teaching professionals who will use the program? + ? -

5. The Curriculum of Explicit Skills

a. Is there a scope and sequence of critical and/or creative thinking skills which teachers can teach independently of other course content? + ? -
b. Do guidelines exist for selecting either the deductive or inductive lesson designs? + ? -
c. Are skills selected with a thoughtful rationale? (i.e. Are the skills implicit in the current course content or measured by currently used district tests?) + ? -
d. Do model lesson designs exist in menu form for student use? (i.e. definition, synonyms, uses, examples, operations, special strategies) + ? -
e. Do model transfer lessons exist to help students use thinking skills across the curriculum and/or outside the classroom? + ? -

INSTRUCTION: Rank order these six components. Put the item that needs most attention as #1.

A. **The Preconditions:** The school has a climate in which faculty and students support and honor skillful thinking without put-downs, negative criticism, or a rigid right and wrong attitude. + ? -

B. **Awareness:** All faculty are up-to-date in the research on effective teaching, cognition and school improvement. + ? -

C. **Basic Training Program:** Faculty are versed in the use of strategies that create a positive expectation for skillful thinking by all, structure interaction, and develop metacognition. + ? -

D. **Peer Assistance/Coaching Teams:** Faculty participate with each other to observe, give feedback and support on use of acquired skills. + ? -

E. **Supervision:** Principals and other supervisors use helping skills to facilitate application of new teaching skills in the classroom. + ? -

F. **Evaluation:** There is a systematic review of student improvement, teacher performance and program outcomes to determine the process of a program's objectives. + ? -

1.________________ 4. ________________

2.________________ 5. ________________

3. ________________ 6. ________________

6. Needs Analysis

a. Given the curriculum and the conditions needed to promote more skillful thinking, have you determined what knowledge, skills or attitude changes are needed?	+	?	-
b. Are you analyzing hard data (measurable facts) to support your beliefs about needs?	+	?	-
c. Can you determine which areas need the first attention?	+	?	-

7. Staff Development

a. Can you identify in-district personnel with the knowledge and skill to assist other staff in promoting more skillful thinking?	+	?	-
b. Can you identify skilled consultants who can build on what can't be taught by in-district personnel?	+	?	-
c. As adult educators, do the instructors have the skills to budge theory into practice by modeling use of effective teaching strategies and/or metacognitive strategies? (i.e., Do they practice what they preach?)	+	?	-
d. Can they teach effectively for transfer to the classroom?	+	?	-
e. Are the learning conditions (time, place, incentives) for the staff conducive to maximum success?	+	?	-

8. Coaching and Peer Support

a. Do trainees have the chance to select peer coaches?	+	?	-
b. Are they prepared to observe, give feed-back, support and problem solve with their team?	+	?	-
c. Are conditions conducive to peer coaching in teams (time, place, confidentiality, incentives)?	+	?	-

9. Supervising and Helping In Transfer

a. Do instructional leaders understand the supervisory role and how it differs from coaching and evaluating?	+	?	-

b. Do supervisors know teaching behaviors to observe and how to determine positive effects? + ? -
c. Do supervisors have the communication and interpersonal skills to build trust? + ? -
d. Are supervisors strong in facilitating problem solving? + ? -
e. Do supervisors model intelligent behavior? + ? -

10. Evaluation

a. Are evaluation criteria clear before evaluation occurs? + ? -
b. Is evaluation delayed until after sufficient practice has occurred? + ? -
c. Are the evaluation results kept confidential? + ? -

"That is a long list," commented George, a member from a small district.

"I hope it is useful," I said. "It includes all that we know goes into a successful program. Most importantly, however, you have to think about how you would answer each question and what you can change to fit your situation. Begin by noting which of the ten areas you have in place and which you need to incorporate into your new plan. Your list might look like this:"

	Area	Fully In Place	Partly In Place	Not In Place
1.				
2.				
3.				
4.				
5.				
6.				
7.				
8.				
9.				
10.				

"I think we are doing several of these things," George said. "I know we have started some coaching without supervisors."

"Good. And you may want to stay with a supervisory coach approach. As you know from the work of Showers and Joyce, coaching is the element that makes the most difference in moving new skills into the classroom. I prefer the peer coaching model. It makes for a lighter load on the principal and it builds collegiality."

"I accept the importance of their research," interjected Mary Anne. "It certainly tells us how much money we have wasted on the old dog and pony shows. Now, I need to think how I can make best use of that research for my district."

"Let me make several suggestions," I said. "First, break the time barrier. All teachers don't need to have the entire inservice at one time in one year. If you want all children learning and all children thinking more skillfully, give yourself three to five years."

"You mean 'Rome was not built in a day' don't you?"

"Yes. If you consider your mission in a five-year plan, you can work backward to see what steps to take each year. When it comes to training and coaching, I like what one teacher called the Amway approach."

"What's that?" asked George.

"Its a staff development pyramid," I commented. "Suppose you have 180 teachers in your district and your mission is that all children learn social skills as well as content. You select cooperative groups for your model. You know what you must do to give your teachers the skills to teach cooperative learning. You know a one-shot inservice on institute day won't do it. You lack the dollars to give everyone the eight days of training that the Johnsons suggest. So you ask Roger Johnson to do an awareness program at the fall institute. You know he'll make a positive impression and stir up interest. As soon as he is done, you announce that you want 20-30 volunteers for a cooperative group training program; you give the times and other details, and wait for the names. For the next two years, the volunteers have their inservice with Roger and David while the others focus on other issues. After two years of inservice, coaching, and creation of classroom lessons, each of the original volunteers initiates a team training program with one to three new volunteers. In small group tutorials, the original volunteers train, coach and support their 'tutees' in the theory and practice of cooperative groups. The pyramid continues until all complete the cooperative group program and cooperative groups are a well established classroom tool as well as a faculty support-team method. For the next two years, the teams work together to refine the method, develop new lessons and evaluate the results—you have put the improvement into practice."

"So the initial financial investment comes in the first two years?" asked another member.

"Yes," I said, "but recognize the danger. I'd suggest that you build in consultation time in

Staff Development Pyramid

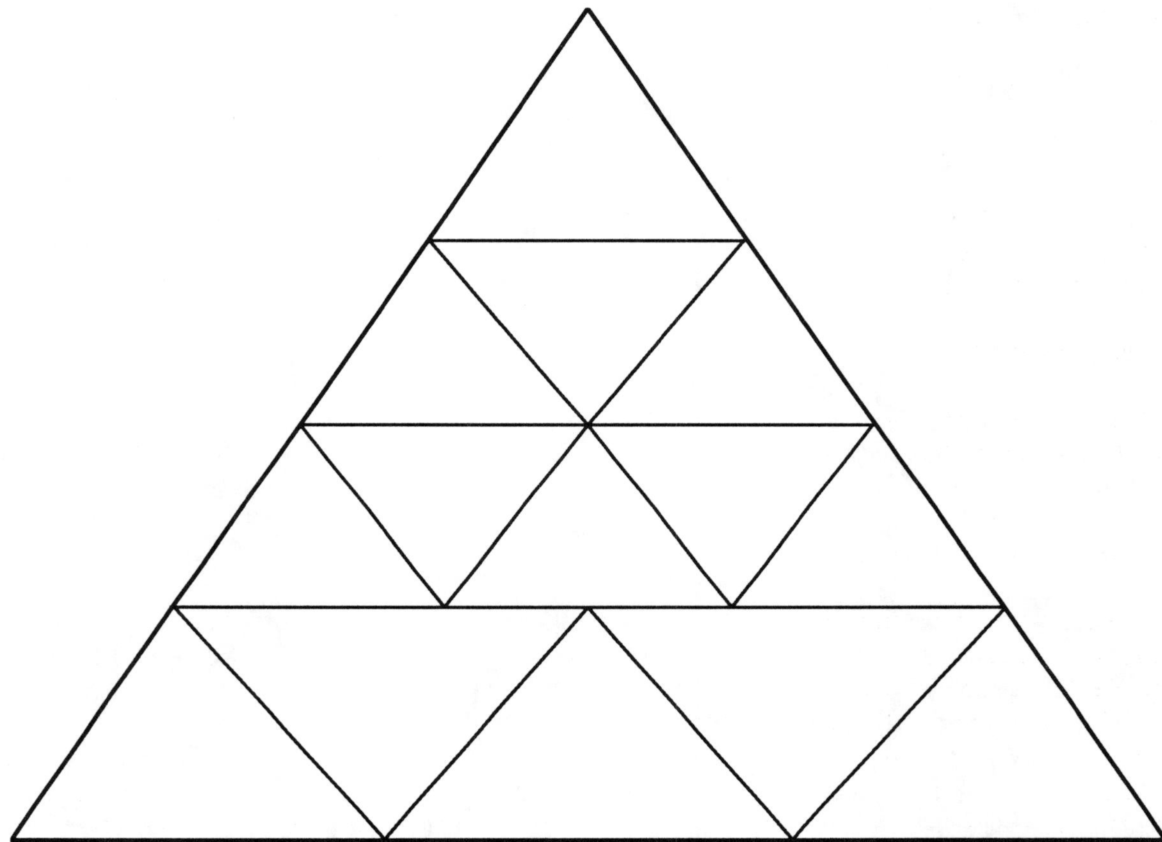

the next few years or some method that assures quality control. The pyramid does reach all, but it also can cause the message to become diluted."

"That's a good point," commented George.

"Now that you have given us this model, what do we do next?" asked Marion.

"For our next meeting, we'll need to consider the first element in a thoughtful plan: the mission. This seems like the best place to end this session. Shall we adjourn?"

Staff Development Model

Peer Coaching Component

(see pp. 16-21 for discussion)

1. Common Training

2. Selection of Peer Partner (Partners/Teams)

3. Commitment to Metacognitive Process (1-2 hours/week)

   (a) Plan together: "That's A Good Idea" (p. 71 & 232)

   (b) Monitor Each Other: Observation Grid(s) (p. 76)

      observations
      videotapes
      audiotapes
      artifacts

   (c) Evaluate Together: Mrs. Potter's Questions (p. 227)

4. Continue (a), (b), and (c) cycle

5. Team Sharing Between Trainings and Every Two Weeks Following Training (1 hour) Use 2-4-8 Focus Interview, (p. 117)

6. Collection of "Artifacts" Evidencing Strategies Practiced

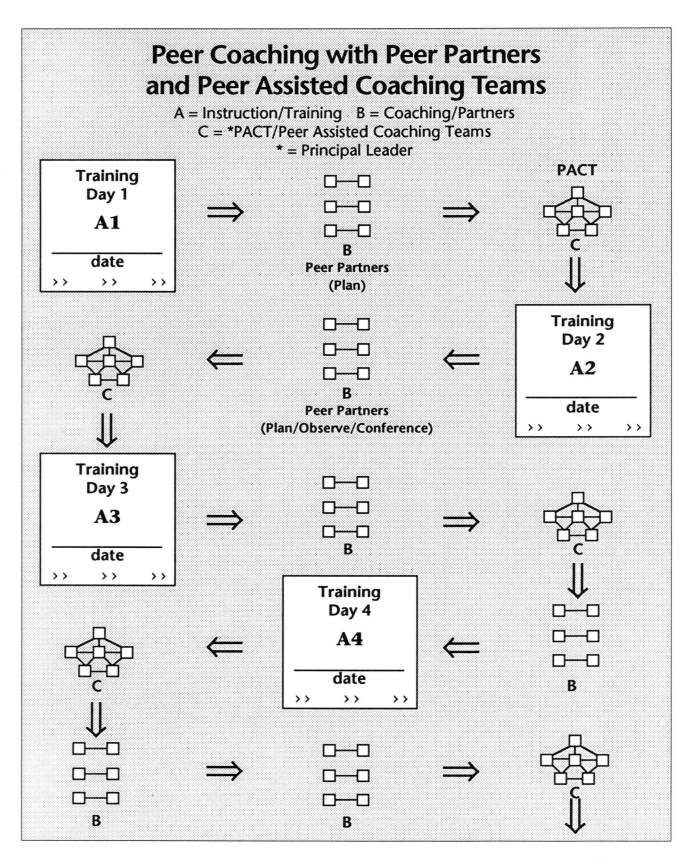

Peer Coaching with Peer Partners and Peer Assisted Coaching Teams

A = Instruction/Training B = Coaching/Partners
C = *PACT/Peer Assisted Coaching Teams
* = Principal Leader

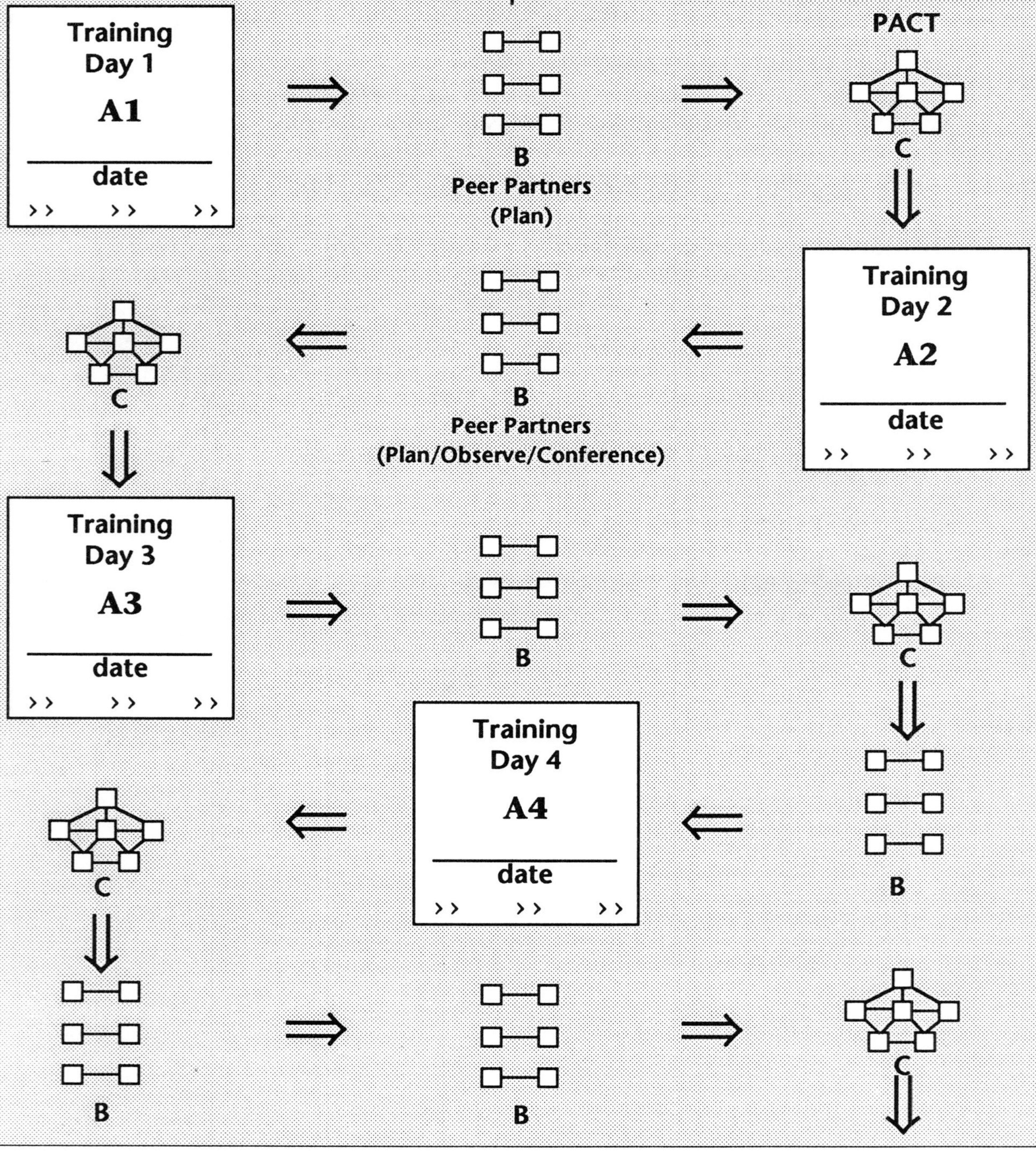

Training Day 1
A1
date
›› ›› ››

⟹

B
Peer Partners
(Plan)

⟹

PACT
C

⟸

B
Peer Partners
(Plan/Observe/Conference)

⟸

Training Day 2
A2
date
›› ›› ››

C

Training Day 3
A3
date
›› ›› ››

⟹

B

⟹

C

B

Training Day 4
A4
date
›› ›› ››

C

B

⟹

B

⟹

C

Transfer of Learning

Model	Illustration	Transfer Disposition	Looks Like	Sounds Like
Ollie the Head-in-the-sand Ostrich		Overlooks	Persists in writing in manuscript form rather than cursive. (New skill overlooked or avoided.)	*"I get it right on the dittos, but I forget to use punctuation When I write an essay."* (Not applying mechanical learning.)
Dan the Drilling Woodpecker		Duplicates	Plagiarism is the most obvious student artifact of duplication. (Unable to synthesize in own words.)	*"Mine is not to question why—just invert and multiply." (When dividing fractions.)* (No understanding of what she/he is doing.)
Laura the Look-alike Penguin		Replicates	"Bed to Bed" or narrative style. "He got up. He did this. He went to bed or He was born. He did this... He died." (Student portfolio of work never varies.)	*"Paragraphing means I must have three 'indents' per page."* (Tailors into own story or essay, but paragraphs in-appropriately.)
Jonathan Livingston Seagull		Integrates	Student writing essay incorpor-ates newly learned French words. (Applying: weaving old and new.)	*"I always try to guess (predict) what's gonna happen next on T.V. shows."* (Connects to prior knowledge and ex-perience; relates what's learned to personal experience.
Cathy the Carrier Pigeon		Maps	Graphs information for a social studies report with the help of the math teacher to actually de-sign the graphs. (Connecting to another.)	Parent-related story. *"Tina suggested we brainstorm our vacation ideas and rank them to help us decide."* (Carries new skills into life situations.)
Samantha the Soaring Eagle		Innovates	After studying flow charts for computer class student con-structs a Rube Goldberg type invention. (Innovates: Invents; di-verges; goes beyond and creates novel.)	*"I took the idea of the Mr. Potato Head and created a mix and match grid of ideas for our Earth Day project."* (Generalizes ideas from experience and and transfers creatively.)

Teacher Levels of Transfer

Ollie
the Head-in-the-sand Ostrich
OVERLOOKS

Does nothing; unaware of relevance and misses appropriate applications; overlooks intentionally or unintentionally. (persists)

"Great session but this won't work with my kids or content"...or "I chose not to use...because..."

Dan
the Drilling Woodpecker
DUPLICATES

Drills and practices exactly as presented; Drill! Drill! Then stops; uses as an activity rather than as a strategy; duplicates. (observes)

"Could I have a copy of that transparency?"

Laura
the Look-alike Penguin
REPLICATES

Tailors to kids and content, but applies in similar content; all look alike, does not transfer into new situations; replicates. (differentiates)

"I use the web for every character analysis."

Jonathan
Livingston Seagull
INTEGRATES

Raised consciousness; acute awareness; deliberate refinement; integrates subtly with existing repertoire. (combines)

"I haven't used any of your ideas, but I'm wording my questions carefully. I've always done this, but I'm doing more of it."

Cathy
the Carrier Pigeon
MAPS

Consciously transfers ideas to various situations, contents; carries strategy as part of available repertoire; maps. (associates)

"I use the webbing strategy in everything."

Samantha
the Soaring Eagle
INNOVATES

Innovates; flies with an idea; takes into action beyond the initial conception; creates enhances; invents; risks. (diverges)

"You have changed my teaching forever. I can never go back to what I used to do. I know too much. I'm too excited."

Student Levels of Transfer

Ollie the Head-in-the-sand Ostrich **OVERLOOKS**	**Dan** the Drilling Woodpecker **DUPLICATES**
 Misses appropriate opportunity; overlooks; persists in former way. *"I get it right on the dittos, but I forget to use punctuation when I write an essay."* (Doesn't connect appropriateness.)	 Performs the drill exactly as practiced; duplicates. *"Yours is not to question why—just invert and multiply."* (When dividing fractions, has no understanding of what she/he is doing.)
Laura the Look-alike Penguin **REPLICATES**  Tailors but applies in similar situation; all look alike; replicates. *"Paragraphing means I must have three 'indents' per page."* (Tailors into own story or essay, but paragraphs inappropriately.)	**Jonathan** Livingston Seagull **INTEGRATES**  Is aware; integrates; combines with other ideas and situations. *"I always try to guess (predict) what's gonna happen next on T.V. shows."* (Connects to prior knowledge and experience.)
Cathy the Carrier Pigeon **MAPS**  Carries strategy to other content and situations. Associates and maps. Parent-related story—*"Tina suggested we brainstorm our vacation ideas and rank them to help us decide."* (Carries new skills into life situations.)	**Samantha** the Soaring Eagle **INNOVATES**  Innovates; takes idea beyond initial conception; risks; diverges. *"After studying flow charts for computer class student constructs a Rube Goldberg type invention."* (Innovates; invents; diverges; goes beyond and creates)

Coaching For Transfer—Teaching For Transfer

A Metacognitive Reflective Model in terms of the new learnings

Am I:

Ollie
Head-In-the-sand Ostrich

Overlooking opportunities

Dan
the Drilling Woodpecker

Duplicating; copying

Laura
the Look-alike Penguin

Replicating; tailoring

Jonathan
Livingston Seagull

Integrating; raised consciousness

Cathy
the Carrier Pigeon

Mapping; strategic planning

Sam
the Soaring Eagle

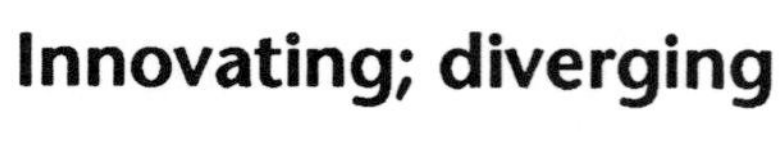

Innovating; diverging

A Word About Transfer

All teaching is for transfer; all learning is for transfer. To extend learning; to bridge the old and the new; and to lead students toward relevant transfer and use across academic content and into life situations, is the mission of the thinking classroom.

In some cases, the transfer of learning is obvious because the learned skills seem close to the skill situation in which they are used or transferred. For example, when teaching "supermarket math"—price comparisons, making change, etc.—the learning situation "hugs" the life situation. The transfer is clear. This transfer is called simple transfer.

However, in other instances, the learning in the school situation seems far removed or remote from the transfer across content or into life. For example, a high school student spends a great deal of time and energy staring at, memorizing and using the Periodic Table of Elements. However, unless the student is destined for a scientific career in which frequent reference and deep understanding of the table is essential, it is difficult for the student to feel that the learning is really useful. Does one really need to know that Au is gold?

Most students do not "see" how this learning is useful. The transfer is complex. They miss the connection between the rigors of learning the elements and the similar rigors of visualizing, practicing, and memorizing other material. Few students note that the analytical skills used in "reading" the table of elements are similar to the critical thinking used in analyzing other charts or graphs. Seldom are students aware that the patterns evident in the table of elements set a model for searching for patterns in other phenomena or constructing similar matrices or grids. The transfer here is remote; it is obscure. The student needs explicit instruction in making these and other connections. In these situations, teachers can help kids make relevant transfer through mediation or "bridging" strategies.

The six transfer strategies which are illustrated next require explicit instruction with students to help them make application, in other words, to help them transfer.

Transfer: The Creative Connection

Mediation Strategies That Bridge Learning

Transfer Strategy #1: Setting Expectations

SET EXPECTATIONS for transfer. Elicit examples of when the information, skill or concept is used in other content or life situations. Ask students how they might use this new learning; how it connects to past experiences; how it might be useful in particular subject areas or life situations.

Transfer Strategy #2: Reflecting Metacognitively

REFLECT ON YOUR TRANSFER LEVEL by asking: Am I...

Ollie		**Head-in-the-sand Ostrich**	Missing appropriate opportunities; over-looking; persisting in former ways?
Dan		**Drilling Woodpecker**	Performing the drill exactly as practiced; duplicating with no change; copying?
Laura		**The Look-alike Penguin**	Tailoring, but applying in similar situations; all looking alike; replicating?
Jonathan		**Livingston Seagull**	More aware; integrating; subtly combining with other ideas and situations; using with raised consciousness?
Cathy		**The Carrier Pigeon**	Carrying strategy to other content and into life situations; associating and mapping?
Samantha		**The Soaring Eagle**	Innovating; taking ideas beyond the initial conception; risking; diverging?

Transfer Strategy #3: Making Connections With Questions
USE BRIDGING QUESTIONS such as:

OVERLOOKING Think of an instance when the skill or strategy would be inappropriate.
"I would not use__________when____________________________."

DUPLICATING Think of an "opportunity passed" when you could have used the skill or strategy.
"I wish I'd known about ____________ when ______________ because I could've______________________________."

REPLICATING Think of an adjustment that will make your application of ______________________________ more relevant.
"Next time I'm gonna ______________________________ ______________________________."

INTEGRATING Think of an analogy for the skill or strategy.
"__________________ is like __________________ because both ______________________________."

MAPPING Think of an upcoming opportunity in classes to use the new idea.
"In__________, I'm gonna use ______________________ to help ______________________________."

INNOVATING Think of an application for a "real-life" setting.
"Outside of school, I could use ________________________ when ______________________________."

Transfer Strategy #4: Modeling

MODEL EXAMPLES of how the skill or strategy has been used by showing or referring to explicit models. Share specific examples through "artifacts" collected from students and/or teachers—people using the ideas.

Transfer Strategy #5: Promote Risk Taking

CREATE CONNECTIONS by promoting risk taking that stretches learning across content and into life. Foster "safe risks" by encouraging students to play with ideas.

SECTION 2

AWARENESS

There is only one way in which a person acquires a new idea; by the combination or association of two or more ideas he already has into a new juxtaposition in such a manner as to discover a relationship among them of which he was not previously aware.

—Francis A. Cartier

Four Elements that Promote Thinking

Climate (Teaching FOR Thinking) Setting a safe climate for thinking by modeling risk-taking and acceptance.	**Explicit Skill** (Teaching OF Thinking) Teaching the thinking skill explicitly to students and bridging skill application into relevant situations.
Structured Interaction (Teaching WITH Thinking) Getting kids to process the information together and interact with the material in experiential activities.	**Metacognitive Processing** (Teaching ABOUT Thinking) Getting kids to think about their thinking and deliberately bring their patterns for thinking to a conscious level.

A Survey of Elements That Promote Thinking

Based on a synthesis of the best educational research available, the four essential elements that promote thinking in the classroom are:

- CLIMATE
- EXPLICIT SKILL INSTRUCTION
- STRUCTURED INTERACTION
- METACOGNITIVE PROCESSING

THE TEACHER IS KEY, for the teacher provides the framework. Ask yourself these questions:

CLIMATE: Does the room arrangement invite interaction, openness, flexibility? What verbal and non-verbal messages are you communicating? Are you modeling "teacher as learner?" Do you LISTEN? Do you energize and motivate? Do you tolerate the noise, movement, and failure that sometimes accompanies a thinking environment? Do you set an atmosphere of expectancy and focus? Do you project high expectations? Do you treat students as thinkers?

EXPLICIT INSTRUCTION: Do you teach the micro-skills of thinking explicitly? Do you define terms, post the objective? Do you vary the learning input to meet different learning styles and different rates of learning? Do you provide opportunities for students to process the material? Do you build in guided practice with monitoring and feedback? Do you value thinking enough to set time priorities to teach the skills?

INTERACTION: Do you structure groups flexibly to accommodate various learning situations and learning styles? Do you model teacher as participant? Do you invite involvement through forced responses? Do you set clear rules and objectives for students to target? Do you assign roles and responsibilities to foster accountability and cooperative efforts? Do you listen, observe and facilitate interaction to foster thinking in the classroom?

METACOGNITIVE PROCESSING: Do you process learning activities with students? Do you help them track their "patterns for thinking" by inviting them to verbalize how they did what they did? Do you lead them into metacognitive processing by providing time to reflect in writing about their thinking strategies? Do you help students make the connections between new learning and past experiences? Do you guide them to extend new learning with relevant situations both in and out of the classroom? Do you bridge learning for students to help them make the transfer? Do you provide visual formats and ask metacognitive questions?

AWARENESS

Elements That Promote Thinking

CLIMATE:

- Room arrangement
- Attitude - verbal and non-verbal messages
- Modeling of teacher as learner
- Openness to listen; energy to motivate
- Tolerance for noise, movement and failure
- Atmosphere - focus and sense of expectancy

INTERACTION:

- Structure of groups - flexible and varied
- Modeling of teacher as participant
- Involvement
- Invitations to respond
- Clear rules and objectives for students
- Assigned roles and responsibilities
- Cooperative efforts

EXPLICIT INSTRUCTION:

- Definition of terms
- Objective
- Input
- Guided Practice - monitor and feedback

METACOGNITIVE PROCESSING:

Level I	*Level II*	*Level III*	*Level IV*
Tacit Use	**Aware Use**	**Strategic Use**	**Reflective Use**
Uses problem solving but does not think about using any particular strategy	Conscious of use and when he/she is using a particular strategy	Organizes thinking by deliberately using a particular strategy	Plans, monitors and evaluates a particular strategy

-Swartz and Perkins

The Four Elements

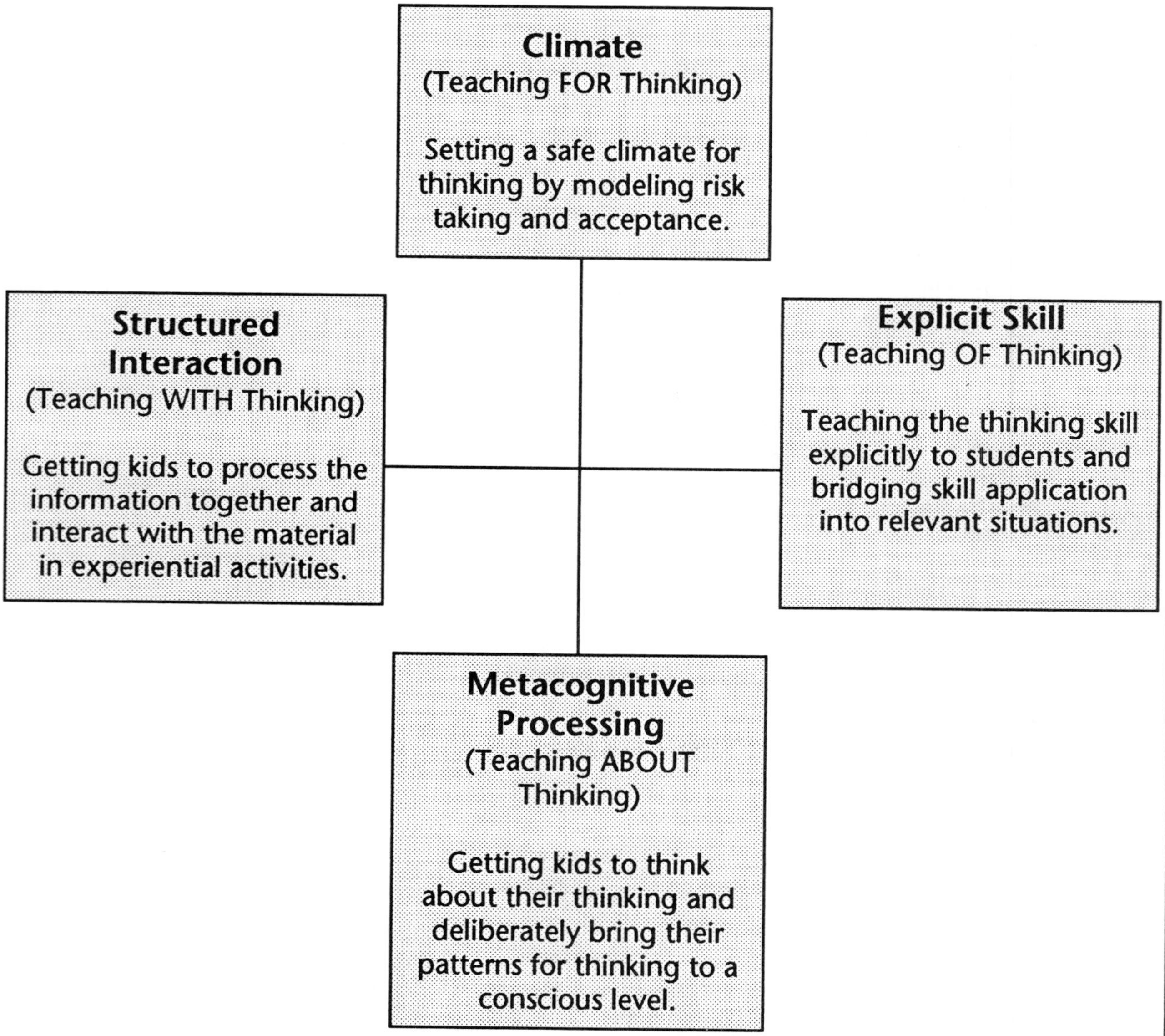

Climate
(Teaching FOR Thinking)

Setting a safe climate for thinking by modeling risk taking and acceptance.

Structured Interaction
(Teaching WITH Thinking)

Getting kids to process the information together and interact with the material in experiential activities.

Explicit Skill
(Teaching OF Thinking)

Teaching the thinking skill explicitly to students and bridging skill application into relevant situations.

Metacognitive Processing
(Teaching ABOUT Thinking)

Getting kids to think about their thinking and deliberately bring their patterns for thinking to a conscious level.

Adapted from
Ron Brandt

Goals of Patterns for Thinking—Patterns for Transfer

For the Instructional Leaders:

1. To identify the essential knowledge and skills of creative and critical thinking necessary for effective instruction in *Patterns For Thinking—Patterns For Transfer.*

2. To communicate that teaching is both an art and a science in which the instructional leader has a major responsibility to enable successful learning.

3. To explicitly teach the skills of creative and critical thinking through specific strategies that have transfer application for the classroom.

4. To establish Professional Coaching Networks that provide team follow-up, support and encouragement for continued instruction in *Patterns For Thinking—Patterns For Transfer.*

For the Students:

1. To understand the essential knowledge and skills of creative and critical thinking.

2. To become cooperative and active participants in a 'thinking classroom' where both creative and critical thinking are valued expectations.

3. To internalize the *Patterns For Thinking—Patterns For Transfer* skills for personally relevant transfer application in problem-solving and decision-making situations across all content and into life situations.

AWARENESS

Goals

What I Know	What I Want To Know	What I Learned

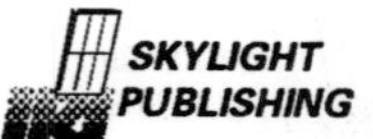

CLIMATE: The People Search

Find someone who:

1. Has read the same book as you this past year.

2. Advocates a political position similar to yours.

3. Can brainstorm 10 *M* words in 1 minute.

4. Can describe what it feels like to be put on "hold" on the telephone.

5. Can explain the difference between inductive and deductive reasoning.

6. Ranks these items the same as you do:

☐ Mind  Body  Soul

7. Can present both sides of an argument in two minutes.

8. Can list the six levels of Bloom's Taxonomy.

9. Can classify teachers into four different groups.

10. Can attribute a mystery story.

11. Can explain the difference between an alligator and a crocodile.

12. Can sequence their steps to problem solving.

FRIENDS: Why Do a People Search?

Focuses on content:

As students move through the various lessons of the day, it becomes critical that the teacher provide a timely focus for the content to be presented. Carefully designed "search statements" lead students toward the target lesson.

Reinforces learning through articulation:

Much of the research in the area of reading suggests that recitation by the student, rephrasing in one's own words, is a powerful way to help place material into long-term memory. By talking with each other, all students have an opportunity to articulate their conceptions.

Invites meaningful interaction:

As a teacher promoting thinking for all students in the classroom, getting them to interact with each other about the material is vital. The activity of "searching" out friends to discuss the lesson content does just this.

Exemplifies a model of "safe-risk" climate:

By structuring the statements on the People Search as open-ended and divergent in nature, students are "safe" risking their interpretations of an answer because there are as many answers as there are student "connections."

Notes value placed on people as resources:

"Cooperation and communication are valued" is the message modeled in this sort of strategy. The teacher is demonstrating the resources available among the members of the group. Students sense that it's not only OK to talk with classmates about things, but it is expected as part of the learning process.

Diagnoses prior knowledge for new learning:

As the teacher participates actively in the "search," she/he senses the readiness of the group and notes whether or not the preconditions to the proposed learning are in place. From the information learned in this activity, the teacher adjusts subsequent plans.

Signals priorities of the unit or semester:

The teacher can flag the primary concepts, objectives and goals of the unit (or semester) through the People Search. The message to students says, "These are the important things. If you understand these, you will have a solid grasp of the material."

PEOPLE SEARCH: Sample Items

MATH SEARCH — Level: Middle

Find someone who:

1. can describe a "Rube Goldberg."
2. can explain why we invert and multiply in the division of fractions computation.
3. has designed a flow chart for a computer program.

TOUCH THAT DIAL (Article) — Level: Senior

Find someone who:

1. knows why politicians like the radio.
2. can explain why radio and records help each other.
3. can give a pro and con argument about radio.

CHEMISTRY — Level: Senior

Find someone who:

1. can explain a chemical change that they experienced today.
2. knows why your water heater is in the basement and not the attic.
3. is inert.

TELLING TIME — Level: Primary

Find someone who:

1. has a digital clock.
2. can draw a clock showing lunch time.
3. can explain the time it takes for a T.V. commercial.

SHORT STORIES — Level: Middle

Find someone who:

1. can give three differences between a short story and a novel.
2. has written a short story and can give you the title.
3. can describe the typical setting for a murder mystery.

BIOLOGY — Level: Primary

Find someone who:

1. has watched tadpoles and can tell you about them.
2. has climbed a pole.
3. has seen a frog in the last week.

GROUPS — Level: Adult

Find someone who:

1. can demonstrate and explain body language.
2. has been a member of an organized team.
3. will discuss the paradox: Alone in a crowd.

As you can see, the creative teacher can use the People Search with great versatility and after sufficient modeling by the teacher, students can create People Searches for selected topics to be studied. Again, the benefits of this strategy are limited only by the imaginative application of each teacher. Share your ideas with your peers and spark even more uses.

AWARENESS

The People Search As: A Pre-Strategy for—Focus

DNA SEARCH

Level: High School

Find someone who...

1. has experienced a spiral staircase or slide.
2. is wearing a zipper.
3. knows someone named Watson.
4. knows what to do with a phosphate.
5. likes to eat sugar.
6. can make up three words with base in them.
7. would be a good pair with you.
8. can name a cell in his body that is reproducing right now.
9. knows an identical twin.
10. has jeans on.
11. knows the difference between a female and male gene.
12. who ate a protein today.
13. can name a commercial product that has an enzyme in it.
14. knows triplets.
15. knows many symbols in Morse code.
16. knows a president of a company.
17. knows someone who uses blueprints.
18. can take the 1st, 5th and 20th letters of the alphabet and construct three different words.
19. can describe how a foreman's job is different from an assembly-line worker's job.
20. can name a substance that bonds things together.

The People Search As:
A Post-Strategy for—Review

AWARENESS

PEOPLE SEARCH "My Furthest-Back Person—'The African'" Level: Jr. High

Find someone who...

1. attended a family reunion last summer.
2. has a living great-grandparent.
3. knows what countries his ancestors came from.
4. can describe what a "family tree" contains.
5. has a relative who learned English as a second language.
6. can locate the Gambia River and Annapolis, Maryland on the map.
7. uses a name different from that on his birth or Baptismal certificate.
8. can list the circumstances in which "oral tradition" might be considered dependable.
9. can defend the African's need to keep his clan name Kinte and not be called Toby.
10. can explain why "My Furthest-Back Person—'The African'" is an appropriate title for this selection.
11. can explain why this selection is included on a unit dealing with determination.

AWARENESS

The People Search As:
A "Sponge" Strategy for—Transition

Level: Elementary

Can you find someone in our room who...

1. knows the difference between Flipper and Charlie Tuna? __________
2. whose mother loves to cook fish? __________
3. can stay under water for 30 seconds? __________
4. owns a green scale? __________
5. knows someone named Gil? __________
6. has touched a fish? __________
7. has met a red snapper? __________
8. can tell a "fish story"? __________
9. can make a noise like a fish? __________

There are one-story intellects,
two-story intellects,
and three-story intellects with skylights.
All fact collectors, who have
no aim beyond their facts,
are one-story men.
Two-story men compare, reason,
generalize, using the labors of the
fact collectors as well as their own.
Three-story men idealize,
imagine, predict—
their best illumination comes
from above, through the skylight.

—Oliver Wendell Holmes

Three-Story Intellect Verbs

3 **APPLYING**

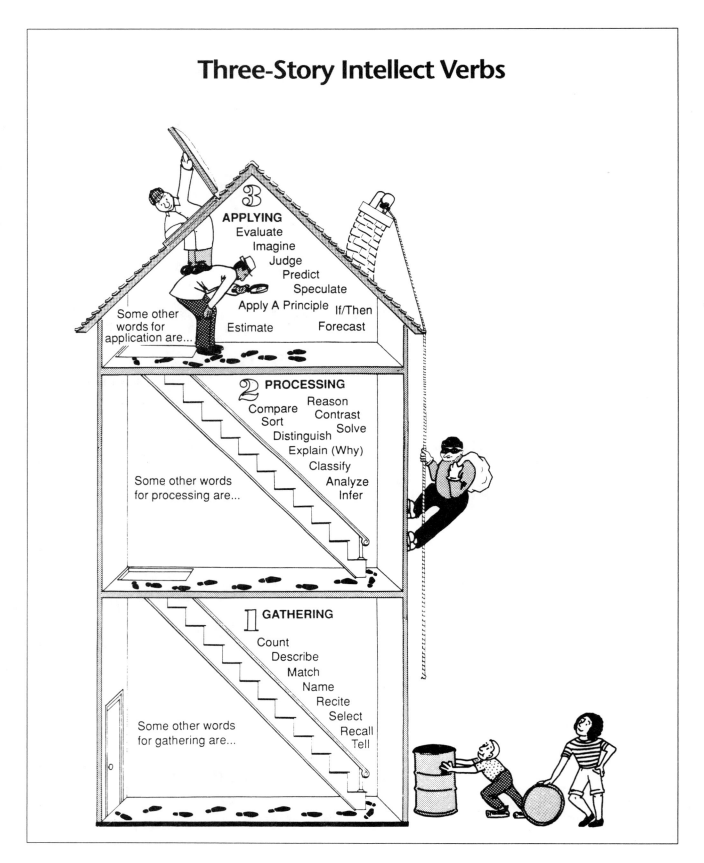

Evaluate
Imagine
Judge
Predict
Speculate
Apply A Principle
If/Then
Estimate
Forecast

Some other words for application are...

2 **PROCESSING**

Compare
Sort
Reason
Contrast
Solve
Distinguish
Explain (Why)
Classify
Analyze
Infer

Some other words for processing are...

1 **GATHERING**

Count
Describe
Match
Name
Recite
Select
Recall
Tell

Some other words for gathering are...

Write Your Own

To form high-quality questions or statements for a People Search, use the cue words on the Three-Story Intellect page. These particular verbs force students into higher mental processes. For example, instead of asking students to list, the statement could require them to rank items. Rank means not only to recall the list but to process that list and place value on each item. Thus, the statement leads to more sophisticated mental processing.

Try to write the Search in such a way that the key issues are spirited "through the back door." The Search should not read like a pre- or post-test or quiz. It should be focused, but fun. For example, instead of asking students studying a DNA unit to define genes, the teacher asks them to find someone wearing jeans. She/he triggers an analysis level of thinking by subtly interjecting a homonym into the Search. Students think of jeans and genes which leads them to compare the two concepts. It requires complex thinking, beyond just recall.

To practice divergent strategies as you create your own People Searches, scan the examples provided. Then, select your topic, select your verbs and write away!

TOPIC OR UNIT OR CONCEPT

Find someone who...

1.
2.
3.
4.
5.
6.
7.
8.
9.
10.
11.
12.

AWARENESS

Enhancing Cognitive Levels of Classroom Interaction

Gathering and Recalling Information (Input)

To cause the student to INPUT data, questions and statements are designed to draw from the student the concepts, information, feelings, or experiences acquired in the past and stored in long- or short-term memory. They can also be designed to activate the senses to gather data which the student can then process at the next higher level. There are several cognitive processes included at the INPUT level of thinking. Some verbs that may serve as the predicate of a behavioral objective statement are:

completing
counting
defining
describing
identifying
listing
matching
naming
observing
reciting
selecting
scanning

Examples of questions and statements designed to elicit these cognitive objectives are:

Question/Statement	Desired Cognitive Behavior
"Name the states which border California."	Listing
"How does the picture make you feel?"	Describing
"What word does this picture go with?"	Matching
"Define the word, 'haggard.'"	Defining
"What were the names of the children in the story?"	Naming
"What did you see the man doing in the film?"	Observing
"Which ball is the blue one?"	Identifying
"How does the Gettysburg Address begin?"	Reciting
"How many coins are there in the stack?"	Counting
"Which words in this list are rhyming words?"	Selecting
"The Mexican houses were made of mud bricks called...what?"	Completing
"Watch what color it turns when I put the litmus paper in the liquid."	Observing

Making Sense Out of the Information Gathered (Processing)

To cause the student to PROCESS the data gathered through the senses and retrieved from long- and short-term memory, questions and statements are designed to draw some relationships of cause and effect to synthesize, analyze, summarize, compare, contrast, or classify the data he/she has acquired or observed. Following are verbs that may serve as the predicate of a behavior objective statement if the desired cognitive behavior of students is at the level of processing.

synthesizing	planning
analyzing	explaining
classifying	grouping
comparing	inferring
contrasting	making analogies
distinguishing	organizing
experimenting	sequencing

Examples of questions designed to elicit these cognitive objectives are:

Question/Statement	Desired Cognitive Behavior
"Compare the strength of steel to the strength of copper."	Comparing
"Why did Columbus believe he could get to the East by sailing West?"	Explaining
"From our experiments with food coloring in different water temperatures, what can you infer about the movement of molecules?"	Inferring
"How can you arrange the rocks in the order of their size?"	Sequencing
"How can you arrange the leaves so that all those that are alike are in groups?"	Classifying
"What do you think caused the liquid to turn blue?"	Explaining Cause & Effect
"Arrange in groups the things that a magnet will and will not pick up."	Grouping
"What other machines can you think of that work in the same way that this one does?"	Making Analogies
"What are some characteristics of Van Gogh's work that make you think this painting is his?	Distinguishing
"What can you do to test your idea?"	Experimenting
"How are pine needles different from redwood needles?"	Contrasting
"How can you arrange the blocks to give a crowded feeling?"	Organizing
"How can we go about solving this problem of the lost playground equipment?"	Planning
"What data are we going to need in order to solve this problem?"	Analyzing

AWARENESS

Applying and Evaluating Actions in Novel Situations (Output)

Questions and statements which cause OUTPUT are designed to have the student go beyond the concept or principle that he/she has developed and to use this relationship in a novel or hypothetical situation. Application invites the student to think creatively and hypothetically, to use imagination, to expose a value system or to make a judgment. Verbs that may serve as the predicate of a behavior objective statement if your desired cognitive behaviors of students is at the level of application include:

applying a principle	imagining
evaluating	judging
extrapolating	model building
forecasting	predicting
generalizing	speculating
hypothesizing	

Examples of questions designed to elicit these cognitive objectives are:

Question/Statement	Desired Cognitive Behavior
"What will happen to our weather if a high-pressure area moves in?"	Forecasting
"If our population continues to grow as it does, what will life be like in the 21st century?"	Speculating
"Since the amount of heat does affect the speed of movement of the molecules, what will happen when we put the liquid in the refrigerator?"	Predicting
"Imagine what life would be like if there were no laws to govern us."	Imagining
"What can you say about all countries' economies that are dependent upon only one crop?"	Generalizing
"Is there a way you can think of to use this bimetal strip to make a fire alarm?"	Applying
"With this clay make a model of a plant cell."	Model building
"What would be a fair solution to this problem?"	Evaluating
"Which of the two paintings do you think is more unique?"	Judging
"From what we have learned, what other examples of romantic music can you cite?"	Applying a principle
"What do you think might happen if we placed the saltwater fish in the tank of fresh water?"	Hypothesizing

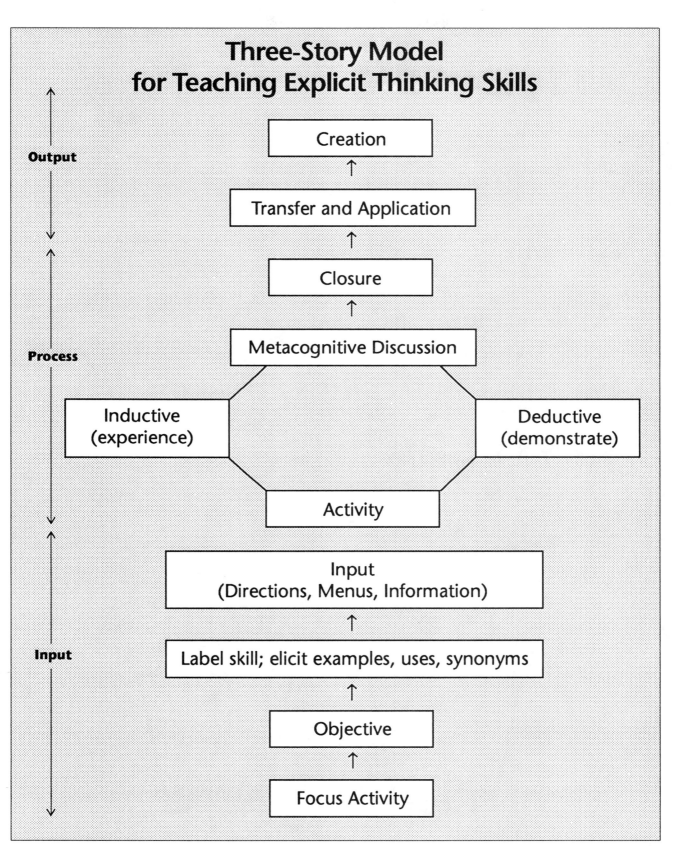

Three-Story Model for Teaching Explicit Thinking Skills

Output

Creation

↑

Transfer and Application

↑

Process

Closure

↑

Metacognitive Discussion

Inductive (experience)

Deductive (demonstrate)

Activity

Input

Input (Directions, Menus, Information)

↑

Label skill; elicit examples, uses, synonyms

↑

Objective

↑

Focus Activity

ATTRIBUTING

TUNE IN; FOCUS

RUN WITH IT; BRAINSTORM

ASSOCIATE IDEAS; PIGGYBACK

IMAGE THE CONCEPT OR ITEM; DEFINE IT

TEST THE ATTRIBUTES

SELECT THE CRITICAL ATTRIBUTES

Attributing

☐ Creative Thinking

☑ Critical Thinking

PROGRAM Skill: Attributing

PASSWORD Acronym: **TRAITS**

DATA BASE Definition: to analyze characteristics, qualities, elements or traits of a concept or item

LIST Synonyms: characteristics, traits, likenesses

SCAN Examples: attributes of mammals; attributes of courage

ENTER When to use:

- to define concept or term
- to distinguish between two similar concepts or items
- to clarify concept in own terms

MENU How to use:

Tune in; focus
Run with it; brainstorm
Associate ideas; piggyback
Image the concept or item; define it
Test the attributes with a specific example
Select the critical attributes necessary to define concept or item

DEBUGGING What to do if:

- cannot separate it from similar concept; *find specific example to use as model; use references or resource material*
- cannot select *critical* attributes; *keep all*
- cannot think of specific example to test with; *get help from someone or continue to add attributes until more clearly defined*

AWARENESS

AWARENESS

VISUAL LAYOUT

Patterns: Attribute Web
List
Concept Map

FILE

Sample Lesson in Language Arts: Literature—A Mystery

Tune in: Think of a mystery on TV or in a book.

Run with it: Brainstorm its attributes—clues, suspense, problem-solution, hero.

Associate: hero, victim, suspects

Image: Imagine and define items—clues lead to climax, but these are several possibilities.

Test: Take a specific mystery. Did it have all these attributes?

Select: Choose defining attributes—problem, hero, victim, suspects, clues, suspense (no victim, therefore eliminate from final list of attributes—can have mystery without victim).

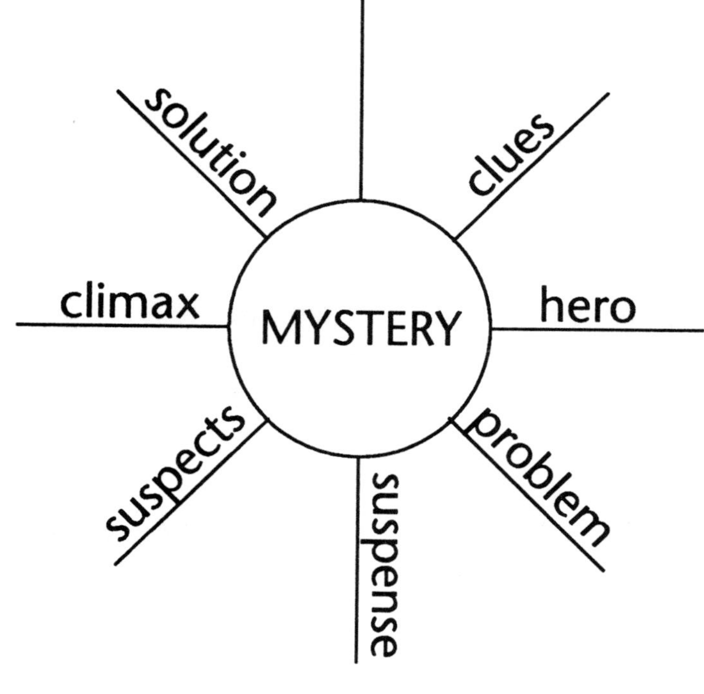

INDEX

Suggested Applications:

MATH	• Metric system • Graphs • Word problems
LANGUAGE ARTS	• Paragraph • Character analysis
SCIENCE	• UFOs • Nutritious foods • Force
SOCIAL STUDIES	• Leaders • War • Geographic location

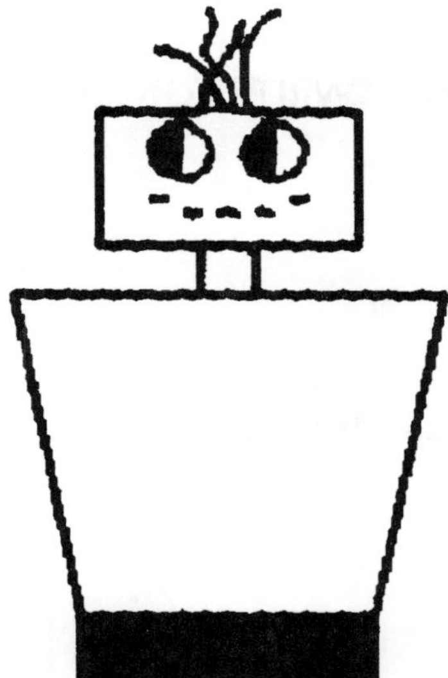

Structured Interaction: Cooperative Groups

Leadership Responsibilities

1. LEADER - "ENCOURAGES GROUP MEMBERS"

2. OBSERVER/TIMEKEEPER - "REPORTS ON GROUP PROCESS"

3. RECORDER - "WRITES ON CHART"

4. MATERIALS MANAGER - "GETS SUPPLIES"

Explicit Thinking Skill: Analysis of Attributes

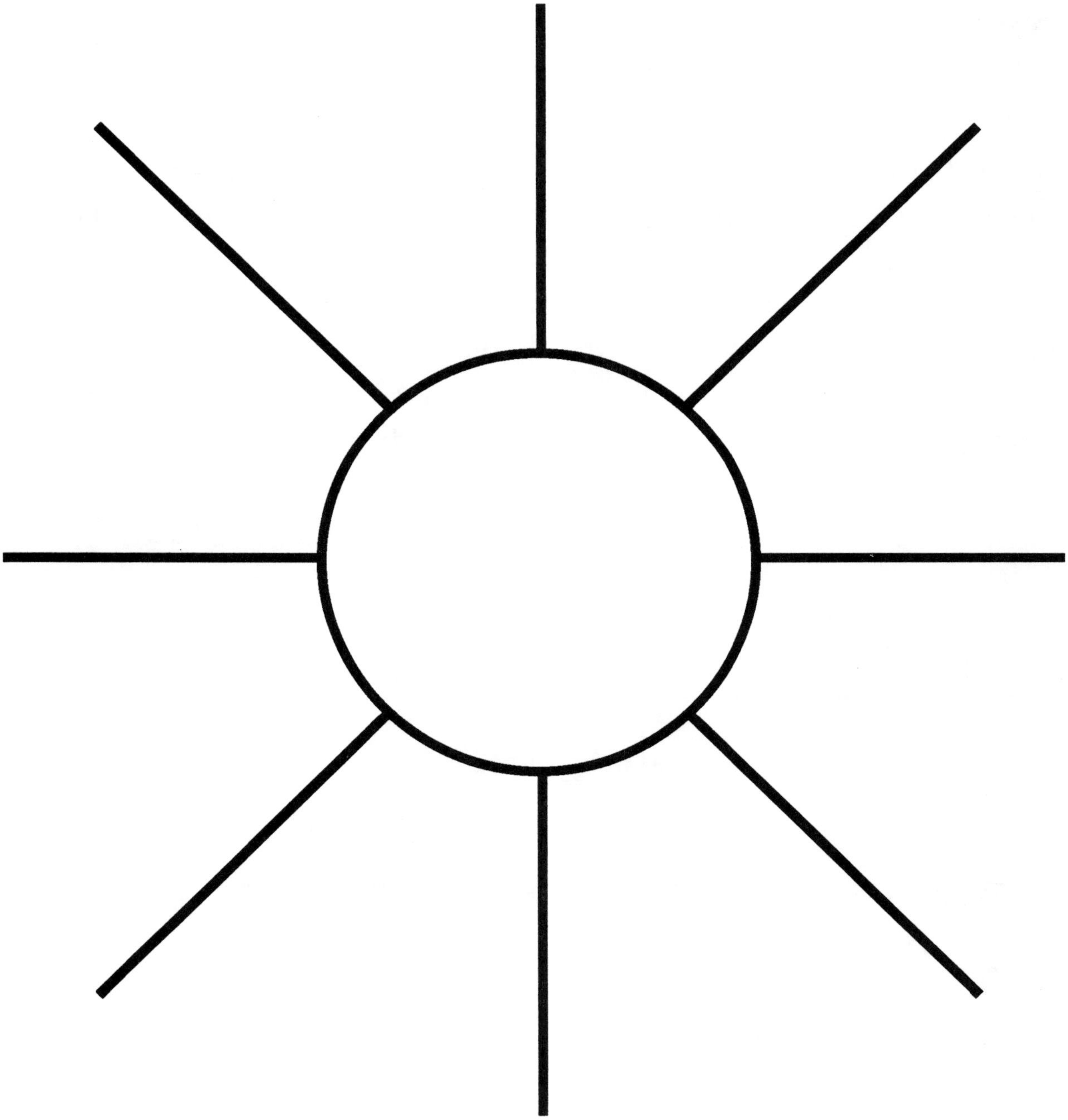

AWARENESS

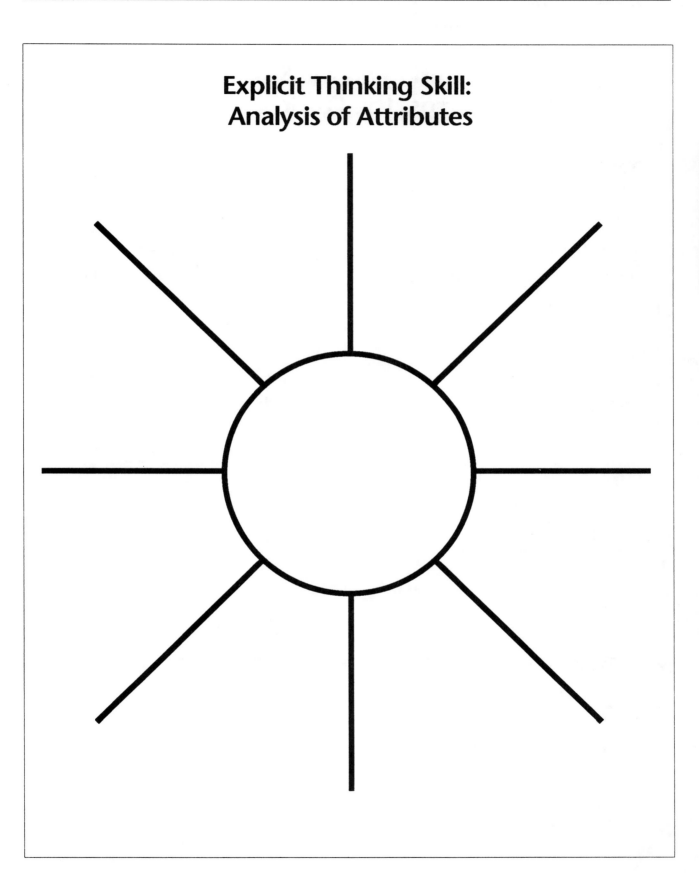

AWARENESS

Bridging the Skill Across the Curriculum

MODEL:
(Some things I already teach and ways I could use this skill to promote thinking.)

Novel: Old Man & The Sea • perform character analysis of boy and man	**Author:** F. Scott Fitzgerald • analyze his style using an attribute web
Mysteries • analyze the attributes of a mystery story	**Poetry:** Limerick • analyze the patterns that make this a specific form

PRACTICE:

__________ •	__________ •
__________ •	__________ •

AWARENESS

That's a Good Idea

1. **D**efer judgment
   Opt for original
   Vast number of ideas
   Expand by piggybacking

2. Response In Turn
   Your Idea
   That's A Good Idea because. . .

3. Pass Rule

4. Keep Going Around

5. Chart

Topic	
Improvement	**Reason**
1.	1.
2.	2.
3.	3.

AWARENESS

Comparisons

1. How is ______________________ like a ________________________? Explain.

2. ______________ is like ________________ because both ________________________ ______________________________________.

3. ______________ is like ________________ because ____________________________ ______________________________________.

4. ______________ is like ________________ because ____________________________ ______________________________________.

Agree/Disagree Statements				
Statement	Before		After	
	Agree	Disagree	Agree	Disagree
1.				
2.				
3.				
4.				
5.				
6.				
7.				
8.				
9.				

The Thinker's Puzzle

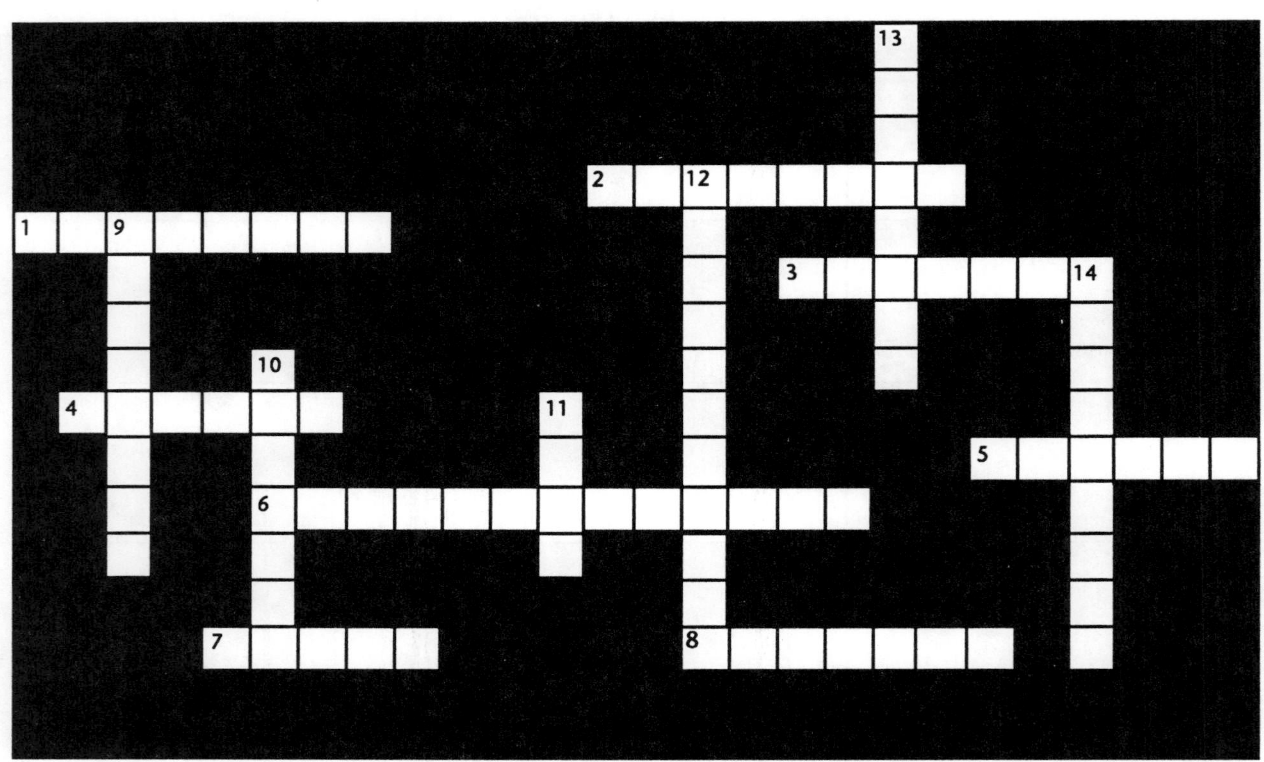

Across

1. Mind Designs
2. Analytical, evaluative thinking
3. Le Penseur
4. Abilities
5. Cooperative Teams
6. Thinking about thinking
7. Directory of operations for skills
8. Support and resource groups

Down

9. More basic than the basics
10. Risk-free Environment
11. Thinkers' notebooks
12. Communication
13. Fluent, flexible, generative thinking
14. Inductive and deductive thinking

AWARENESS

Quick Reference Lesson Planning Sheet

Consider these strategies . . .

CLIMATE FOR THINKING

- Student Repeat Directions
- Room Arrangement
- Hurrahs!
- Wait Time
- Multiple Answers
- Mobility
- Humor
- Expectations
- Student Responses
- That's a Good Idea!
- DOVE
- PACTS

SKILLS OF THINKING

- Brainstorm
- Predict
- Visualize
- Attribute
- Classify
- Prioritize

FOR	OF
WITH	**ABOUT**

- P.M.I.
- Mrs. Potter
- Log
- Wraparound
- What?
- So What?
- Now What?
- Bird's-Eye View

METACOGNITION ABOUT THINKING

STRUCTURED INTERACTION W/ THINKING

- Pairs
- Peer Review
- People Search
- Think/Pair Share
- 2-4-8
- Human Graph
- Coop.Groups
- Triad

- Thought Tree
- Venn Diagram
- Concept Map
- Rank Ladder
- Metaphor
- Web
- Hex Message
- Sequence Model
- Analogy
- Story Grid
- KWL
- D/M
- P/S

AWARENESS

Observing for Thinking

CLIMATE (For)	EXPLICIT SKILL INSTRUCTION (Of)
STRUCTURED INTERACTION (With)	METACOGNITION (About)

SECTION 3

CLIMATE

We must have ... a place where children can have a whole group of adults they can trust.

—Margaret Mead

Skillful Thinking in the Classroom

Just as it is necessary to build a tall building on a solid foundation, it is necessary to build skillful thinking in the classroom on two preconditions: (1) the teacher's mastery of the content and (2) the teacher's effectiveness in creating and managing positive conditions for thinking. Without a teacher who has mastered the subject, be it social studies, language arts, math or science, the students will lack a model who thinks about the content. Thinking skills do not work in a vacuum. They are not content free. They are immersed in content. Just as the coach, with experience and knowledge of the game, introduces the right skill at the right time for each player, the skilled teacher does the same for her thinking students.

A second important element is the teacher's skill as an effective classroom manager. The most effective thinking skills instruction won't cure a chaotic or disruptive classroom. Nor will it bring to life a classroom that is controlled through fear. At the very least, the teacher must be conducting a classroom in which students know and follow basic rules and there is a strong, on-task atmosphere well-grounded in respect and responsibility.

Given these preconditions, the soil is ready to plant the seed for critical and creative thinking. The thinking classroom is a classroom in which the teacher purposefully gives priority to teaching students multiple ways to think about what they are learning. In a concrete sense, this means she will structure opportunities for guided practice of the thinking skills, and teach the students how to transfer these skills into more difficult content. She will shift the emphasis in the classroom from a content/product orientation to a content/thinking process approach.

We live in a time of information overload. Faster than we can grasp the information that rains down on us each day, radical new discoveries wash away traditionally accepted theories.

In 25 years, the computer has shrunk in size from a two-story building accessible only to high level graduate students to a tiny micro-chip hidden in every car, thermostat and electrical appliance that is sold. Mail, not long ago trapped in week-long delivery schedules across town, now flies electronically around the world in minutes. Mass production jobs disappear from the want ads and are replaced by calls for computer programmers, technicians, and high-tech engineers.

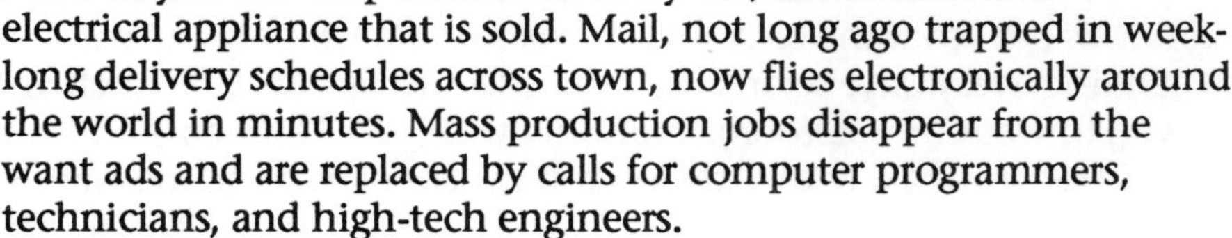

While the work, home, and leisure worlds have changed in the last two decades more rapidly than we could anticipate, only one world has remained essentially the same. Almost immune to improvement and innovation, the school seems forever trapped in the information acquisition model begun with the Gutenberg Press. The schoolhouse has done all it can to ignore the real power of the computer. Using a pre-chip mentality, schools change the curriculum solely by adding more: more information (Compare a high school U.S. History text of 25 years ago with one published this year. Note how much more information is jammed into the same course which 25 years ago couldn't cover all the information.); more courses (everyone who suffers from the "facts are learning"

disease wants to plug another course into the curriculum; driver's education, substance abuse, parenting, and so on); more of everything...except perhaps quality.

Most serious teachers are frustrated with the "cover it" mentality which has resulted from the idea that "more is better." "In the same amount of time, cover everything in the curriculum including what we added this year" translates to "don't slow down if students are struggling. Don't stop for an in-depth look at an important skill or concept. Don't investigate." There is no time. "Mrs. Smith's class," says the complaining parent, "is four chapters ahead." And what about the departmental exam that covers the whole book? Or the supervisor who asks: "Shouldn't you be further...?"

John Goodlad addressed this rat race in *A Place Called School*. As his researchers saw it, there are few classrooms in which the teachers do more than pump out information to their students. They saw teachers who talk, students who listen. Teachers construct scantron tests, students check off the facts. Ultimately, nationally standardized tests tell us that these same students cannot problem solve, think critically or argue logically to support a position.

To prepare our young people for the possibilities and probabilities of the future that few of us can imagine, the wisest course seems to be a curriculum that triggers their critical and creative thinking. The computer will store more information better than the most brilliant learner. By causing students to think, question, wonder, explore, analyze, debate, hypothesize, create and use wisely the avalanche of information they will encounter every day, an in-depth curriculum that focuses on thinking skills will provide more fertile ground for their intellectual growth in a high-tech world.

Given such a curriculum, every classroom teacher will have a major responsibility to promote every student's skills for thinking. The teaching technology exists by which any of us can change our classroom from the present pool of passivity to an action lab of active thinking.

However, rather than ask teachers to reinvent the wheel, we need only recognize, as Ron Edmonds did "that the technology exists. We need only the will." That technology, which is expanding every day, begins with the effective teaching research and includes methodologies proven to work in classrooms, not only with gifted students, but with students with learning disabilities, students with little interest in school, high school students, and kindergarten students.

Anyone who has been in school must concede that as teachers, we possess an almost absolute power within the classroom. Bruce Joyce says that "teaching is the second most private behavior." According to Marilyn Ferguson in *Aquarian Conspiracy*:

"Even doctors, in their heyday as godlike paragons, have never wielded the authority of a single classroom teacher, who are the purveyors of prizes, failure, love, humiliation, and information to a great number of relatively powerless, vulnerable young people."

Based on this belief that the teacher is without exception the key figure in the classroom, let's consider some important implications: the impact of teacher expectations, the roles the teacher plays in a "thinking classroom," cognitive research and the important methodology available for promoting skillful thinking.

1. **Expectations:** Thomas Good's research on teacher expectations offers convincing evidence that when teachers *expect* high quality learning, students sense these subtly disguised expectations and tend to live up to (or down to) them.
If and when teachers believe that all students *can* think and all students *need* to think, that message *is* communicated to the students. Teachers who value thinking challenge all students to stretch. These teachers cause students to interpret, analyze, translate, hypothesize, predict, apply, synthesize and evaluate what they learn. They expect students to discuss, debate, answer higher level questions, prove, write, think aloud and critically and creatively attack the ideas shared by the teacher, the texts and peers.

These teachers are *mindful decision-makers*, who take the time to dig deeply into carefully selected key ideas; who force thinking responses from all students; who ask probing questions and expect thoughtful answers from all students; who develop all students' thinking skills; and find new methods to challenge even the most reticent. In short, teachers' expectations for excellence in all students is modeled repeatedly in overt and deliberate teaching behaviors.

The key to high expectations, however, is more than commanding students to "think harder" and "think harder again." The tell-tale sign of high expectations in a classroom is the teacher's behavior toward low performing students. These are the students generally perceived as not doing their work, hiding in the back of the classroom, clowning around or regularly off task for one reason or another. Good's research indicates that teacher perception of student behavior is a major shaper not only of overt misbehavior, but also of self-concepts, achievement motivation and levels of aspiration.

Just as Henry Higgins was able to change Eliza Doolittle's self beliefs, so too every classroom teacher has an expectation impact on students. Some students learn from repeated praise, attention and success that they are expected to do very well. They strive to live up to that expectation. Others, year after year, get the signals that they are slow, awkward and poor workers. After a while they learn to act as they are expected.

Good and others have traced specific teacher behaviors which communicate to many students that not much is expected in the classroom. For one reason or another, very often through conscious stereotypes of race, sex or class, the teacher perceives certain students to be low academic performers. As a consequence, he communicates that low performance is all anyone can expect. These low expectations are communicated in a number of subtle ways.

What else does the research show about the low performers? Teachers smile at them less often, make less eye contact, call on them less, praise them less, give them less feedback, demand less effort and criticize them more. In the meantime, the same teachers give more wait-time, more cues and more follow-up questions to the students perceived as being more active learners.

The low performers find seats farther away from the teacher. This makes it easy for them to avoid monitoring and to slip into off-task behavior. In the meantime, those who see themselves as the high performers grab the front row. Some call this the Sunday Church Syndrome. If you don't want to be there, hide in the back pew and exit fast.

Although it may seem that teachers who promote thinking by all students must do everything except divide the Red Sea, their challenge is considerably less. Starting with the belief that all children can learn to think more critically and creatively, the effective teacher need do little more than add to her repertoire of skills and methodologies that promote skillful thinking. For examination, these are divided into four categories: teaching FOR thinking, by setting the climate; teaching OF thinking, by presenting the explicit skill: teaching WITH thinking, by structuring the interaction: and teaching ABOUT thinking, by metacognitive processing. But first, let's look at another key factor in the thinking classroom.

2. **Teacher Roles:** What roles do teachers play that demonstrate the value they place on thinking? To promote genuine "thinking" in the classroom, teachers take tremendous risks. As a high school physics teacher said: "In a thinking classroom, the sage must abdicate the stage." The teachers who foster thinking in the classroom make a conscious decision to give up their autonomy in that classroom. They relinquish "center stage" and instead assume several enabling roles. They are leaders who assume various, strategically effective roles dictated by circumstances. Marilyn Ferguson described the classroom leader in this way:

   "The open teacher...establishes rapport and resonance, sensing unspoken needs, conflicts, hopes and fears. Respecting the learner's autonomy, the teacher spends more time helping to articulate the urgent questions than demanding right answers....The teacher is...a midwife to ideas...a steersman, a catalyst—a facilitator—an agent of learning...."

   In addition, the works of Blanchard & Hersey (*Situational Leadership*) and Peters and Austin (*Passion for Excellence*) portray leadership roles within the same fluid framework of constantly shifting identities.

   Catalyst/Motivator: Motivation is ultimately intrinsic, but there are extrinsic strategies that set conditions to invite youngsters into the learning situation, that excite their curiosity and entice them to investigate further. As Dr. Madeline Hunter comments about motivation, "You can lead a horse to water, but you can't make him drink...but you can add salt to his oats." The catalyst/motivator role presumes that "first you've gotta hook them."

   For instance, at a recent mind-brain workshop, the trainer captured the curiosity of the participants. By suggesting that following a demonstration on "eye movements" the attendants would be able to "tell if someone was lying," he "hooked" them into the learning situation about to take place, a discussion of neuro-linguistic programming.

   Teacher/Educator: Instructional input, teaching methodology, development and implementation of lessons are the components of this role. The teacher demonstrates and models explicit skills as the instructional expert who presents content for student absorption. This role epitomizes the act of teaching as most of us conceive it.

   For instance, teaching the skill of classification explicitly, the teacher defines the terms, states the objective, provides instructional input through lecture, media or discussion, structures interaction for students to practice the skills, monitors, reinforces and gives immediate specific feedback.

   Facilitator/Coach: When facilitating thinking, the teacher is making it easier. She helps guide, gives specific direction, and coaches with focused attention on particular skill needs. The facilitator/coach is visible, on-the-scene, moving about to observe previously taught skills. The

leader in this role senses when *and* when *not* to intercede in the process; she's front and center when needs arise, but she assumes a low profile when the situation seems to be progressing well on its own. In this role she teaches by guiding the 'book group' as they process a novel; by clarifying the "trouble-shooting" as needed.

Counselor/Cheerleader: This role adheres to the "fluff them up" theory of positive reinforcement for developing student behaviors. It involves active listening, encouragement, 'cheering,' support and meaningful feedback. The counselor/cheerleader role is most often a one-to-one interaction, but there are instances in every classroom when group guidance, direction and support become necessary.

For instance, when a student shifts from an involved participant in discussions to a quiet, uninvolved by-stander, the sensitive teacher notes the variance and finds a private time to talk with the student. Similarly, a student successfully mastering long division is positively reinforced for his success.

Confronter/Disciplinarian: Although this is not a coveted role in the thinking classroom, it is at times a necessary one. The effective leader handles occasions that call for confrontation, routinely and skillfully as they arise. For instance, during a brainstorming session, one particular student consistently violates the DOVE Guidelines. The effective teacher notes this pattern of behavior and confronts the student appropriately.

Champion: Dr. Benjamin Bloom in *All Our Children Learning*, prods us to "imagine a classroom learning session which is so powerful that many students have almost total memory of it twenty years later...peak learning experiences...reveal the conditions which are essential to creating them...a charismatic instructor does much to create an atmosphere for peak experiences...(if) the students regard the teacher as one who is communicating some fundamental truth or...some way of viewing phenomena which is both unique and of great moment."

Peters and Waterman advance a similar idea of the necessity of this key figure in *In Search of Excellence*. They note that *without* committed champions, a handful of dedicated people with "know-how," energy, daring and the staying power to implement an idea, the idea dies. Teachers who believe in a "thinking classroom" display persistence and courage of heroic quality. They are zealous volunteers who present powerful role models to young people. These teachers are "insanely" good at what they do and what they do is create classrooms that cause students to become intensely involved in their thinking. The role these teachers play is truly one of CHAMPION OF COGNITION.

3. **Cognitive Research:** More than twenty years ago, Mary Budd Rowe introduced the research on wait time. More than fifteen years ago, Roger and David Johnson introduced us to the research on cooperative learning. In the past ten years, other researchers including Berliner, Good, Brophy, and Resnick have shared the results of their studies about other teaching strategies which marked specific ways to increase student achievement. In the last five years, the research of Resnick, Winograd, Brown and others on cognition, have provided us with an understanding of the reasons why strategies have worked. This evidence we call cognitive research.

What is cognitive research? It is the study of those effective teaching strategies which help students process information so they extract meaning from it. It includes what the teacher does to help students understand what they read or hear, solve word problems in math, think critically and creatively in all contents, transfer knowledge and skill to new areas, and think about their thinking in purposeful ways.

Cognitive research has special meaning for the improvement of learning. Because the research has shown us that learning is an active process that contributes to both long term and short term memory, we can no longer argue that learning is the result of rote recall or the artificial linking of bits of information. Rather than place emphasis on drill and practice, the teacher who operates from a cognitive perspective has the assurance that the time spent in processing information through wait-time, higher order thinking discussions and cooperative groups is the more valuable instructional activity for all students. Moreover, there is growing evidence that such processing time is a must for the lower achievers.

Interestingly, some of the best cognitive research has come from the area of reading. When it was noted that poor readers seemed to lack the flexible and fluent attack strategies of the better readers, used ineffective problem solving strategies and spent little time preparing for the reading task, the reading researchers began to look for instructional ways to correct the difficulty. Subsequent research suggested that the teacher could improve reading by cognitive instruction that encouraged the student to draw on the reader's knowledge base, provide the student with new learning strategies for thinking about reading, and refine the student's thinking skills with corrective feedback.

No piece of research has more value to us in this regard than the studies of metacognition. By teaching students to plan purposefully how they intend to think through a reading task and use learned strategies, how they can check or monitor their strategic reading and how they can self-evaluate and refine their thinking after the task, the researchers noted how much greater the successes were in reading achievement. More importantly, as students master the PME strategies (planning, monitoring, evaluating), they learn how to control their learning process and take charge of the reading tasks. The more closely we examine cognitive research, the more sharply it brings into focus the importance of taking the time to help students process information. This suggests the value of taking time to provide explicit instruction about thinking skills, teaching of thinking, and the development of student strategies in questioning and visualizing, as precursors of effective thinking about thinking. In specific terms, the cognitive research tells us why wait-time, higher order questions, teacher acceptance, a positive peer climate, cooperative groups, and the other effective teaching strategies worked to increase student achievement. These methods worked because they provided the structure, the time and the expectation for students to think about what they were learning, to make mental connections, and to transfer new insights into new situations.

If we take full advantage of cognitive research, it is important that we consider the time trap. Cognitive processing, to facilitate concept development in the content or to improve metacognitive strategies for use with course content, takes time. It takes time to structure the strategies and it takes more time for the students to practice. Where do we get the time? There are several possibilities.

(a) Cut down on drill and practice. See short drill and practices as a preparation for metacognitive discussion or as a check for individual progress after intense metacognitive work.

(b) Save dittos and workbooks for a rainy day. If you check most of your workbooks, they are asking students to *recall* information at least 90% of the time. Instead, take more time to focus students on the key concept of lesson, plan with them how they are going to apply information processing strategies and thinking skills, monitor their progress and evaluate how they thought through the task. Instead of covering the pages and answering the recall questions at the end of each chapter, ask higher order questions focused only on the critical concepts.

(c) Keep quiet. Before you begin intense work using effective teaching strategies, tape record several half hours of class time. Count the amount of time you use talking and the amount of talk time for students. The more you talk, the less time is available for students to process. If you are a long-winded lecturer, remember that the most attentive mind has little chance of absorbing more than 15-20 minutes of straight talk. Carefully select the most important information and spend at least half the class time to structure student processing of that information.

(d) Re-examine the curriculum and prioritize the most important information. Remember, most standardized tests do not ask for material recall. They test application, analysis, problem solving and other thinking skills. If you are concerned that you can't cover what is "required," recall your days as a "crammer" and what little recall of those facts you now have. If you still want more memory, know that time taken for processing will pay better results in recall and in transfer than many facts crammed for a test.

Most importantly, as students increase their ability to think effectively, they become more efficient in all their learning. At the minimum, wait-time will give you more attending for questions, more hands raised to process information and more active participation. It has been shown that cooperative grouping, when correctly used, increases achievement as well as student attention to task. Add to this the higher expectations for thinking and the attendant concentration by more students, and you have reduced off-task time. Thus, you spend less time correcting student misbehavior and more time with higher order learning. As lower achieving students master the thinking strategies and apply these to all class work, you will see even greater "time savings."

4. **The Methods:** What is it that the teacher does to help students think about their thinking and form their own patterns for thinking? First, the teacher sets the conditions which promote thinking in the classroom. Second, the teacher introduces students to the explicit skills and structures time for the students to practice the skills. As they explore the thinking skills, the teacher uses a variety of techniques that facilitate thinking about thinking.

(a) *The Thinking LOG:* As far back as Leonardo da Vinci, philosophers, poets and inventors have kept daily records of their reactions. They sketched, recorded anecdotes and traced how they were thinking. By using a LOG, students have a private place to play with their ideas, trace patterns of thought and try out, risk-free, new ways to develop their thinking.

(b) *The Lead-In:* Like leaves from a tree, new ideas sprout from short terms provided by the teacher. The stems prime the pump and help students expand their thinking on a topic. Short stems, such as "I think..." to longer stems are successful metacognitive starters.

(c) *The Wraparound:* Allowing each student a turn to comment on an idea helps students share perceptions and appreciate multiple ways to think about a topic.

(d) *Visual Formats:* Graphs, charts, matrices, +/-/? lists, and other visual formats help students structure how they are thinking and provide an easily recalled guide to use in new situations.

(e) *PME:* Questions to prepare, monitor and evaluate one's own thinking guide students through a clear, metacognitive framework. Whether drawn from Bloom or some other taxonomy, these questions make an easy to use tool for checking and improving the quality of one's thinking.

(f) *Creative Problem Solving:* Thinking skills are artificial tools for helping students understand the complexity of the thinking process. When the skills are used as a part of a purposeful process such as CPS, the tools take on a special value especially when facing complex problems. The process reminds us of the tools we have at our disposal so that we can think about which tools will most help us select the best solution.

Teaching For Thinking

The teaching for thinking, actively promoting all students to think about the subject matter, falls into two major subdivisions. In the first, the teacher takes time and care to create the conditions which encourage all students to think in the classroom. In the second, the teacher uses a variety of strategies to develop students' attitudes about themselves as problem solvers.

The Climate For Thinking

Many students acquire bad habits and bad attitudes about thinking in the classroom. They expect the teacher to do all the work. The slower the student, the more deeply ingrained are these non-thinking attitudes. By high school, where tracking further reinforces non-performance especially among basic students, a teacher might rightfully wonder if any thought is possible. As many teachers using the teaching for thinking strategies can attest, even in those students whose self-beliefs about their own capabilities are the most negative, changes do occur. This is not to say that roses will spring instantaneously from rock, but extra care and extra work will eventually bring change.

What are the most effective tools available if a teacher wants to set the climate for thinking?

1. ***Discussion Guidelines:*** Fears of ridicule, failure and being wrong prevent many students from active participation in classroom discussion. Over the years, many have learned that school success is a fast track to oblivion, "Don't get caught thinking." The norm is to keep quiet and let the teacher and one or two nerds do the work. To break this norm and to reassure students that they don't have to worry about being shot down by the teacher or their peers, establish guidelines for expected behavior during discussion. Needless to say, these will build upon any rules already in place to promote positive classroom behavior. The DOVE Guidelines are practical and easy to remember.

D = DEFER JUDGMENT! Do not use put-downs or make positive or negative judgments about others' ideas.
O = OPT FOR OFF-BEAT! As a thinker, be different. Try different ways, seek a new combination.
V = VAST NUMBERS ARE NEEDED! Go for quantity. From quantity comes quality.
E = EXPAND! Piggyback or hitchhike on others' ideas.

Post these guidelines and discuss each point. Students can keep a copy of the guidelines in their LOGS.

2. ***Structured Questions For Discussion:*** If students learn to identify the types of questions they are being asked, they will more quickly cue into the type of thinking they are expected to do. Although Benjamin Bloom did not create his cognitive taxonomy for this purpose, categories of his questions can help teachers stimulate thoughtful discussion.

After sharing with the class the DOVE Guidelines, the teacher can initiate a discussion of the guidelines' meaning and application by asking sample challenge questions from the taxonomy.

(a) In your own words, explain each of the letters.
(b) How do you think the ideas of DOVE will help you during classroom discussions?
(c) What reason do you think I have for insisting on everyone following these guidelines?
(d) What would happen if you had to follow the DOVE Guidelines in every class?
(e) Agree or disagree with the idea that it is important to discuss what you are learning in class.

Following the discussion about DOVE, label for the students the type of CHALLENGE questions you asked.

(a) Checking for Understanding: "in your own words, explain..."
(b) Application: "how can you..."
(c) Analysis: "what reason..."
(d) Synthesis: "what would happen if..."
(e) Evaluation: "agree..."

Post a chart with the DOVE Guidelines and a chart with the CHALLENGE questions on a bulletin board. Let the students know that you expect all to live by the DOVE Guidelines and that you will be asking all to take turns answering the CHALLENGE questions.

3. ***Wait-Time:*** Asking questions, even in the structured sequence described above, will not accomplish the goal of involving all students in the discussion. With the questions must go the strategic use of what the science researcher Mary Budd Rowe called "wait-time."

If there is a single strategy that will yield immediate and dramatic increases in student involvement and interaction, that strategy is "wait-time!" What is wait-time? It is simply: SILENCE! SILENCE! SILENCE! MAGICAL SILENCE! That's it! Silence! Wait 3 to 10 seconds after asking a question. Wait! Just wait! Count silently! Grit your teeth! Pick your fingernail! But wait! And watch what happens. Not only will the length of student response increase, but the probability of clarification, extension, justification and on-task conversation will increase too. Students will begin to listen to each other. Expecting immediate teacher verification and not getting it, classmates nervously will support and defend their own or each other's points of view. They will elaborate and give personal, relevant examples. They will begin to bridge the new concept to past learning and they will demonstrate evidence of THINKING! Just by your silence student participation will noticeably increase.

Although "wait-time" is not new, it is essential to the "thinking classroom." The research documents the effect of "rapid fire" questioning patterns. Students soon learn that the teacher really isn't interested in thoughtful answers, only quick answers. The effective teacher will communicate that effective thinking by all is a pre-eminent expectation. Thus, that teacher will:

(a) Wait 3-10 seconds after each question before calling on any responder.
(b) Wait 3-10 seconds after the last response before introducing a new question.
(c) Seek multiple responses to the same question, even when recall is used.
(d) Move close to a student who doesn't usually answer.
(e) Ask the question to the class, wait, and then call on the first student.
(f) Establish eye contact and cue the students.

(g) If the student's answer is incomplete, continue questions or paraphrase the response and ask for clarification.
(h) Reinforce the correct response and/or the students' willingness to "hang in there."

4. ***Forced Responses:*** In a BBC program aired on PBS, Private David Jones, a wounded British soldier, faces his class at a private school. His natural order of questions modeled the forced responses. "Suppose," he asked, "that the royalists had won the war. How would history be recorded differently?" The class was silent. Jones waited. Finally, he called on a boy in the last row. "Dobson?" Dobson shook his head. "I don't know, sir."

   Jones rephrased the question. Dobson was silent. Jones waited. "Would the winner's point of view predominate?" "I think no, sir." "Why do you say that, Dobson?" "Because, sir, history is history." "What do you mean by that?" "Well, sir, the facts never change." "Anything more?" "Yes, sir, I believe..." and Dobson continued. When he finished, Private Jones said, "That was good thinking, Dobson. That is what you are here for."

   Forced responses are specific enabling behaviors which will encourage all students to think actively about *all* questions. "When I ask a question, I expect all to try for their best answer." To assist the *reticent student* the teacher can prompt involvement and break habits of apathy and passivity.

   The teacher can encourage responses with techniques that encourage all to participate successfully.

   (a) *Seat Assignments.* As often happens in church, persons who want a fast exit sit in the back rows. The devout seek the front pew. Likewise, in school students who don't like class, feel inadequate or prefer to be elsewhere, seek seats or lab stations far removed from the teacher if given the opportunity. The eager students go front and center.

   Students learn early in their school careers that teachers attend most to the students with quick answers. To avoid teachers' academic attention, unmotivated students pick the far seats, avoid eye contact, don't raise their hands, and answer as briefly as possible.

   To counteract this well-learned, active avoidance, effective teachers will use planned strategies which keep the avoidance close at hand.

   (1) Assign seats by performance. Place high performers in the back, low performers to the front.
   (2) Move around the room. Be sure avoiders are seated in major paths with quick access.
   (3) Let students elect their seats. Each week, place your desk on a different side of the room.
   (4) Start multiple responses by calling on students most removed from you.
   (5) Use the wraparound calling on each student in turn.

   (b) *Signals.* Signals force all students to take a *public position on a question.* If students are sure you will call upon them they will be more inclined to listen to your questions, your instructions, your information. When a signal is accompanied by an attitude on your part that says: "I expect everyone to think, in fact, I'm ecstatic when everyone thinks!" you will find up to a 100% increase in what the students have to say.

There are several practical signals for use in a thinking classroom:

(1) Pre-announced "All Hands." "Think about your *best* answer to my question. When you have answer, raise your hand. When I see *all hands up* I'll call on several students for responses." This leaves open that the "several" may be students who have not raised a hand.

(2) "Thumbs ups." Pre-teach the signal. When you want a response, ask for thumbs up, sideways or down. Everyone must select and signal one option (post cards, palms out, colored cards, etc., also work).

(3) "Hands up." Pre-teach this signal. When students are working on a task, either together or alone, you will raise your hand to interrupt or end the task. When students see your raised hand, they will end their tasks, raise their own hands, and focus attention to you. After you have explained the process, ask all students to signal with "thumbs up" how well they each understood, call on one to paraphrase the instruction, gather other responses if needed to have the full answer, reinforce appropriately and end with the entire class practicing "hands up."

(c) *Equal Responsibility to Answer.* Active students who quickly raise hands have the most chance to be called on. In some programs, one or two students can give 95% of all answers as they dialogue with the teacher. The effective teacher calls on all students equally and without a predictable pattern. Thus, every student knows that any question may be his/her question and must be ready to answer. Your dependency on the "quick answering" student will be broken.

There are several ways to build the equal response habit:

(1) Put all names in a hat. Ask a question, pull a name.

(2) Never call a name before a question.

(3) Set a random pattern in you gradebook each week. Check off each name that answers. Work through the whole class.

(4) Use the wraparound with multiple answers. Ask a question; and have each student in turn make a response or say "I pass."

(5) Make your classroom into a Bingo board. Keep numbers in a bingo bin, spin and draw.

In addition to spreading initial questions around the classroom, be sure you spread your extending question. Extending questions ask students to clarify answers, analyze, and evaluate. Usually the most verbal students get this attention. Low participators learn to give superficial grunts because they are never asked to extend.

Some examples of good *extenders* are:

"Can you give me an example of __________?"
"Tell me how..."
"How is that similar to __________?"
"How is that different from __________?"

"What might you do differently when _________?"
"In your own words, _________."

When extending a student response, you will use congruent body language to communicate patience and acceptance of the student's effort to think. When necessary use nonverbal (head nods, eye contact, smiles) and verbal encouragers to draw the student out. Above all, recall that every student must have the equal chance, the equal responsibility to answer all questions.

(d) *Selective Reinforcement.* The most destructive myth about reinforcement is that every student needs reinforcement for every answer. Rubbish. When a teacher spends half her time saying "good," "wonderful," "excellent" to every student response, she is having no more positive effect than static in a radio opera. At best, the static is blocked out. At worst, it is a waste of time and energy.

Effective reinforcement is selective. The teacher picks a *single accomplishment that a specific student makes* and carefully reinforces that behavior each time it is repeated. For instance, rather than reinforcing all students all the time for raising hands to answer, the teacher will give special note to the student who has been reticent until this question, "I'm glad that you attempted to answer, Marcia. Your analysis was very complete." When Marcia becomes a regular hand raiser, the teacher will stop the reinforcement for that behavior. In short, the teacher selects reinforcement for specific, appropriate instances of new, *developing behavior.* When students are learning to think, it is best to reinforce the thinking process, not the answer.

5. ***Hurrahs and Other Indicators of Acceptance.*** Driekurs has shown us the importance of acceptance, especially during the tumultuous years when we are forming our self concept. When there is no feedback for expected effort or the only feedback comes as criticism, it is easy to doubt one's own worth. When others give us positive strokes, earnestly for a job well done, we are sparked to continue the effort. Within the thinking classroom, where frequent risk taking is not only encouraged, but expected, it is doubly important that we know our ideas and efforts at thinking are recognized. A variety of techniques, appropriately selected, will encourage students' positive feelings about the value of their thinking.

Recognition of real effort or meaningful achievement is a basic emotional response. We want to feel appreciated and valued. We need positive strokes from others to signal recognition of that worth. When this recognition is earnest and appropriate, it invariably sparks further effort. Within the thinking classroom, where frequent risk-taking is not only encouraged, but expected, recognition is a must. It sets a non-threatening tone; an accepting climate, where encouragement and regard for all students is a priority.

Techniques that provide recognition can focus on both groups and individuals.

(a) *Hurrahs!*
The 'hurrah' is a wonderful often spontaneous action to signal recognition of another or to energize the group as a whole.

(1) *North Country Hurrah*
An enthusiastic, but silent waving of the hands overhead, in shivering fashion,

constitutes the North Country hurrah.

(2) *Standing "O"*
Place both arms overhead in a classic ballet position creating a "standing ovation," or the standing "O."

(3) *Give A Hand*
To give a hand, place the right arm across the chest and over the opposite shoulder. Then "pat" yourself on the back for a job well-done.

(b) *Encouraging Statements:* Encouragement occurs before the event: praise comes after. You encourage a five year old to balance on her two wheeler as you push/hold her down the street. When finally, she takes off peddling frantically without your steady hand (and sore back!), you praise her accomplishment. Encouragement communicates your belief in the student's capability. "I know you can do this next problem. It's difficult, but you have done tougher problems correctly."

(c) *Post-it Note:* A brief, specific, positive note of praise "posted" on a student paper or desk is a 'warm fuzzy' that is usually saved and reread many times. It also models communication through writing.

(d) *Equal Help:* Help is often construed by students as something they receive outside the classroom, after school. It is shunned because student norms have dictated for eons against seeking help. Helping is easily seen as "brown nosing." Some teachers even see students seeking help as manipulators. "Oh, she's just trying to get my attention." or "He's trying to get a better grade." Far worse, some students avoid help because they believe getting help has something to do with being bright or dumb. "If anybody knew I couldn't do those problems, well...." As a teacher, you must help students overcome this fear by encouraging your students to seek help.

Help starts in the classroom. If a teacher does more than pour information into empty student heads for regurgitation (a recent study showed that in many classrooms, up to 89% of the time is spent this way!), the teacher will provide structured discussion time. That time will help the teacher analyze what student "thinking" difficulties are and *help* the student. If any student is having difficulty *applying* knowledge (i.e., basic math skills to word problems), transferring knowledge (i.e., making generalizations), seeing relationships (i.e., how is a literary character similar to current government leaders), the teacher will help the student with the thought processes. The teacher will not worry about "how" much time this is taking away from my lesson plan."

Such help may come in guided individual practice as the teacher walks around the classroom and monitors especially those students who might have difficulty, in cooperative group reviews or in all class discussions in which mistakes are analyzed and corrected.

Most importantly, all students, especially the learners who have the most learning difficulties, will *perceive* that the teacher does provide equal help for all.

(e) *Dignifying Responses:* Every student will not answer every question appropriately. Rather than embarrass a student by put downs ("That's a stupid answer."), sarcasm ("You might try studying."), guilt trips ("Don't you realize what you are doing to yourself?"), or personal insults ("You are dumb, aren't you?"), an effective teacher will dignify the responses by noting the correct part of the answer ("Tom, you're correct about the number of accidents recorded in 1985."), and ask other students to build on that ("And, who can clarify the major causes?"). If the student is totally off on a single right answer, at least acknowledge the effort *with* sincerity. You may avoid this trap, however, by *always* seeking multiple answers and then selecting the correct answer. For instance, if you asked students to solve this word problem, you would dignify responses this way. "I'm going to list several answers on the board." As you get each answer say "Thank You" and record it. "Now I'm going to compare answers." Select but don't identify the correct answer and work through the problem to show the correct process. Ask the students with the incorrect process/answer to show you what they could correct in their own example. Reinforce them for identifying the change because you "have caught them thinking."

(f) *Focusing on Concerns:* Just as teachers may come to school with concerns and problems which make it hard to focus on the day's task, students may also be hindered from their day's task of learning. Without turning every class into a counseling session, the effective teacher helps students with these concerns.

(1) *Academic Concerns:* Homework assignments, questions about yesterday's class discussion, a due reading assignment—each can block a student's concentration on the here and now lesson.

(2) *Personal Concerns:* A family death, finances, lost materials, a stolen bike may dominate a student's feelings as the day begins.

The easiest approach is the preventive approach. At the beginning of the day, or the start of the class, the teacher can ask for Comfort, Concerns and Continuity: "What issues, problems, or concerns are you experiencing which will keep you from giving full attention to today's lessons?" sometimes students will identify that they are worried about a coming special assignment or test; other times, it may be forgotten lunch money, a medical appointment. More often, there are no responses to the 3 C's, but the effort is appreciated.

In deciding how to answer concerns, the teacher must make several decisions. The first is centered on the issue what is best for the student, the second on what is best for the class and the third is based on time.

a. *The Student.* Is a full answer needed now? or can it be saved for a private tete-a-tete? If the latter is true, indicate a short answer now and a complete answer at a specific time and place. "Kate, my short answer is that all buses will leave at 5 p.m. If you need a longer explanation, see me at the door on the way to lunch."

b. *The Class.* Will the entire class benefit from the public response? Is it a general concern that needs a public response? If so, decide on how much time you will need to allot.

c. *The Time.* All effective discussions are a question of time. The formal concerns session is best limited to five minutes. Obviously, a major concern that involves many students will need more time.

A Special Note: It is important to recall that concerns are a feeling issue. Therefore, it is best to focus on the feeling, not the event. If you provide only solutions to a problem, without checking for a changed feeling tone, the concern will remain. If the student's feelings are sufficiently strong and not resolved, you can bet no thinking will occur that day!

Obviously, a formal five minute, 3C session at the beginning of the day will not eliminate concerns or issues that might arise in a day. The 3C sessions is designed to give students a comfortable time to bring up issues. As issues arise during the day you can help the student decide whether the concern can wait until the next morning, or must be resolved at once. As with concerns identified in the morning session, you will want to (a) reflect on the feeling, (b) focus on the concern with a "what do you want," (c) and check that the feelings behind the concern are resolved.

(g) *Talking Up:* A crucial variable in each of the behaviors described in this unit is *tone*. Tone of voice, as in "don't speak to me in that tone of voice!" is subtle. A slight inflection can change a warm praise into a sarcastic bite. The effective teacher communicates with a warm, business like tone. Sarcastic and sardonic tones which have the purpose of putting a student down or hurting the student are unnecessary and ineffective. While "cuts" may silence a student for a moment, more likely they will silence a student for a long, long time. More effective than talking down, is talking up...finding the positive thing to say to each student.

How long you will have to work with any given class to set the conditions for thinking will depend on the learning history and the personalities of each class. If you are in high school or junior high, the time variable may even depend on the period of the day. What you do with you first period of class may differ drastically from what works sixth period. It will also depend on how students are grouped in your school, their past experiences and parental attitudes.

Given your success with setting the conditions for thinking you can increase the challenge to think. By increasing the students' familiarity with higher order questions and by asking more and more extending questions of all the students, you will improve their discussion skills and promote greater quality in how they think about your course content. BEWARE!!! You will also increase the amount of time you spend on each lesson.

Extending Student Thinking: (More Questions)

As you spend more time with discussion in your course, you and the students can refine question asking skills. They will soon discover that there are many words which structure responses to questions. When asked in a sequence the question cues resemble the rungs of a ladder. The "lower" questions are easy to reach; the higher require more complex thinking.

F Evaluation
E Synthesis
D Analysis
C Application
B Comprehension
A Recall

(A) Can students recall factual information?
(1) A memorized list (short).
(2) A memorized definition.
(3) A memorized sequenced list by time, by importance, and by anagram.

(B) Can students understand concepts?
(1) Translate into own words.
(2) Paraphrase simple statements.
(3) Explain in own words "what this means to me."

(C) Can students apply a concept?
(1) Relate the day-to-day use of the concept.
(2) Describe uses of the idea in school or home situations.

(D) Can students analyze a concept?
(1) How object is like another? (physical example)
(2) How the objects are different?
(3) How object is like another? (abstraction)
(4) How to classify objects?

(E) Can students think creatively?
(1) Make a change in an idea?
(2) Predict what would happen if you...?"
(3) Forecast consequences?

(F) Can students evaluate?
(1) Tell why they like __________?
(2) Explain which is best __________?
(3) Judge which is most __________?
(4) Decide __________?

There are innumerable question keys at each level. Here is a chart for your reference.

Sample Questions and Key Words To Use In Developing Questions

I. **Knowledge** (Eliciting factual answers, testing recall and recognition)

Who
What
Why
When
Where
How
How much
Recall
Describe
Define
Memorize
Select
Which One
Name
Point Out
Label
List
Reproduce

II. **Comprehension** (Translating, interpreting, and extrapolating)

State In Your Own Words
What Does This Mean
Select The Definition
State In One Word
What Part Doesn't Fit
Read The Graph Table
This Represents
Explain
Define
Locate
Give an Example
Condense This Paragraph
Explain What Is Happening
Explain What Is Meant
What Restrictions Would You Add
What Exceptions Are There
What Are They Saying
Indicate
Tell
Translate
Outline
Summarize
Select
Match
Identify

III. **Application** (Using in situations that are new, unfamiliar to students)

How Would You Use
What Is The Use For
Tell What Would Happen
Choose The Statements
Tell How Much change
Make A Lesson
Demonstrate How
If...How
That Apply
There would Be
Show How
Apply
Construct
Explain
Identify

IV. **Analysis** (Breaking down into parts, relating parts to the whole)

Distinguish
Diagram
Similar
Like
Chart
Plan
Dissect
Contrast
Cause For
Arrange
Separate
Conclude
Outline
Different

Graph
Classify
Compare
Differentiate
Reason For
Investigate

What inconsistencies, Fallacies
What Literacy Form Is Used
What Persuasive Technique
What Relationship Between
What Is The Function Of
What's Fact, Opinion
State The Point of View Of
What Ideas Justify Conclusion
What Assumptions
What Motive Is There
What Conclusions
Make A Distinction
What Is The Premise
Implicit In The Statement Is The Idea Of
What's The Theme, Main Idea, Subordinate Idea
The Least Essential Statements Are
What Does Author Believe, Assume
Deduce
What Statement Is Relevant, Extraneous To
Related To, Not Applicable
Categorize

V. **Synthesis** (Combining elements into a pattern not clearly there before)

Write
Create
Tell
Make
Do
Choose
Hypothesize
Plan
Compose
Combine
Estimate
Invent
Build
Make A Film
Solve
Make Up
Dance
Advertise
What If
Design
Develop
Invent
Forecast
Construct
Blend
How Would You Test
Propose An Alternative
Solve The Following
Formulate A Theory
How Else Would You
What Different If
State A Rule
Imagine
Infer
Predict

VI. **Evaluation** (Judging according to some set of criteria and stating why)

Appraise
Editorialize
Which Is Best
Choose Why
Judge
Decide
Verify
Evaluate
Criticize
Rate
Dispute
Find The Errors
Defend
Value
Grade

What Fallacies, Consistencies, Inconsistencies Appear
Which Is More Important, Moral, Better, Logical, Valid, Appropriate, Inappropriate

A social studies lesson using higher order questions might look like this:

The Causes of The Black Plague

I. **Anticipatory Set:** (3 minutes) Describe to the students what happened last year when half the school had the flu.

II. **Input:** (20 minutes)
1. Define the word "plague."
2. Give examples of various plagues.
3. Lecture on the Black Plague
   A. Causes
   B. Effects
   C. Major Statistics

III. **Discussion:** (15 minutes)
1. In your own words, describe the causes and effects of the Black Plague (Comprehension)
2. What would result today if the Black Plague struck this school? (Application)
3. Graph the death tolls for three counties struck by the plague. (Analysis)
4. If you were the county medical doctor, how would you help a plague victim? (Synthesis)
5. Defend the people who wouldn't help the plague victims. (Evaluation)

The same procedure will work with stories. Primary students might discuss a fairy tale.

The Three Little Pigs

I. **Anticipatory Set:** (3 minutes). Ask the students to predict what would happen to them if their house was blown away.

II. **Input:** (5 minutes). Read the story, "The Three Little Pigs."

III. **Discussion:** (15 minutes)

1. Recall key facts. (Recall)
2. In your own words, tell what happened to the pigs. (Understanding)
3. What would you do if a bad person knocked on your door? (Application)
4. How were the pigs' houses different? (Analysis)
5. What would have happened if a police officer were present? (Synthesis)
6. Explain why you think the pigs were good thinkers or bad thinkers. (Evaluation)

VII. **Closure:** Check predictions made earlier in class.

All children need time to reflect on information. The more we know about metacognition, the thinking about thinking, the more we recognize the importance of structuring time for students to think about the information we provide. Yes, this will mean less information and more discussion. When we provide that time by asking well-structured questions, we are teaching *for* thinking.

In *Catch Them Thinking*, we have integrated the many strategies which promote skillful thinking in the classroom. The more of these strategies you have in your repertoire the more you will succeed in promoting more skillful thinking by all your students.

Asking Questions

KNOWLEDGE: Can students RECALL information?

???

COMPREHENSION: Can students EXPLAIN ideas?

???

APPLICATION: Can students USE ideas?

???

ANALYSIS: Do students SEE relationships?

???

SYNTHESIS: Can students combine ideas and CREATE a new entity?

???

EVALUATION: Can students make JUDGMENTS and support them?

CLIMATE

THE THINKER'S PENCIL bookmark...

PATTERNS FOR THINKING

EVALUATION
Decide
Rank
Defend
Verify
Critique

SYNTHESIS
Hypothesize
Infer
Predict
Imagine
Estimate
Invent

ANALYSIS
Compare/Contrast
Make an analogy
Classify
Sequence
Give cause

APPLICATION
Apply
Demonstrate
Illustrate
Generalize
Show how

PATTERNS FOR THINKING

EVALUATION
Decide
Rank
Defend
Verify
Critique

SYNTHESIS
Hypothesize
Infer
Predict
Imagine
Estimate
Invent

ANALYSIS
Compare/Contrast
Make an analogy
Classify
Sequence
Give cause

APPLICATION
Apply
Demonstrate
Illustrate
Generalize
Show how

Ask the Right Question

BACKGROUND In marketing, a basic operating principle is "ask the right question and you will get chaos." To learn how to ask the right question, the one that will give the answer we want, is a difficult skill to master. When asking the question in the context of skillful thinking, what we want is responses that show the students are applying thinking skills well. This means the students recognize what type or level of thinking is being asked (Critical or Creative? Analytical? Evaluative?) and how to use the needed mental operations.

To help students recognize what they are being asked to do as thinkers and to facilitate using different thinking skills, it helps that they learn labels, definitions and samples as "mental coat hooks" on which to hang their thinking patterns. One highly successful method is to teach the students patterns of questions. Although it is not the only approach, nor was it compiled for this purpose, Bloom's cognitive taxonomy serves as a useful tool.

THINKING SKILL: INVESTIGATING

FOCUS ACTIVITY On the overhead, display this saying:

"Even if you are on the right track, you will get run over if you just sit there." Will Rogers

Ask the following questions. Allow wait time. Seek multiple responses to each question. In the last question, encourage students to supply a rationale or proof of the judgments. Don't forget DOVE.

1. In you own words, explain the key idea of the quote.
2. What would result if you were to use this idea with you school work?
3. What assumptions does Rogers make about life?
4. Propose your own theory about life.
5. Agree or disagree with Rogers. Give proof for your answer.

OBJECTIVE To identify four (4) patterns for asking questions.

INPUT Give each student a copy of The Thinker Pencil.

They can include the page in their notes or cut out the pencil for a bookmark. You may also want to make a larger poster copy of the pencil and keep it displayed in the front of the room. Discuss the importance of asking the right question and the value of thinking about information in a variety of ways. Questions not only seek answers, but if open ended, they will stimulate thinking.

When you give out the pencils, spend some time reviewing the vocabulary or assign students to use the dictionary. Check for understanding.

Ask the Right Question

ACTIVITY Instructions:

1. Select a story, paragraph from student text, popular song, a short video documentary, news editorial, a non-fiction article from a magazine, etc., and give a copy to each student.

2. Assign the students to groups of three. Give each group a sheet of newsprint, tape and markers. Select recorder, leader and time keeper.

3. Allow 15 minutes for the task. Each group will invent 4 questions, one from each group on the pencil about the story or article. (You may want each group to use a different article.) The recorder will write the question on the newsprint.

4. Post the questions and instruct each group leader to walk through the questions, labeling the type of question being asked (i.e., analysis, synthesis, etc.) Give feedback and modify.

METACOGNITIVE DISCUSSION Ask the following questions. Seek multiple responses.

1. Explain in your own words and give an example of the following: application, analysis, synthesis, evaluation.

2. Explain how you might use each of the different levels of questions if you were a teacher.

3. What are some sound reasons for learning the different ways to think?

4. What would happen to you if you had to answer analytic and evaluative questions in every class?

CLOSURE In your LOG, write an editorial in which you defend the current way grades are given in your school (or some other practice of student interest).

CLIMATE

CATCH THEM READY TO THINK

Fat and Skinny Questions

1. Start with a **TOPIC.**
2. **BRAINSTORM** a list of questions that would help them learn about it.
3. **EVALUATE** questions: FAT questions get FAT answers!
   Skinny questions get "Yes," "No," "Maybe so!"

Topic: Earthquakes	Easy	Hard	Skinny	Fat
1. When do they happen?	X		X	
2. How do we get rid of them?		X		X
3. Where do they occur?	X		X	
4. Can we control them?		X		X

4 . **CHOOSE** the best questions (the FAT ones).

5. **SEQUENCE** the FAT questions.

6. State **GOAL.** (When answered, what will you know?)

7. **ADD**, modify, revise.

8. **RESEARCH.**

9. Review and **ASSESS.** (Were the FAT questions helpful in directing your research?)

Setting the Climate: Teacher Expectations

THE AVERAGE CHILD

I don't cause teachers trouble
my grades have been okay.
I listen in my classes
and I am in school every day.

My teachers think I am average
my parents think so too.
I wish I didn't know that
cause there is lots I would like to do.

I would like to build a rocket
I have a book that tells you how,
Or start a stamp collection
well no use in trying now.

'Cause since I found I am average
I am just smart enough you see
to know there is nothing special
that I should expect of me.

I am part of that majority
that hump part of the bell
who spends his life unnoticed
in an average kind of hell.

—Anonymous

Response Strategy: Wait Time

AVERAGE TEACHER

- Wait time #1 = 1 second
- Wait time #2 = .9 seconds
- Asks three to five questions in a minute, sometimes ten questions a minute
- Asks 400 questions in short class session
- Repeats (mimics) every student response
- 25 percent of words are *very good* and *wonderful*
- Rewards indiscriminately
- Looks for the answer

Why do teachers do these things?

Pacing? Control?

Result: The focus is on the teacher, not on the content.

How To Use Wait Time

1. Wait at least three seconds after asking a question to let the student begin a response. Say to yourself, "One thousand one, one thousand two, one thousand three...." It sounds simple, but the silence can be deafening the first few times.

2. Wait at least three seconds after any response before continuing the question or asking a new one. This second wait time recognizes the possibility that the student may wish to elaborate on the initial response.

3. Avoid verbal signals—positive or negative—in asking questions. Among the most common cues are "Isn't it true that...?" and "Think!"

4. Eliminate mimicry, i.e., repeating the response a student has just made.

5. Eliminate verbal rewards ("OK," "Fine," "Good," "Right") and negative sanctions (the typical "yes, but..." pattern, in which the teacher completes the answer or restates the question).

Benefits of Wait Time Strategy

STUDENT BEHAVIOR

1. The length of the students' responses increased.
2. The number of freely offered and appropriate student responses, unsolicited by the teacher, increased.
3. Failure to respond—"I don't know" or no answer—decreased.
4. Inflected responses decreased, thus students appeared to be more confident in their answers.
5. The number of speculative responses increased, thus students appeared to be more willing to think about alternative explanations of the subject matter at hand.
6. Children worked together more at comparing data.
7. Children made more inferences from evidence.
8. The frequency of questions raised by students increased.
9. The frequency of responses by students who were rated relatively "slow" by their teachers increased.

Periodically, have a peer coach sit in on one of your class discussions and record the number of times students initiate questions. Is this increasing over time?

Benefits of Wait Time Strategy

TEACHER BEHAVIOR

1. Teachers became more flexible in their responses—i.e., more willing to listen to diverse answers and to examine their plausibility.

2. Teachers' questioning patterns became more manageable; questions decreased in number, but showed greater variety and quality.

3. There was some evidence that teachers raised their expectations of students who had been rated as relatively "slow."

CLIMATE

Try This

Tape-record a class discussion. Check the number of questions you ask and how long you pause between questions.

Plus/Minus/Intriguing	
P(+) Plus	
M(-) Minus	
I(?) Intriguing	

CLIMATE

Tips for Teaching Thinking

Teach	thinking by modeling; demonstrate and label critical and creative thinking as it occurs.
Expect	all students to think skillfully; be aware of implied messages; believe that *all kids can think.*
Ask	questions that cause "something" to go on inside the student's head.
Create	cooperative groups for processing information; invite student-to-student interaction.
Help	students process strategies metacognitively; help them think about their learning and thinking by planning, monitoring and evaluating with them.

Tolerate	noise, movement and "failures"; a thinking classroom is a "busy" place.
Have	fun! Your enthusiasm for learning is contagious in the classroom; the kids will catch it.
Invite	multiple responses to carefully designed, divergent questions; ask "Why?"
Nurture	thinking by arranging your classroom to encourage intense, involved student interactions.
Keep	silent! Use "wait time," a three- to ten-second pause, after asking a question; let them think.
Insist	on intelligent behaviors by guiding students to make their own decisions and solve their own problems.
Never	stop moving. Teacher mobility in the classroom impacts positively on student interaction.
Give	the kids responsibility for their own learning; don't tell them; involve them.

The Listening Post

BACKGROUND

To make it easy for students to share thinking, it helps if they develop listening and speaking skills. As we listen to each other, our bodies and behaviors tell the person speaking more than we realize. By sensitizing students to helpful and non-helpful listening behaviors, we lay the groundwork for more productive classroom discussions.

THINKING SKILL: ACTIVE LISTENING

FOCUS ACTIVITY

Divide students into pairs. Designate the taller student in each pair as B; the other A. Have all Bs attend to the first instructions.

1. Think of a time in your life when you had something important to tell your friends, but no one would listen. Prepare to describe that event to your partner. What did you want to say? Who didn't listen? What happened?
2. Bs recall the story while the As are given their instructions.
3. As will recall what it takes to be a good listener (i.e., you look at the person (eye contact), you nod your head, you look interested, you lean slightly forward, you don't interrupt, you smile). Good listening takes hard work.

OBJECTIVE

To identify helpful listening behaviors.

INPUT

On the overhead or board list behaviors. Ask the students to tell you what they see or note when someone is listening to them. Demonstrate or provide the clues they need.

ACTIVITY

Instructions:

1. Check that the storytellers are ready.
2. Check that the others have an idea of what behavior is expected of a good listener. After they assent, tell them that they are to work with the assigned partner, but they may *not listen to* the partner. They are to behave the opposite of how a good listener behaves as long as they follow these simple rules: (1) stay in room; and (2) nobody gets hurt.
3. Encourage the storytellers to follow the same rules and try to get their story told.
4. After two minutes, signal the students to stop, return to their seats and attend to you.
5. Instruct the non-listeners to apologize and shake hands for their misbehavior.
6. Ask the storytellers to describe the non-listening behaviors they experienced. Make a master list.

The Listening Post

METACOGNITIVE DISCUSSION

1. Change the pairs. Invite students to pick a different partner. Give instructions to the new pairs.

   A. Study the non-helpful behaviors. Make a joint list of the opposite behaviors which would tell you that someone *was* listening to you. (3 minutes)

   B. Take your partner and make a foursome with another pair.

   C. Share your lists and find the helpful behavior you all agree upon. Make a master list of the agreed upon items. (6 minutes)

2. On the board construct an unduplicated list from the sub-groups. Ask a variety of students to select the item that is most important. Each will explain his/her selection. Encourage all to practice the items as they listen to each speaker.

3. Discuss the value of helpful listening behaviors in classroom discussions.

CLOSURE

In the LOG, invite students to list the helpful listening behaviors they do best, the helpful behaviors they might work to improve, and at least one situation in which they might practice the helpful listening.

OR

Ask students to vote on a classroom code of conduct built on the helpful listening behaviors. Each item from the master list that receives a unanimous vote will be in the code. Ask for volunteers to prepare a code card to hang or duplicate the code for each individual's LOG.

PACTS

BACKGROUND The positive climate necessary for skillful thinking is included with skillful communication. The five basic communication pre-skills encourage the positive interaction which marks the clear interchange of ideas.

PRE-SKILLS Paraphrasing, affirming, clarifying, testing options and sensing

FOCUS ACTIVITY Write the word "compact" on the overhead or board. Follow with the synonyms contract, agreement, charter, or PACTS. Explain the definition of "compact" as a formal agreement between two people or an agreement or pact to ***com***municate with others. Share examples from history such as the "MayFlower Compact." Ask several students to explain the word "compact" with their own examples. Conclude by highlighting on the overhead or board how the word PACTS and Com = Communication Pacts.

OBJECTIVE To identify helpful listening behaviors.

INPUT On the board or overhead display the word:

P
A
C
T
S

Note to the student that the word is a tool which will help them remember five key skills that will help them communicate more successfully. Fill in each letter, define the skill and demonstrate with an example. Encourage the students to write their menu in their LOGS.

P = Paraphrase or play back. Ask a student to read this. "In a paraphrase, I repeat the key ideas stated to me. I don't add my own ideas or change the ideas to say what I want. I am like a recorder that plays back what it has recorded." Demonstrate paraphrasing by labeling what you are going to do and then paraphrase the above statement. Conclude by asking several different students to paraphrase a short statement that you have selected from today's newspaper.

A = Affirming or appreciating. Ask a student to read this statement. "Affirming means that I tell a person I like what they are doing, saying or thinking." Label that you are going to affirm the student for reading the definition. "_*(name)*_, I liked how _*(adverb)*_ you read that statement." Conclude by asking several students to make an affirmative statement to another student. Affirm their efforts.

C = Clarify or check on specific details. Ask a student to read this statement, "Clarifying means to check what someone means by asking the person to describe in more detail, give an example, or be more specific about words we don't understand." Identify that you are going to model a clarifying question so that they have a specific example. "If I were to clarify or make more clear the word clarify, I would say "please give me an example of clarify." If I wanted you to clarify

PACTS

the word difficult, I might say, "describe a job you had to do which you thought was difficult." Then you might tell me about last night's homework. As a result, we would both be clearer in understanding what you meant. Conclude by asking a student to read this sentence. "Thinking is fun." Ask other students to ask clarifying questions.

T = Testing Options or trying out ideas. Ask a student to read this statement. "Testing options means to help the person I am talking with explore different possible answers." Identify that you are going to model this skill. Ask a student "What is one skill you have learned?" Affirm the answer and repeat the last question. Conclude by telling students that you are going to affirm helpful communication behaviors you have observed in the class. After you give each one, tell them that volunteers may use the "T" skill with you until you signal a stop. Start with "the first helpful skill I have observed being used is...."

S = Sensing or seeking out feelings. Ask a student to read the following. "Sensing or seeking out feelings means that I try to capture how a person is feeling about the idea. Is the person angry, sad, happy? When I sense a feeling I not only listen to the words but I listen to the tone of voice and watch the body language." Tell the class that the reader will repeat the description and that you will ask them to paraphrase the statement. After the second reading and several paraphrases, invite students to ask clarifying questions about "S." You will also want them to practice the "T" by asking you to demonstrate different emotional tones and non-verbal behaviors so that they can "sense" the tone.

Conclude with a summary review and check for understanding.

ACTIVITY Instruction:

1. Divide the class into groups of *three*. If there is one four, divide it into two pairs. In each trio, have students label themselves as Piff, Poof & Pop.

2. Indicate that each of the following tasks will rotate at your signal. Display the tasks on the overhead, or give each trio a worksheet as well as the check chart.

   A. Observer (Start with POP): listens to the dialogue but focuses on the listener. Each time the listener uses a PACTS skill, the observer will check the chart.

   B. Listener (Start with POOF): listens to the speaker and practices PACTS as appropriate.

   C. Speaker (Start with PIFF): Talks for 1 to 2 minutes on one of the listed topics and then responds to the listener.

   (1) My dream vacation...
   (2) A hero I admire...
   (3) A place I'd love to travel...
   (4) My favorite sport...
   (5) The food I hate the most...
   (6) A topic of my choice...

PACTS

D. Check that all understand the task by asking different students to paraphrase the instructions for each role.

3. Review the check chart.

Name	P	A	C	T	S
PIFF ______________					
POOF ______________					
POP ______________					

4. Each five minutes, rotate the jobs. Affirm positive behaviors at the end of each round.

CLIMATE

METACOGNITIVE DISCUSSION Encourage the students to continue the PACTS practice through this discussion. Ask the following questions. Extend responses with modeling of PACTS.

1. When someone is talking with you and paraphrases your ideas, what happens with your thinking? What other reactions do you have?
2. When someone asks you to clarify, what happens with your thinking? What other reactions do you have?
3. What are the benefits to your thinking when you use PACTS in your communication?
4. How might a PACTS skill hinder your thinking?

CLOSURE In you LOG, list some situations in which you could improve your communication by using PACTS.

OR

In your LOG, pick one situation in which an historic or literary character you know might have benefitted by using PACTS. Explain your choice.

OR

With a partner, select the PACTS skill which you want to continue practicing and explain how it will help your communication in a specific situation. Let each be on focus for three minutes and practice as you listen.

NOTE: With less mature students, you may want to break this lesson into smaller units, shorter time and more guided practice. For each PACTS skill, you may select age-appropriate vocabulary, short recordings, video tape news items, or daily editorials. Encourage all students to use the skills as you give corrective and affirmative feedback.

2-4-8 Focus Interview

INSTRUCTIONS:

1. Have students select a partner, preferably a person they do not know or have not worked with on a day-to-day basis. Partners should take their materials and sit together.

2. When all students are in matched pairs, introduce the signal systems for this training:

   (a) "Hands Up." When the teacher wants to stop the group activity, he/she will raise a hand. If you see this, stop what you are doing (finish the sentence, please!) and raise your hand. As you see other hands go up, do likewise and focus on your teacher. When everyone is silent, the teacher will give the next instruction.

   (b) "Thumbs Up." In many instances, you may be asked to vote. Signal a "yes" with thumbs up and a "no" with thumbs down.

   (c) "Timeout." In the midst of an activity, a group discussion or a lecturette, you may get lost. Don't assume you are at fault. Give the T for timeout and check out the confusion or misunderstanding with your teacher or classmates. At times, the teacher may signal timeout to focus on an issue or check for understanding.

3. Each pair should then identify the speaker (i.e., "Picker-Pickee," "Larger shoe size," "Long-distance traveler") and the helper for the first task.

4. The speaker will interview his/her partner, without taking notes, for the introduction. In the interviews, there are two absolute rules; everyone has the responsibility to say "I pass," and everyone has the right to rebound (i.e., ask the interviewer the same question). Here are some interview questions:

   - Name?
   - Thinking Skills lesson you tried?
   - Experience?
   - Positive aspects?
   - Challenges?

   As the interview works, the interviewer should listen actively to the responses. Eye contact, positive body language, paraphrasing responses to check out what was said, etc.—all are important.

INTERVIEWERS BE ADVISED: You will soon be asked to introduce your partner to another matched pair. Listen intently and store up the important ideas, so you can repeat the experience and concerns you hear.

5. At the end of five minutes, signal a switch within each pair. The interviewer will now be interviewed.

6. At the end of the second five minutes, signal the end of the interview. Instruct partners to stay together and match with another pair.

7. Have the students introduce their partners to the small group and repeat their partner's classroom experience—each member of the foursome will do an introduction. Then, have each foursome match with another set of four.

8. Have the students repeat the introductions but this time introducing *someone different*—each of the eight students will make an introduction. By the end of this activity, each student will have heard seven applications of some aspect of this training.

9. Process the 2-4-8 activity.

   (a) What are some thoughts or feelings you experienced? (PMI)
   (b) What is the value of this activity?
   (c) What are some other ways you might use 2-4-8? (e.g., Primary—Show & Tell, Intermediate—Book Reports, High School—Research Projects)

10. Introduce the LOG.

    Date/time each entry.
    Use lead-ins in the first person:

    I learned...
    I discovered...
    I'm pleased...
    I'm proud...
    I wonder...
    I feel...
    I'm concerned...
    I hope...

SECTION 4

SKILLS

Natural abilities are like natural plants that need pruning by study.

—*Francis Bacon*

Teaching Of Thinking

Dr. Barry Beyer is the leading advocate for teaching explicit thinking skills which he calls "the teaching of thinking." In this approach, the teacher identifies 4 - 8 thinking skills which are already included in the subject matter. For instance, classification is taught implicitly in Biology, problem solving is implicit in math word problems, attributing in character analysis of a novel. Although the best students are able to grasp these thinking skills which are buried in the content, most students seldom recognize or master them. As a result, when they have to use the skills without teacher direction, the students can only guess at what to do. Beyer argues that formal instruction in explicit thinking skills will give all students the tools to do more skillful thinking.

What goes into this formal instruction? First, there is a formal lesson design. As we have used it in the 50 strategic lessons, the design includes:

1. **A FOCUS ACTIVITY** This is the advanced organizer or anticipatory set that Rowe's research showed to be so important in helping students focus their attention on the topic at hand. In this case, the activity will focus concentration on a specific thinking skill such as comparing or predicting.

2. **THE LESSON OBJECTIVE** This will spell out to students what they will learn in this lesson. It is important that the teacher communicate the objective, both by sight and by sound, to the students before the lesson and as much as necessary during the lesson. Effective teachers follow the adage: "This is what I am going to teach you. This is what I did teach you." As often as students ask "What are we doing?" that is how often it is necessary to reinforce the objective.

3. **INPUT** Students need solid information about the thinking skill. If it is their first introduction, they will need a clear definition with synonyms, an explanation of when and how the thinking skill is used, an easy way to remember the mental operations used in the thinking process, and a demonstration of how one uses the skill in a thinking task. The task selected should make it easy for them to focus on the key mental operations of the skill without confusing the thinking process with the course content. For instance, biology students would best learn classification by grouping types of clothes or popular music. After having grasped the classifying rules and procedures, they can apply the rules to botany and zoology.

   For students who have a working knowledge of the thinking skill, a more inductive approach will benefit them. Rather than give the definition and operations to the students, you might set up an experiment which requires them to think through the task or problem solve. Then you would use questions to help the class generalize a definition and list the operations they used. For instance, in social studies, you might provide the class with data that indicates a number of social trends. From the data, the class would predict future events. When they have completed the task, you would review how they solved the problem and develop acceptable rules for making logical predictions.

4. **STRUCTURED ACTIVITY** Under your close supervision, the class would practice or apply the information they had received about the thinking skill. This important step is too often overlooked. In fact, it is as important for you to structure the practice, observe what students do and give corrective feedback as it is for you to give them the information about the thinking

skill. Until they have the opportunity to use the information and refine its use, they have no skill. If a teacher is not going to take this practice and feedback time, she might as well *not* take the time to fill the students' heads with useless definitions, synonyms, and uses of the thinking skill.

5. **METACOGNITIVE DISCUSSION** Once the students have had the opportunity to try out the skill, they need the opportunity to process what they have done. This mental processing, thinking about their thinking, we call "metacognition." This is the tool that reading researchers now are able to think about thinking, the chances are very high that students will not tie the pieces together and find meaning in what they are thinking about. Without this meaning, they will have very little chance to retain or to transfer what they have learned to content areas.

   As a method for promoting metacognition, the stems ("I think..." "I wonder..." "I learned...") are an easy first step. Using Bloom's Taxonomy with the higher level questions focused on the thinking accomplished in the structured task ("How might you use the predicting skill in your job?" "What would happen if you used the 5 step problem solving model...") is a second method. A third approach is the PME model: planning, monitoring and evaluating how we think.

Planning your thinking

1. What is your thinking goal? Is it achievable? Believable? Conceivable?
2. How will you think to get there?
3. How will you sequence your thinking tasks?
4. What problems will occur?
5. How will you overcome these problems?
6. What will give you the most trouble in your thinking?
7. Predict what will happen...
8. How will you know you have succeeded in this thinking task?

Monitoring your thinking

1. Where are you in the sequence of mental operations?
2. What surprises did you discover? How did you handle the surprise in your thinking? What did you decide to do?
3. What mistakes did you make in your thinking? How did you adjust? Recover?
4. What have you learned new about your thinking patterns?
5. What have you reinforced about what you do well?

Evaluating your thinking

1. What did you think about?
2. What operations/skills did you use?
3. If you did this thinking task over, what would you do differently?
4. What did you do well? Goal/Skill use?
5. What are you unsure about?
6. How accurate was your thinking?
7. How precise was your thinking?
8. How fluent was your thinking?
9. How flexible was your thinking?

6. **CLOSURE** Before ending a lesson on a specific thinking skill, it is advisable to check carefully to ascertain how well students have mastered the skill. If necessary, repeat input, structured activity and the metacognitive discussion. You may want to have students explain the definitions and operations, change the activity and use different questions. When you have ample evidence that at least 80% mastery is present, move to the lesson closure. At its best, an effective closure will help students key on the critical learnings about the skill in a way that will encourage strong retention for future use. At the worst, closure will be a quiz which communicates that the skills can be filed for future use.

The formal lesson, however, is only the first step in the explicit instruction of the thinking skill. Once students have a mastery of what the skill is and how to use it, they are ready for transfer lessons into one or more subjects. The transfer lesson will follow the same design principles as the introductory lesson. The teacher will make instructional decisions about which components (focus, input, etc.) to include and which to pass over in each transfer lesson. For instance, the classification transfer lesson to Biology may require no more than a review of the introductory lesson. The review would serve as focus and input. Very quickly, the students would begin a classification activity using 40 words provided on the overhead. After a brief metacognitive discussion, they might start a second classifying activity, using lab equipment. Each time, they would think about how they were classifying and find ways to improve that thinking skill. Ultimately, the teacher might challenge them to classify objects that have no relationship to Biology to test their grasp of the classifying skill itself.

These components are not selected by accident. The more we learn about the secrets of cognition, the more apparent it becomes that each piece contributes to the quality of thinking about the content. The secret of success in learning springs from the students' ability to take information and cognitively integrate the new with the old. This leads to meaning. Each piece, like the components of a computer menu, plays an important part in helping all students learn how to structure the pieces into a meaningful whole. Given solid instruction, visual formats, clues and intense practice, each gets the chance to integrate the single skills into a personally meaningful mental construct.

The danger inherent in the teaching of thinking is that the discrete skills remain single and isolated. There is little value in this approach if students are not given the opportunities to practice and transfer the thinking skills into the course content and to integrate the single skills into a cognitive whole.

Teaching An Explicit Thinking Skill

To accomplish these goals, we will be engaged in doing exactly what the signs erected near highway repair projects often state is going on:

Temporary Inconvenience
Permanent Improvement

What may appear to be a temporary inconvenience—time away from teaching subject-matter—will turn out to be a permanent improvement as students are explicitly taught the skills of critical and creative thinking, the skills that transfer across content and into life.

Barry Beyer, Ph.D.

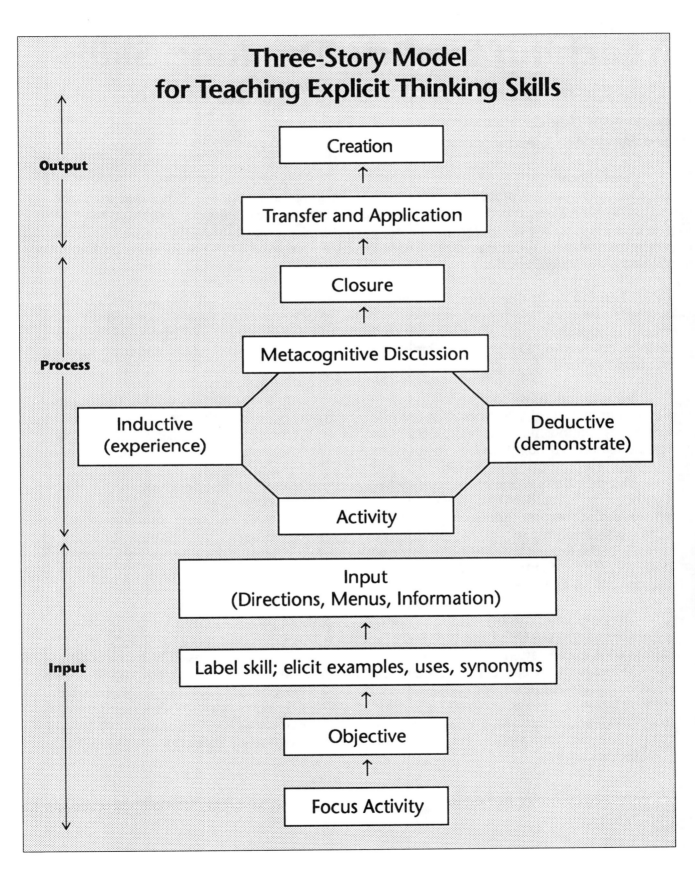

Three-Story Model for Teaching Explicit Thinking Skills

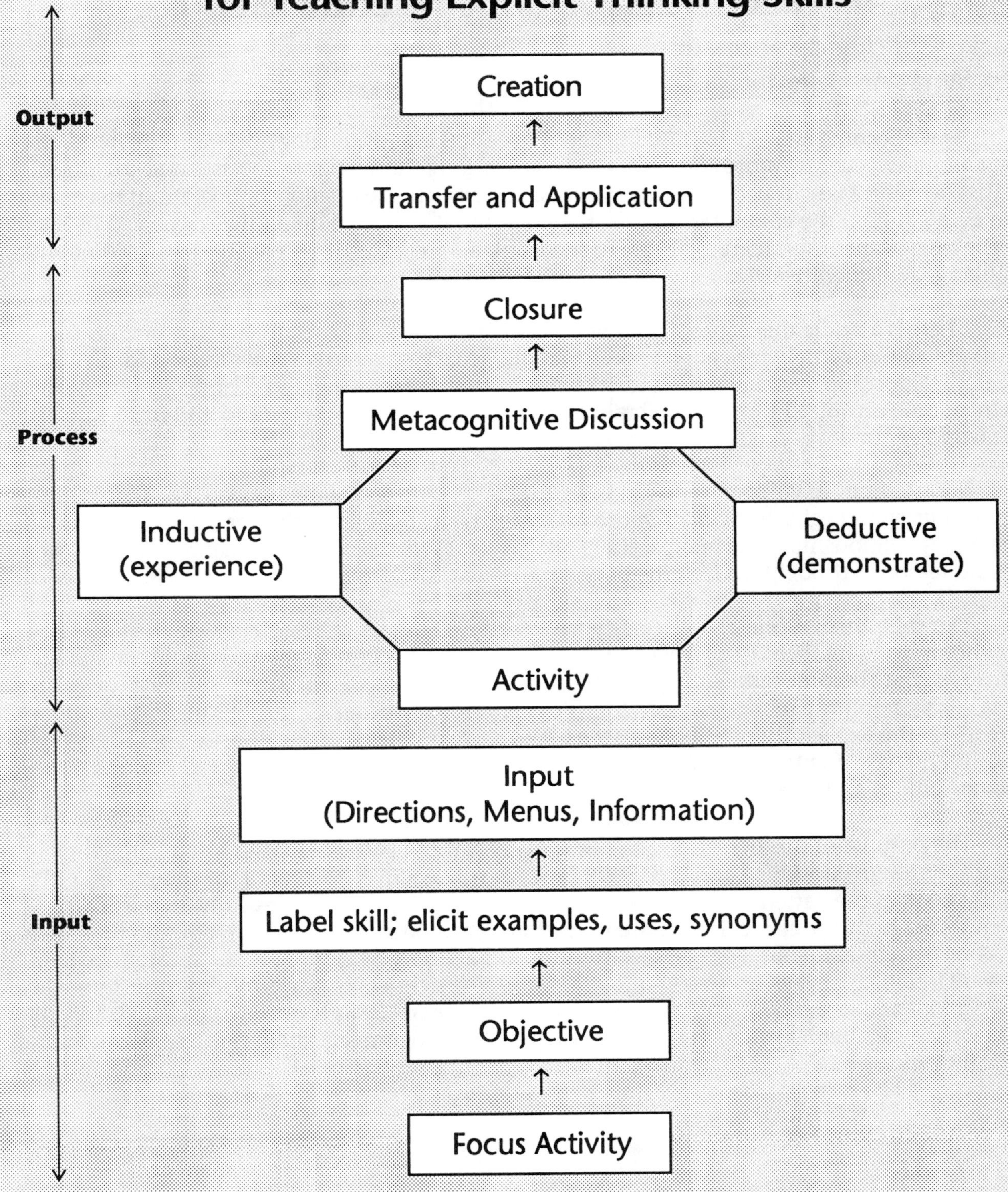

Teaching Explicit Thinking Skills

Questions Teachers Ask About "Mental Menus"

Background and Rationale:
Just What Are Mental Menus?

As we become attuned to thinking about our thinking, the analogy between the mind and the computer becomes more and more obvious. Tracking the thought processes and cognitive paths the mind takes in performing thinking skills is much like the flow of operations needed to run a program on the computer. So, too, the menus that are called up on the screen can be likened to the mental menus that are available to our thinking processes, if we consciously think about our thinking, metacognitively.

There is a riddle that states: "Your brain is smarter than you are." In fact, the brain is the most marvelous computer of all. It seeks structure, perceives patterns, recalls associations and creates relationships. Actually, if we trust our brain to guide us, it *seeks* to channel information for us into some organized format. The brain invites order to help us understand and make sense of the world about us.

For example, as we are faced with a circumstance, our mental menus pop up. Almost intuitively, our brain begins to reorganize the data by sequencing, prioritizing, grouping, and building analogous relationships. The brain seeks to analyze and synthesize as it evaluates data that lead toward reasoned thought. In fact, the brain "shifts" to the appropriate menus almost on its own.

Our task, then, is one of consciously tracing this phenomena by articulating the processes that occur; to bring them to a level of awareness. Once we become adept at racing these thought processes, they become familiar patterns for thinking, Then, as we encounter situations, we can consciously select the model or menu for thinking through the task. Thus our mental menus are essentially the explicit thought patterns we use to solve problems, make decisions and design creatively. These mental menus become the patterns that we can deliberately call upon as we become critical and creative thinkers.

The purpose of this book is to provide models of those patterns for thinking: our mental menus! Through continued and consistent practice with models, teachers and students become skillful users of the patterns. Over time, applying the thinking skills successfully, by sprinkling them throughout the curriculum content, teachers and students will begin to develop their own versions of mental menus. For you see, this little book is only a beginning. The substantive benefits are found, as always, as we begin to draw upon the richness of our own resources from within as we adopt and design and experiment on our own. *Mental Menus* is merely the catalyst to ignite the creative capabilities inherent within us to think metacognitively about our creative and critical thought processes.

Content: Just What Skills Are Covered In Mental Menus?

To model the use of concrete examples that clarify abstract concepts, we have selected the computer as the basis of our metaphor: Mental Menus. The menus are elaborations of the cognitive processes that occur as we engage in critical and creative thinking.

To extend the computer metaphor further, the skills are presented within the framework of computer lingo. This glossary of terms illustrates the terminology used throughout the book.

Mental Menus: A Glossary of Terms

Program: the explicit thinking skill
Password: an acronym of the skill concept
Data Base: a definition of the skill
List: a list of synonyms for the skill
Scan: a look at specific examples of the applied skill
Enter: when to use the skill
Menu: directory of operations used in doing the skill
Debugging: trouble-shooting; what to do if...
Visual Layout: formats, structures, patterns to use with the skill
File: a specific example of a classroom application of the skill
Index: a list of suggested subject area applications for practice

The Explicit Skills

Twenty-four explicit thinking skills are extensively developed in *Teach Them Thinking* (Fogarty and Bellanca, 1986). These skills are divided into critical thinking and creative thinking skills. The authors differentiate between this duality of skill categories in this way.

Critical Thinking Skills require analytic, evaluative processing while Creative Thinking Skills dictate synthesis and a generative model of thinking. However, a word of caution is warranted here. Although we have purposefully separated the skills, in reality they are often used almost simultaneously as we process an idea. So the division is somewhat artificial as we consider a more holistic approach to problem-solving, decision-making and creativity.

With that thought in mind, the specific skills illustrated within this framework are outlined here:

Critical Thinking Skills:

1. Attributing—TRAITS
2. Comparing/Contrasting—SAD
3. Classifying—CLUE
4. Sequencing—SORT
5. Prioritizing—RANK
6. Drawing Conclusions—DRAW
7. Determining Cause/Effect—CHAINS
8. Analyzing for Bias—BIAS
9. Analyzing for Assumptions—ASSUME
10. Solving for Analogies—SOLVE
11. Evaluating—RATE
12. Decision-making—JUDGE

Creative Thinking Skills:

1. Brainstorming—THINK
2. Visualizing—IMAGE
3. Personifying—LIVE
4. Inventing—SCAMPER
5. Associating Relationships—RELATE
6. Inferring—INFER
7. Generalizing—RULE
8. Predicting—BET
9. Hypothesizing—THEORY
10. Making Analogies—MAKE
11. Dealing With Ambiguity And Paradox—DUAL
12. Problem-Solving—IDEAS

Each skill cluster includes a target skill as the center and several related skills in the outer cluster circles. The target skill provides the foundation upon which to build more complex or associated skills. For example:

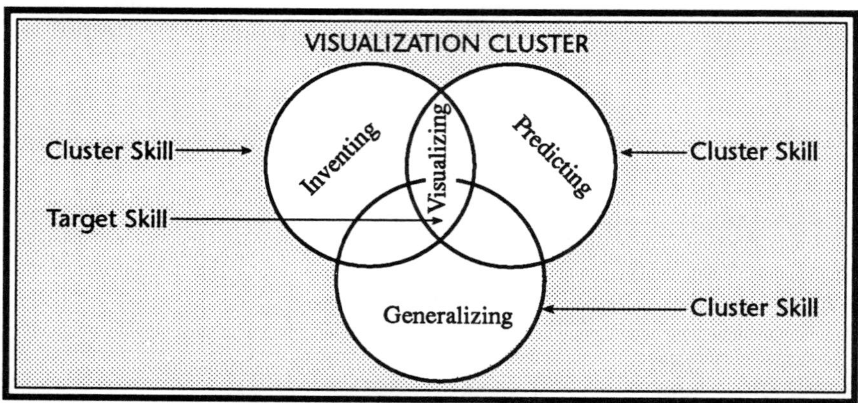

Visualization is the *target* creative thinking skill that will ease the learning of our cluster skills such as inventing, predicting and hypothesizing. Once students have had practice visualizing and imaging, for instance, they can more readily form predictions by "seeing" the possible or probable outcomes.

However, the skill of prediction also seems to fit into the INFERENCE CLUSTER, since predicting is often based on inferences drawn from available data. Other possibilities include placing the prediction skill in a BRAINSTORM CLUSTER, as we consider the generative process involved in making predictions. Therefore, predicting can be included in any one of the three clusters or in all three or in other clusters you create.

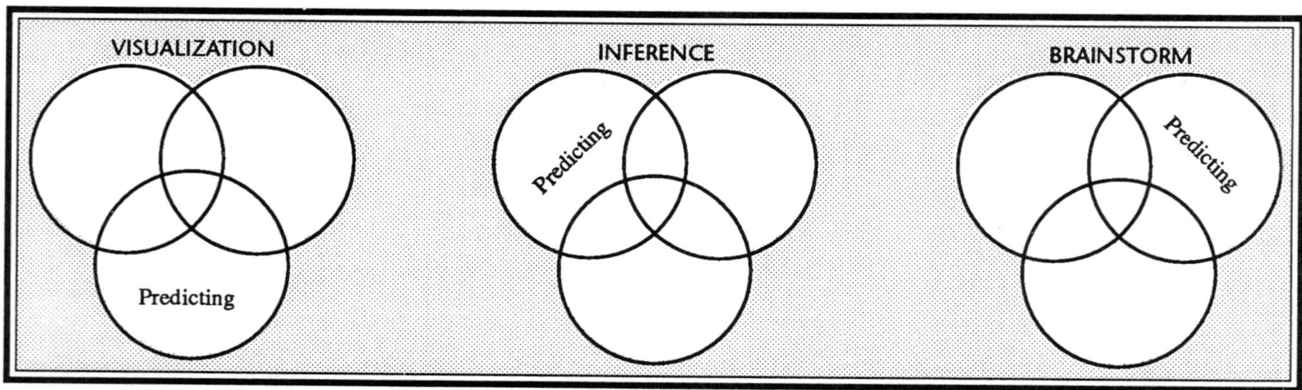

The cluster arrangements are intentionally presented as arbitrary, permitting fluid constructs of skill clusters as deemed appropriate. Yet, by using the idea of clusters, you have a guide to lead you in the selection of a few appropriate skills to work on in the classroom. Much like selecting foods from the four basic food groups, you can be assured that you are sampling different skills from different clusters and giving students a "well-balanced" curriculum in the area of thinking skills, without being mandated to use the skills in a structured order. Again, you must decide what skills are most appropriate to "plug into" your curriculum. The cluster curriculum is merely a suggested one that may help in articulating a scope and sequence of thinking skills as you develop a comprehensive integration of thinking skills into your classroom.

SKILLS

The Cluster Curriculum

CRITICAL THINKING SKILLS CLUSTER

CREATIVE THINKING SKILLS CLUSTER

ATTRIBUTE CLUSTER
Classifying
Attributing
Comparing and Contrasting
Sequencing

SEQUENCE CLUSTER
Prioritizing
Sequencing
Finding Cause and Effect
Drawing Conclusions

ANALYSIS CLUSTER
Drawing Conclusions
Analyzing for Assumptions
Analyzing
Analyzing for Bias

EVALUATION CLUSTER
Solving Analogies
Making Decisions
Evaluating
Analyzing for Bias
Analyzing for Assumptions

PROBLEM SOLVING
DECISION MAKING
CREATIVE IDEATION

VISUALIZATION CLUSTER
Predicting
Inventing
Visualizing
Hypothesizing

INFERENCE CLUSTER
Predicting
Inferring
Generalizing
Hypothesizing

PROBLEM-SOLVING CLUSTER
Inferring
Problem Solving
Making Analogies
Dealing with Ambiguity and Paradox

BRAINSTORM CLUSTER
Personifying
Associating
Brainstorming
Inventing
Visualizing

GENERATIVE AND PRODUCTIVE SKILL CLUSTERS

GENERATIVE AND PRODUCTIVE SKILL CLUSTERS

SKILLS

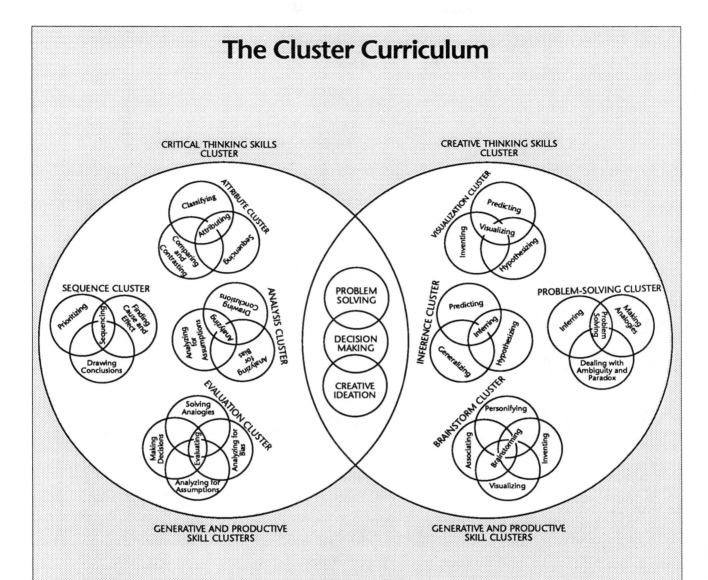

The listings are not intended to suggest a hierarchial structure, although certain skills do seem to logically fall into a cluster of sorts. For instance, attributing must precede skills such as comparing and contrasting and classification since these latter skills are ascertained through determining attributes. Therefore, attributing is a target or foundation skill for other thinking skills. The diagram illustrates suggested skill clusters.

Skill Introduction

Just How Do I Introduce Thinking Skills To My Class?

THINKING IS
like the ability to move or
perform as a ballerina
or athlete...left to our
own devices, the body does
not move with style and grace
...so too, left to our
own devices, the human
intellect does not function
very well... We must
educate for intelligent
performance...with
rehearsal, practice, and coaching.

A thinking skill is just that—a skill—and like any skill it requires explicit instruction to fully develop the inherent intellectual talent. To introduce an explicit thinking skill, the skill itself becomes the focus of the lesson. The content used to develop the lesson is merely a vehicle to present the skill. That content should be familiar to the students. Once the skill has been taught explicitly, it can be applied with new content as students interact to process the material.

For example, in the introductory skill lesson on classification, the science content of the states of matter is somewhat familiar to intermediate students. Therefore, we can focus the objective on the *skill* of classification. Once students have had ample opportunities to practice the skill, classification can be applied to new learning.

In short, the explicit skill lesson highlights the skill itself. This introductory lesson helps bring the skill to a conscious level so that students become acutely aware of the processing involved.

Within the explicit instruction, the introductory lesson includes:

- a stated objective
- a definition of terms
- examples of the applied skill
- informational content
- modeling
- guided practice with the skill
- independent practice
- transfer applications
- metacognitive processing

A sample lesson outlines the format used to develop each thinking skill.

Making Analogies

☑ Creative Thinking ☐ Critical Thinking

PROGRAM Skill: Making Analogies **PASSWORD** Acronym: MAKE

DATA BASE Definition: Creating metaphors to visualize ideas.

LIST Synonyms: metaphors, similes

SCAN Examples: Reasoning by analogy to make abstract concept more concrete: rage as thunder; sun as love

ENTER When to use:
- to grasp abstract concepts
- to present ideas in unique ways
- to communicate a complex thought

MENU How to use:
Make a comparison of two unlike things.
Acknowledge similarities.
Keep the similarities in mind and infer a relationship.
Express the relationship as a metaphorical image.

DEBUGGING What to do if:
- can't find similarities: keep brainstorming using all your senses or change comparison.

VISUAL LAYOUT Patterns: Thought Trees
________ is like _______ because both ________.

FILE Sample Lesson:

History — Courageous People from History (Courage)

<u>Focus</u>: Make a comparison; courage and rain.
Acknowledge similarities: both can appear unexpectedly.
Keep similarities in mind and infer a relationship: courage appears like a sudden shower of rain — out of nowhere.
Express a relationship as a metaphorical image: courage, like a summer shower, often appears quite unexpectedly.

INDEX Suggested Applications:

<u>Math</u>
- Figural Analogies
- Numerical Analogies
- Concepts of: fractions, measurement, decimals,geometric shapes

<u>Language Arts</u>
- Concepts of: love, lonliness, isolation, grief, equality, sanity, humor, anger, joy

<u>Social Studies</u>
- Concepts of: war, diplomacy, poverty, geographic locations, capitalism, events

SKILLS

Making Menus in the Classroom

STEP 1: PROGRAM : Skill: Select a thinking skill.

STEP 2: DATA BASE : Definition:
Develop a definition of the skill with the students using their own wording.

STEP 3: LIST : Synonyms:
Elicit synonyms from the students.

STEP 4: SCAN : Examples:
Cite a concrete example of an application of the skill. Have students think of other applications.

STEP 5: ENTER : **When to use:**
List appropriate instances in which the skill is used.

STEP 6: MENU : **How to use:**
Outline the operations used to perform the skill. Then, use a word symbolic of the skill and rewrite the operations in the form of an acronym.

STEP 7: PASSWORD : Acronym:
Develop an acronym as a memory aid *after* you track the necessary operations in Step 6.

STEP 8: DEBUGGING : **What to do if:**
Explore possible snags in performing the skill and decide on possible alternatives that allow you to proceed.

STEP 9: VISUAL LAYOUT : Patterns:
List graphic organizers that provide an aid in using the skill.

STEP 10: FILE : Sample Lesson:
Develop a sample skill lesson using subject area content.

STEP 11: INDEX : Suggested Applications:
Think of further applications in other subject area content: plug the skill into relevant topics.

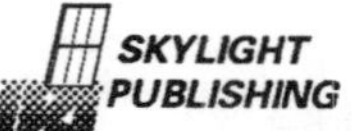

Using an Inductive or Deductive Strategy

Another consideration is which strategy to use to introduce the explicit thinking skill: an inductive strategy or a deductive strategy.

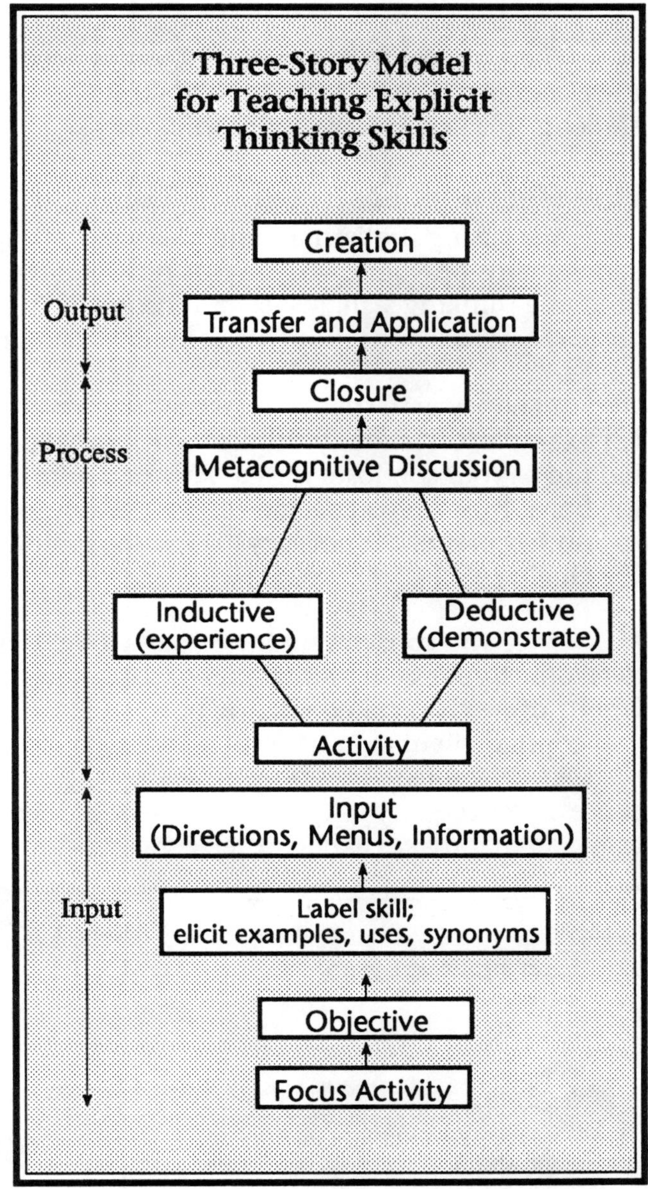

Inductive lesson design is based on the concept of inquiry. Using the inductive strategy, specific bits of information are assembled until a generalization results. Inductive techniques, much like a detective accumulating clues, require seeing patterns and making associations from scattered information and generating a statement that encompasses the suggested results. Students experiment and reflect, apply and review the learning when using an inductive method.

Inductive strategies are appropriate for most classroom lessons since the bulk of our "learning in life" is obtained inductively. Inductive strategies, however, require more skilled teaching and more effective classroom management.

On the other hand, a deductive strategy can be useful in some situations. In the deductive method, a general statement is outlined and demonstrated and then information is processed to determine if it "fits the rule." Doctors use deductive techniques when diagnosing an illness. They try to match the symptoms with known profiles of specific diseases. In essence, they begin with a broad definition and slot the specific facts to the known patterns until they find the "perfect fit." Thus, they can make the diagnosis and decide on treatment and prognosis.

To use the deductive techniques in the classroom, the teacher explains and demonstrates and then has the students apply the content to the defined structure. In the last stages, the students reflect on the learning.

Deductive strategies are most effective when the skill is especially difficult or complex and/or when the learners are novices or lacking in similar experiences. For example, when introducing the skill of inventing which includes *nine* separate strategies, it is best to plan a deductive lesson in which you first, *explain* fully the nine strategies, *demonstrate* their use and then have students *apply* the new information.

Extending the Skill Lessons

How Do I Create And Generate Menus In The Classroom?

There appear to be two distinct steps necessary to begin creating and generating menus in the classroom. The first step involves teacher readiness,while the second step concerns guiding students in the development of thinking skills. The two steps in this process are explained here.

How Teachers Learn Explicit Thinking Skills

After using the formats and ideas set forth in *Mental Menus*, you will want to try developing some menus on your own. There is no secret recipe! To begin to articulate the thought patterns used in a thinking skill, just start a mental listing of what you do when you think critically or creatively. Track your thoughts consciously and be aware of the components of the process.

A good way to start is to take a moment the next time you have an unexpected "challenge." For example, consciously think about your thinking as you figure out what to do when you have a flat tire or your son loses the car keys or you're out of mayonnaise and the tuna fish is already in the bowl. How do you decide whether or not to take the promotion even though it means moving to another part of the country? Track your thinking processes. How do you go about dealing with the challenges and occurrences that arise in life?

Once you consciously trace your thought processes in this fashion, you are on your way to developing your own mental menus. For example, delineate your method for handling an avalanche of newly dictated grading policies. How do you organize the unfamiliar guidelines? How do you connect them to your "old" ways? How do you go about assimilating them into a manageable manner for implementation? Answering these questions will lead you into the metacognitive processing necessary to the development of Mental Menus. It brings to an awareness level the thinking that makes explicit the very patterns for thinking that you already use.

SKILLS

Skill: CLASSIFICATION

An Inductive Lesson	A Deductive Lesson
① Introduce the skill (label, define, give examples, uses and synonyms.	
③ Label the groups and classify the words according to those labels. Explain why you place items in particular groups as you proceed.	② Provide students with a list of words from the science chapter. Ask them to "group" the words in some way. Allow time for processing of their activity, facilitating as necessary.
③ Guide students to reflect on the classification they made. Display the "groupings" and discuss the variations. Elicit "rules" for classifying from students.	② Explain the concept of classification using a list of words from the science chapter. Proceed systematically through the list and find classification labels that are appropriate.
④ Have students apply the learning about classification in a social studies or reading lesson.	
⑤ Review the skill of classification and elicit other applications of the skill.	⑤ Guide students to reflect on the classifications they made and discuss *how* we classify things.

How Students Learn Explicit Thinking Skills

Skilled thinkers think about their thinking. To help all students become skillful thinkers who can track their own thinking, the "paired partners" strategy provides a possible beginning.

In "paired partners" the students take turns articulating the steps they use in solving a problem. Just by asking for a verbal recitation of the process, students are forced to track their thinking. And, again, with many practices they become skilled at doing this. In no time at all, the teacher will be able to elicit Mental Menus from the students as new thinking skills are introduced.

Application

Just How Do I Use These Skills In My Classroom?

Once the explicit thinking skill has been introduced, using the skill in the normal course of lesson follows. Learners need practice, rehearsal and coaching with a new skill.

Practice and rehearsal can be achieved by "bridging" the skill into content areas. For example, the skill of classification can be used with science units, social studies concepts, spelling words or in grouping the stories in a reading unit.

Frequent application of the skill, using the content *already* included in the curriculum, is the most effective application of the thinking skills. In this way, thinking skills do not become an "add-on" to the curriculum, but merely strategies to help students process the material already slotted for study.

With practice, you will find many opportunities to "plug-in" thinking skills. For example, after teaching the skill of analysis by attributing, you can "plug in" the attribute web as you go about your regularly scheduled lessons.

As you work with a piece of *literature*, you can ask students to use the attribute web to analyze the leading character. During the *social studies* lessons, students can develop attribute webs of the various geographic regions as they analyze the material presented in the text. A *math* unit on fractions can be introduced with the attribute web as a diagnostic strategy to determine the prior knowledge of students. An additional application of the skill of attributing can be bridged into the *science* lesson. Student webs can be used to analyze the attributes of mammals as you study the biology unit. The webs below suggest the range of applications for this one skill.

To vary the application of the analysis attribute web, the whole class can develop a web or students can work in small groups to produce a finished web using the same target concept. Also, the jigsaw puzzle model can be used in which each small group is assigned a "piece" of the total "picture." For instance, in social studies, five different groups would work on five different webs: the southwestern, northwestern, midwestern, southern, or northeastern regions. Then the five webs are presented to the class and the jigsaw puzzle "picture" takes form.

As teachers provide lots of practice with a skill, students will begin to transfer these mental patterns into other relevant situations as they become more skillful thinkers.

Accompanying the continuous and consistent practices with the skills, immediate, specific feedback is required, as well as frequent opportunities for metacognitive processing of the skill applications.

The Thinking Log and thoughtful discussions using higher level questioning can lead students comfortably into the metacognitive areas of thinking about their thinking.

The Thinking Log can be used effectively at various spots throughout a lesson. To spark kids' interest, review past learning, or to get them to focus on the concept, you can have them make a log entry *before* the lesson actually begins.

To capture spontaneous student reactions, you might have them go to their logs *immediately following* the processing activity. This need only take a minute or two and can be an effective

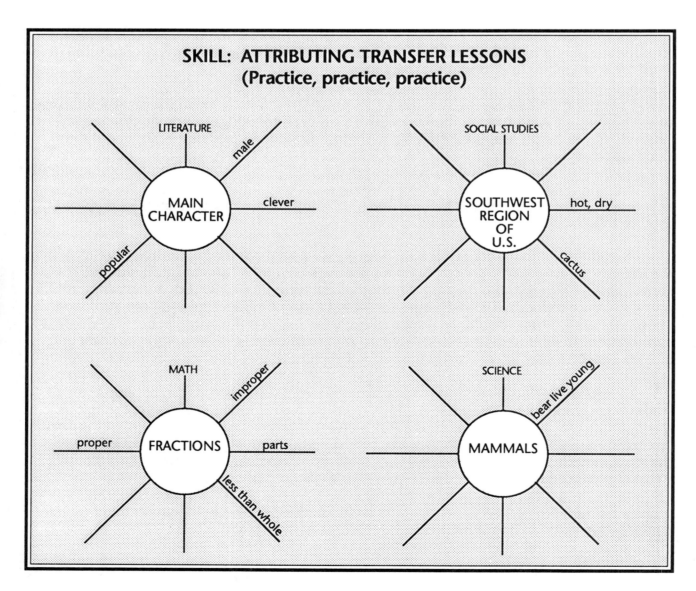

SKILL: ATTRIBUTING TRANSFER LESSONS
(Practice, practice, practice)

LITERATURE
MAIN CHARACTER
male
clever
popular

SOCIAL STUDIES
SOUTHWEST REGION OF U.S.
hot, dry
cactus

MATH
FRACTIONS
improper
proper
parts
less than whole

SCIENCE
MAMMALS
bear live young

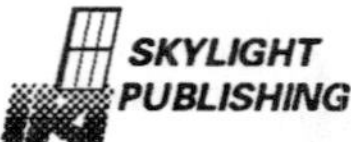

"sponge" activity during *transition* times.

Another natural opportunity for log entries is as a closure task *after* the lesson has been completed. This gives students a moment to reflect on the "big idea" presented during the lesson.

Regardless of when you use the logs, they can become a viable tool to record student thinking and by suggesting a variety of lead-in statements you can gently push students to higher level thinking and metacognitive processing.

To illustrate the use of lead-in statements, note the thinking levels required by these lead-ins:

I believe.................................Evaluation
I wonder.................................Analysis
Suppose.................................Synthesis
I think...................................Comprehension
I question...............................Evaluation
Comparing.............................Analysis
What if...................................Synthesis

Students may also be led toward visual processing in the log. By suggesting that they diagram or graph or "map" their perceptions of an idea, students begin to use graphic patterns to chart their thinking.

If opportunities are given, students will learn to use their log as yet another method for tracking new thinking.

Conclusion

What Do I Do Now?

Now, select a Mental Menu most generic to your content...and begin there. Don't be in a hurry to bombard the student with *lots* of skills. Get one going first. Do it right! Take the necessary time to introduce it explicitly and give ample practice applications with the skill. Process it! Plug it into your lessons until it becomes an automatic pattern for thinking with the students.

Teaching an explicit thinking skill begins with a thorough introduction of the components of skill. But mastery of the skill requires lots of short, busy practices at first, followed by a variety of opportunities to apply the new skill to meaningful situations.

Much like the child who learns to swim, the student must be led gently into skillful thinking. Each component of the skill is tackled separately and eventually the actions are strung together until the body moves easily through the water. Teaching for skillful thinking follows the same pattern.

A reasonable approach to new things is always the wisest. We consider a thorough development of two or three skills a year a reasonable goal. If these two or three skills are elaborated and integrated properly, students will have a good start toward becoming productive problem-solvers, mindful decision-makers, and creative thinkers.

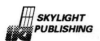

Lesson Model

Focus Activity:

Objective:

Content Input:

Metacognitive Processing:

Closure:

Contrasting Inductive and Deductive Reasoning Strategies in Teaching

Adapted from Strategies For Teachers (Eggen, Kauchak, and Harder, 1979)

Inductive Teaching

Miss Jones wanted her students to develop some understanding of magnetism, so she began an activity by passing out pairs of bar magnets to groups of four in her class. She told them to use the magnets by trying them out on things in their desks. In addition, she gave each group an envelope containing a plastic button, a penny, a nail, a piece of plastic and a staple. After the groups had worked for a while, Miss Jones said, "Let's try to describe some of the things you found about the magnets. What kind of things have you noticed?"

"My magnet is bigger than Jimmy's," Debbie began.

"The magnets are shaped like blocks of wood," Tommy added.

"Mine is yellow," Billy observed.

"They're all different colors," Susie added.

"The paint is coming off mine," Jimmy noted, pointing to his magnet.

"The magnets will stick to some things, but not to others," said Jeannie.

"Yeah, it won't pick up my spelling book or my paper," Jimmy added.

"But it will pick up a paper clip and a ball point pen."

"Good!" said Miss Jones. "It sounds like you've been hard at work and have made some observations. Is there some way we can put some of our observations together to describe things that the magnets have in common?"

"Well," Julie suggested hesitantly, "all the magnets pick up some things but not others."

"Fine," Miss Jones smiled. "Let's organize your observations into a list of things magnets will and won't pick up." With the help of the class Miss Jones then wrote the following lists on the board.

ATTRACTED TO MAGNETS	NOT ATTRACTED TO MAGNETS	
Ball point pen	Books	Desk top
Paper clip	Paper	Glasses
Spiral part of notebook	Clothes	Ball point pen
Desk bottom	Skin	

"What do you notice about our observations?" asked Miss Jones.

"There are more things that magnets don't pick up than they do," said Sam.

"All the things that magnets stick to are metal," replied Harry.

"Some pens are attracted to magnets and some aren't," added Marsha.

"Some pens are metal," Julie noted.

The lesson continued with Miss Jones helping the students clarify their ideas. Finally, she asked, "Would someone summarize in one statement what we've found here today?"

Billy raised his hand. "We've found that magnets are attracted to some things but not others, and the things magnets are attracted to are called metals."

"Excellent," Miss Jones praised. "Now, everyone take a new envelope of things and predict which items in the envelope the magnets will be attracted to."

She then passed out a new assortment of articles for the students to categorize. The students did this, the results were discussed, and the lesson completed.

Now, let's contrast Miss Jones' lesson with that of another teacher, Mrs. Holt, who also did a lesson on magnets and magnetic attraction.

Deductive Teaching

Mrs. Holt began her lesson by asking, "Class, who remembers what we've been studying in science? Jimmy?"

"Well, we've been studying the properties of different kinds of things."

"Can you give some examples so the others will know what you mean?"

"Well, like we talked about water and how it can freeze and get hard and we talked about how it can evaporate. And we talked about different ways we can talk about things like hard and soft and color and smell."

"Good, Jimmy," said Mrs. Holt. "You remembered a lot. Yes, we've been talking about different properties of objects around us. Today we are going to talk about a different way to describe things, and to understand this we will use something that we call magnets. These are magnets and I'm going to pass two of these out to each of the small groups."

After passing out the magnets, Mrs. Holt continued. "Today we're to learn an additional way to classify objects, by using these magnets." With that she put the following generalization on the board.

MAGNETS ARE ATTRACTED TO SOME OBJECTS AND NOT OTHERS, AND THE THINGS MAGNETS ARE ATTRACTED TO ARE CALLED METALS.

"I want everyone to read this statement and to try and understand what it means because we'll be using it in our lesson today. Let's look now at the statement on the board. What does the word attract mean?"

"It kind of means pull or pull toward you, I think," Susan offered.

"Okay," Mrs. Holt smiled. "How about metal? Can someone give me an example of a metal?"

"The leg of my desk!" Billy waved excitedly.

"My lunch bucket," Tommy added.

"Very good," Mrs. Holt praised. "Now look again at the statement. I'm going to show you an example." She picked up a book, "Now do you think the magnets you have will stick to a book? Beth?"

"No."

"Why not, Beth?"

"Because books are made of paper, not metal."

"Good, now why don't you see what will happen if you place your magnet on the desk top."

"Nothing happens," said Mike.

"Now, how about paper clip? Will the magnet stick to the paper clip?"

"I think so," said Jill, "because paper clips are made of metal."

This lesson continued with Mrs. Holt having the students try their magnets out on objects such as pens, clothes, desks and their own skin. She then asked the students to each name one object they hadn't yet discussed that the magnet would attract and one object the magnet would not attract.

She concluded her lesson by giving the children envelopes containing various objects and asking them to predict which objects would be attracted to the magnets. This was followed by discussion.

DEFINITION

Inductive Reasoning: specific —(*experiential*)→ general
(specific clues lead to a generalization)

Deductive Reasoning: general —(*direct*)→ specific
(rule stated; does it fit the rule)

SKILLS

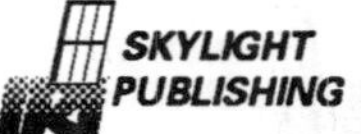

Exercises

In the following exercises, determine if the people are using inductive or deductive reasoning, or both. If it is inductive, identify the data that were used to arrive at the concept of generalization. If it is deductive, explain the syllogism.

1. Two children were looking at the sky on a clear, moonless night.
   "What's that bright star up there?" Jimmy asked.
   "It's not a star, it's a planet," Susan responded.
   "How do you know?" Jimmy wondered.
   "It isn't twinkling," Susan said. "Stars twinkle but planets don't, so it must be a planet."

   A. Was Susan using inductive or deductive reasoning?____________________

   B. If inductive, explain why; if deductive, describe the deductive syllogism.

   ____

   ____

2. Jimmy and Susan were playing with a toy ukulele one day.
   "Hey," Jimmy said, "the shorter the string, the higher the sound."
   "How do you know?" Susan asked.
   "Well," Jimmy responded, "when I place my left hand here on the string and pluck it, it makes this sound." Plunk. "When I place my hand here, it makes this sound." Plonk. "When I place my hand way down here, it makes this sound." Plink.

   A. Was Jimmy using inductive or deductive reasoning?____________________

   B. If inductive, explain why; if deductive, write the deductive syllogism.

   ____

   ____

3. A small boy was looking at pictures of animals with his dad.
   "This is a cheetah," his dad pointed out. "And this is a leopard."
   "Gee, Dad, they all look like kitties," Billy noted.
   "That's right, Son, they're all in the cat family," his dad said. His father then showed a picture of a hyena. "Is this animal in the cat family?" his dad asked.
   "He doesn't look like a kitty," Billy said, "so it must not be."

A. Was Billy using inductive or deductive reasoning?____________________

B. If inductive, explain why; if deductive, describe the deductive syllogism.

____

____

____

4. A math teacher was drilling his third-grade class on the 9s multiplication tables. He put the following problems on the board:

   9 X 3 =　　　　7 X 9 =

   4 X 9 =　　　　2 X 9 =

   After the students answered the problems, one student raised her hand and said, "Hey, the individual digits in the products all add up to 9; like 2 and 7 are 9, and 6 and 3 are 9."

   A. Did the student use inductive or deductive reasoning?____________________

   B. If inductive, explain why; if deductive, describe the deductive syllogism.

   ____

   ____

   ____

SKILLS

5. A child who has learned to like dogs goes to the zoo. Seeing the bears, he tries to approach the cage to pet them.

   A. Did the student use inductive or deductive reasoning?____________________

   B. If inductive, explain why; if deductive, describe the deductive syllogism.

   ____

   ____

CREATIVE THINKING SKILLS

BRAINSTORMING

TARGET CONCEPT AND START LIST

HITCHHIKE ON IDEAS; ASSOCIATE

IMAGE; VISUALIZE

NOTE CATEGORIES; ADD MORE

KEEP REVIEWING TO GENERATE MORE

SKILLS

Brainstorming

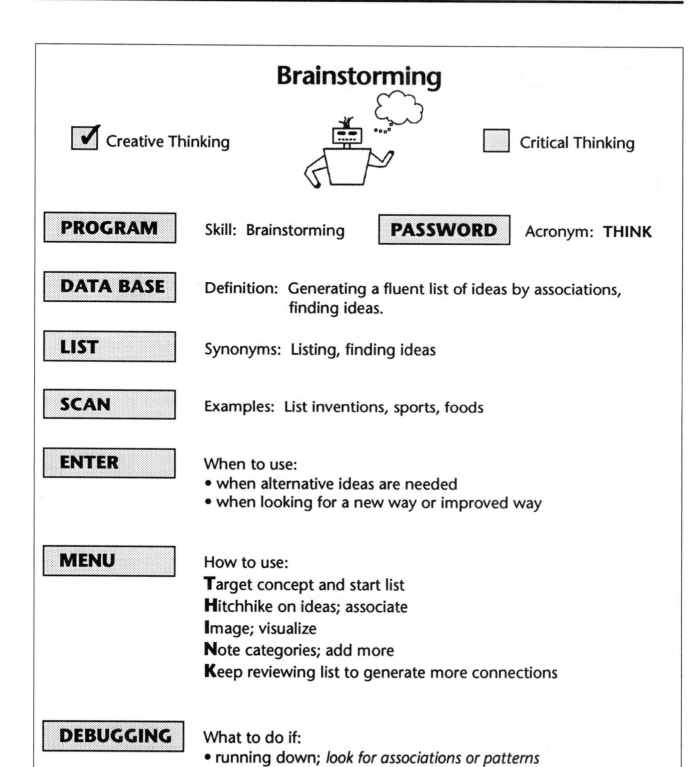

☑ Creative Thinking ☐ Critical Thinking

PROGRAM Skill: Brainstorming

PASSWORD Acronym: **THINK**

DATA BASE Definition: Generating a fluent list of ideas by associations, finding ideas.

LIST Synonyms: Listing, finding ideas

SCAN Examples: List inventions, sports, foods

ENTER When to use:

- when alternative ideas are needed
- when looking for a new way or improved way

MENU How to use:

Target concept and start list
Hitchhike on ideas; associate
Image; visualize
Note categories; add more
Keep reviewing list to generate more connections

What to do if:

- running down; *look for associations or patterns*
- large quantity of ideas; *categorize*
- exhausted ideas; *leave it for a time, then go back*
- want more; *review list*

VISUAL LAYOUT

Patterns: Concept Map
Clustering
Thought Trees
List
Web

FILE

Sample Lesson in Science: Birds

Target concept and list: *robin, sparrow, wren, ostrich, sea gull, parrot, duck, crow*

Hitchhike; make associations:
duck → mallard → Donald → Daffy → geese

Image; visualize: *"See" birds in your mind's eye*

Note categories:

Small	*hummingbird*
Domestic	*chicken*
Cartoon	*Road Runner*
Edible	*cornish hen*
Sports Teams	*Orioles*
Prey	*eagle*
Color	*blackbird*

Keep reviewing to generate more; "Bridging or Plugging-In"

INDEX

Suggested Applications:

MATH
- Terms Used in Measurement
- Tesselations
- Fractions

HISTORY
- Chinese Contribution to Modern World
- A Democratic Society
- Profiles of Courage

LANGUAGE ARTS
- Words for Alliterations
- Physical Traits to Develop a Character
- Research Topics for Women in Literature

SCIENCE
- The Solar System
- Electricity
- Inventions

PREDICTING

BASE ON FACTS

EXPRESS PROBABILITIES AND POSSIBILITIES

TENDER YOUR BET; TAKE A GUESS

SKILLS

Predicting

☑ Creative Thinking ☐ Critical Thinking

PROGRAM Skill: Predicting

PASSWORD Acronym: **BET**

DATA BASE Definition: Anticipating what comes next

LIST Synonyms: forecasting, guessing, anticipating

SCAN Examples: Predicting weather, trends, outcomes

ENTER When to use:
- for focused, attentive reading
- in experiments
- in anticipating outcomes of decisions

MENU How to use:

Base on facts
Examine probabilities and possibilities from clues
Tender your bet; take a guess

DEBUGGING What to do if:
- cannot find obvious clues; *infer from feelings, tone, sensing or intuition*
- guessing wrong; *keep trying*

The Captive

I haven't slept in days, maybe in weeks. My waking hours are spent pacing up and down this 12-by-12-foot chamber of horrors. Why couldn't they have just killed me, put a bullet in my head? But no, for the rest of my life I have nothing but four walls and barred windows to look forward to.

It's a nightmare. I've tried to understand it, but I can't. What have I done, what laws have I broken to warrant this solitary confinement?

It seems so very long ago that I was happy. Certainly we had problems, maybe more than most, but she stood by me all the way. Then came the baby and more problems, but we were in love and would have overcome all obstacles.

Then it happened, I was out for a walk as was my custom after dinner. The sun was shining on my face and the wind was blowing through my hair. I was tired. I'd had a long, hard day, and shortly would return home for a leisurely evening with my family. The events that followed are even now vague in my memory.

Suddenly I felt a piercing pain in my side, and I began to run. I didn't know why I was so afraid, but I knew that I was running for my life. Finally, I could run no more. I fell on my face and lay there. Soon there were men holding guns all around me. They were looking down at me. Everything went black.

The next month was spent moving from place to place. People were yelling at me, pointing at me, accusing me. There were times I thought I was completely insane, that everything happening around me was a nightmare.

I have murdered no one, so why am I here? I have stolen nothing. To the best of my ability I have obeyed the laws, yet for reasons I do not understand, I am to spend the rest of my life in a prison. What have I done?

When I was young I heard about places like this—stories told late at night in whispered voices about the cold, damp dungeons and whip-wielding monsters that inhabit them.

It was common knowledge, the older ones said, that maggot-infested horse meat was the only food given to the captives—and that, only once a week—and dry bread soaked in sewer water. For the crime of even making a sound, one could be stabbed through the bars with long spears, leaving not fatal wounds, but deep slashes of painfully exposed flesh. If only I had known the truth, which is so much worse.

I am never allowed to leave this room and can communicate with no one. I can hear my fellow prisoners on both sides, but I cannot talk to them. They both speak different languages. The guards ignore me and what little communication they have between themselves is also in a foreign tongue.

All day long people are coming and going past my cell. They do not come in. They just stand outside, look at me, then leave. They speak the same language as the guards. In the beginning, I tried to get them to understand me, but like those whom I first came in contact with, they were deaf to my pleas. So now I am quiet. Somehow I know that I have been sentenced to remain here for the rest of my life, and I don't know why.

They have even robbed me of my name. All my life I have been known as Iflan. Even though I can't understand their language, I have picked up two rather unimportant facts. Through the repeated use by my guards and the constant daily spectators, I have learned the name of my prison and the new name I have been given.

Hypothesize: What is the name of the prisoner? What is the name of the prison? Validate your ideas.

SKILLS

Reading To Validate

Base on facts
Express probabilities and possibilities
Tender your bet; take a guess

Then: **READ** to validate
SCORE
REVISE; readjust; refine your idea
BET again based on new information

	+/-
BET #1	
BET #2	
BET #3	
BET #4	
BET #5	

Scoring

+ Score a (+) if your "bet" has not been invalidated in the reading, if it's still a possibility.
- Score a (-) if the reading suggests a different direction than the thinking in your bet.

VISUAL LAYOUT

Patterns: Chart

Focus:
- Gather facts by reading 1st paragraph
- Look for clues to possible or probable outcomes
- Guess, based on your clues
- Prove by stating clues (or reading to verify)
- Repeat "BET" throughout the piece

FILE

Sample lesson in Literature: "The Captive"

INDEX

Suggested Applications:

MATH
- Probabilities
- Estimations
- Stock Market

LANGUAGE ARTS
- Short Stories—Predict Endings
- Write a Scenario of the Future
- Have Students Predict their Future Careers and Support Prediction

SCIENCE
- Weather Predictions
- Predict the Next Breakthrough in Medicine
- Predict Changes in Physiology that we Might Expect in the Future
- Lab Experiments

SOCIAL STUDIES
- "Turning Points" in History (What if...)
- Current Events: International Event—Predict Actions and Outcomes
- Prepare a Newscast for the Year 2000

VISUALIZING

IMAGE FINAL GOAL

MENTALLY PICK A STARTING POINT

ADD, STEP BY STEP, TO YOUR FINAL GOAL

GRAPH YOUR STEPS

ELIMINATE POSSIBLE BARRIERS

SEE THE FINAL IMAGED GOAL

Visualizing

☑ Creative Thinking

☐ Critical Thinking

PROGRAM Skill: Imaging/ Visualizing

PASSWORD Acronym: **IMAGES**

DATA BASE Definition: Seeing or imagining a picture of an idea or concept; visualizing in the mind's eye; making mental images

LIST Synonyms: imagining, picturing, seeing, imaging

SCAN Examples: dreaming; visualizing a place you've visited; imagining yourself winning a race

ENTER When to use:

- at the beginning stages of an idea or goal, trying to visualize a final outcome or product

MENU How to use:

Imagine final goal
Mentally pick a starting point
Add, step by step, to your final goal
Graph your steps
Eliminate possible barriers
See the final imaged goal

DEBUGGING What to do if:

- cannot see an image; *picture "putting it together" using color and all your senses*
- cannot trace path; *leave it, come back later*

SKILLS

VISUAL LAYOUT Patterns: _____ is like ____ because ____.

FILE

Sample Lesson in Science: Gravity

Imagine what would happen if gravity stopped for one second every day. Imagine what things would be like. What would land surfaces look like? How about the oceans and the rivers? Create a scenario depicting this concept. (From *A Whack On The Side Of The Head* by Roger von Oech, Ph.D., 1983)

Imagine the final goal: Using all your senses, picture a scene in detail of that one minute of *no* gravity.

Mentally go back and pick a starting point: See the same scene *with* gravity.

Add, step by step, to the moment of no gravity: See, in detail, the changes that occur.

Graph your steps: Mentally chart your steps until you have a vivid and detailed picture.

Eliminate possible barriers to your mental picture: Concentrate on each separate aspect, then pull it together.

See the final imaged goal: See the finished picture of your scene of that one moment of no gravity.

SKILLS

INDEX

Suggested Applications:

MATH	• Infinity
SOCIAL STUDIES	• Life in Another Country • America as a Communist Society
LANGUAGE ARTS	• Descriptive Passages • Characters in a Novel
SCIENCE	• Prehistoric Times • Life on Another Planet • Sea Community

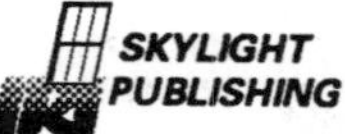

CRITICAL THINKING SKILLS

ATTRIBUTING

TUNE IN; FOCUS

RUN WITH IT; BRAINSTORM ATTRIBUTES

ASSOCIATE IDEAS; PIGGYBACK

IMAGE THE CONCEPT OR ITEM; DEFINE IT

TEST THE ATTRIBUTES

SELECT THE CRITICAL ATTRIBUTES

Attributing

☐ Creative Thinking

☑ Critical Thinking

PROGRAM Skill: Attributing

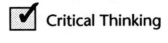

PASSWORD Acronym: **TRAITS**

DATA BASE Definition: Analyze characteristics, qualities, elements or traits of a concept or item.

LIST Synonyms: characteristics, traits, likenesses

SCAN Examples: List attributes of mammals, attributes of courage

ENTER When to use:

- to define concept or term
- to distinguish between two similar concepts or items
- to clarify concept in own terms

MENU How to use:

Tune in; focus
Run with it; brainstorm
Associate ideas; piggyback
Image the concept or item; define it
Test the attributes with a specific example
Select the critical attributes necessary to define concept or item

DEBUGGING What to do if:

- cannot separate it from similar concept; *find specific example to use as model; use references or resource material*
- cannot select *critical* attributes; *keep all*
- cannot think of specific example to test with; *get help from someone or continue to add attributes until more clearly defined*

SKILLS

VISUAL LAYOUT

Patterns: Attribute Web
List
Concept Map

FILE

Sample Lesson in Language Arts: Literature—A Mystery

Tune in: Think of a mystery on TV or in a book.

Run with it: Brainstorm its attributes—clues, suspense, problem-solution, hero.

Associate: hero, victim, suspects

Image: Image and define items—clues lead to climax, but there are several possibilities.

Test: Take a specific mystery. Did it have all these attributes?

Select: Choose defining attributes—problem, hero, victim, suspects, clues, suspense (no victim, therefore eliminate from final list of attributes—can have mystery without victim).

SKILLS

INDEX

Suggested Applications:

MATH	• Metric System • Graphs • Word Problems
LANGUAGE ARTS	• Paragraph • Character Analysis
SCIENCE	• UFOs • Nutritious Foods • Force
SOCIAL STUDIES	• Leaders • War • Geographic Location

SKILLS

CLASSIFYING

COLLECT DATA

LABEL GROUP

USE PATTERN

EVALUATE PATTERN

SKILLS

Classifying

☐ Creative Thinking

☑ Critical Thinking

PROGRAM Skill: Classification

PASSWORD Acronym: **CLUE**

DATA BASE Definition: To sort into groups on the basis of common characteristics (attributes).

LIST Synonyms: grouping, putting into sets, sorting, categorizing

SCAN Examples: grouping rocks, books, animal species

ENTER When to use:
- if data is unorganized
- if there is a lot of data

MENU How to use:

Collect data
Label similar items in group
Use pattern to add others
Evaluate pattern

DEBUGGING What to do if:
- items don't fit; *label miscellaneous*
- data in category vary; *add sub-groups or regroup*
- item fits more than one; *reclassify with new, broader or more focused labels*
- begin to run out of items for one label; *switch to another*

VISUAL LAYOUT

Patterns: Venn Diagram
Morphological Grid
Matrix
Charts

FILE

Sample Lesson in Science: Chemistry—Liquid, Solid, Gas (Phases of Matter)

Collect Data:

wood	soft drink	milk
coffee cup	air	iced tea
paint	muddy water	ice
sugar cube	carbon dioxide	mercury
table salt	T-bone steak	blood
sea water	cough syrup	popcorn

Label similar items in a group:

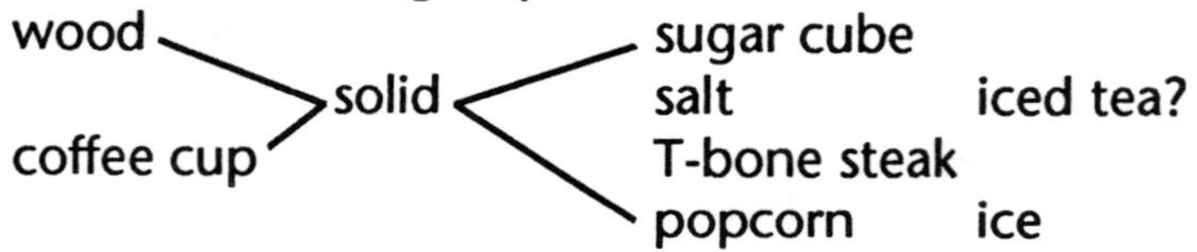

Use pattern to add others:

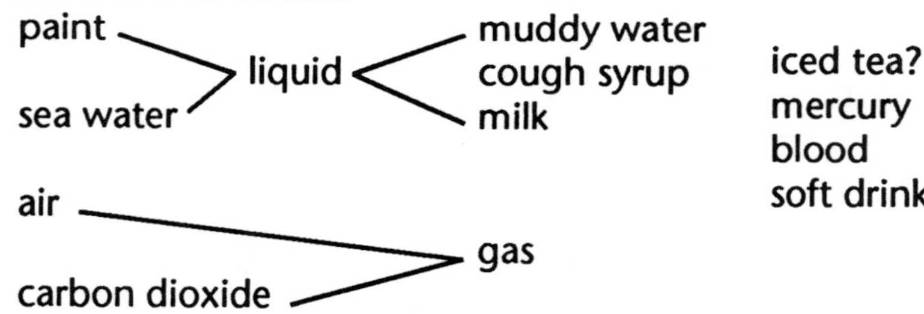

Evaluate pattern:

Question: Where does iced tea fit—solid or liquid?; decide to keep it in *both* categories.

Evaluation: Classifications are ok; double check for gases because there are only two.

SKILLS

INDEX

Suggested Applications:

MATH	• Types of Triangles • Types of Graphs • Prime Numbers
LANGUAGE ARTS	• Dewey Decimal System • Tall Tales, Myths, Fables • Homonyms, Synonyms, Antonyms
SCIENCE	• Trees: Coniferous/Deciduous • Rocks: Sedimentary/Metamorphic/Igneous • Heterogeneous/Homogeneous Matter
SOCIAL STUDIES	• Causes of War: Economic/Political/Social • American Indians • Political Ideologies

PRIORITIZING

REVIEW ALL ITEMS

ADAPT CRITERIA

NOTE TOP AND BOTTOM ITEMS

KEY IN ON 'MIDDLE' OF LIST

Prioritizing

☐ Creative Thinking

☑ Critical Thinking

PROGRAM Skill: Prioritizing

PASSWORD Acronym: **RANK**

DATA BASE Definition: Rank ordering according to determined value

LIST Synonyms: ranking, ordering, selecting

SCAN Examples: with homework, the ordering of assignments, or in packing for a trip, selecting the most important items

ENTER When to use:
- in planning
- for evaluating
- if selecting options
- when deciding

MENU How to use:

Review all items
Adapt criteria: time, value, deadline, energy, mood, goal
Note top items and bottom items on list
Key in on 'middle' of list

DEBUGGING What to do if:
- items seem equal; *review criteria, choose one*
- unsure of one item; *rank it 'down' if unsure, probably* ***not*** *a priority*

VISUAL LAYOUT

Patterns: List
Rank Ladder
Criteria Matrix

FILE

Sample Lesson in Language Arts: Composition

Rank the following according to their importance to writing:

1. quality of content
2. grammar
3. subject
4. format (poetry, novel, etc.)
5. emotional appeal
6. spelling
7. knowledge
8. length
9. first sentence
10. style
11. ending
12. title

Review items: number 1-12 on paper

Adapt criteria: set goal—to communicate one's ideas through writing

Note top and bottom of list:

Top	*Bottom*
1. content	10. knowledge
2. title	11. length
3. emotional appeal	12. spelling

Key in on "middle":

4. first sentence	7. format
5. style	8. ending
6. subject	9. grammar

(Discuss why!)

SKILLS

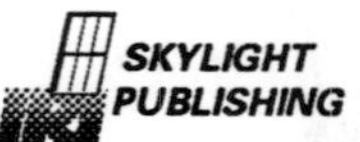

INDEX

Suggested Applications:

MATH
- Stock Market
- Topics of Relevance (Chapters in Book)
- Consumer Education: "Best Buy" in Product Line

SOCIAL STUDIES
- Attributes for Presidential Candidate
- Funding for Federal Programs
- Occupations for Societal Benefits

LANGUAGE ARTS
- Selecting a Research Topic
- Best Commercials on T.V.
- Authors Studied

SCIENCE
- Funding Areas for Medical Research
- Importance of Inventions (List)
- Components of "Wellness" (Health)

Transfer—The Creative Connection

All teaching is for transfer, all learning is for transfer, to extend learning; to bridge the old and the new; to lead students toward relevant transfer and use across academic content and into life situations, is the mission of the thinking classroom.

In some cases, the transfer of learning is obvious because the learned skills seems close to the skill situation in which it is transferred. For example, when teaching "supermarket math"—price comparisons, making change, etc.—the life situation "hugs" the learning situation. The transfer is clear.

In other instances, however, the learning in the school situation seems far removed or remote from the transfer across content or into life. For example, a high school student spends a great deal of time and energy staring at, memorizing, and using the Periodic Table of Elements. However, unless the student is destined for a scientific career in which frequent reference and deep understanding of the table are essential, it is difficult for the student to feel that the learning is really useful in his life. Does he really need to know that Au is gold?

Most students do not "see" the connection between the rigors of learning the elements and the similar rigors of visualizing, practicing and memorizing other material. Few students note that the analytical skills used in "reading" the table of elements are similar to the critical thinking used in analyzing other charts or graphs. Seldom are students aware that the patterns evident in the table of elements set a model for searching for patterns in other phenomena. The transfer here is remote; it is obscure. The student needs explicit instruction in making connections.

In these situations, teachers can help kids make relevant transfer through mediation or "bridging" strategies.

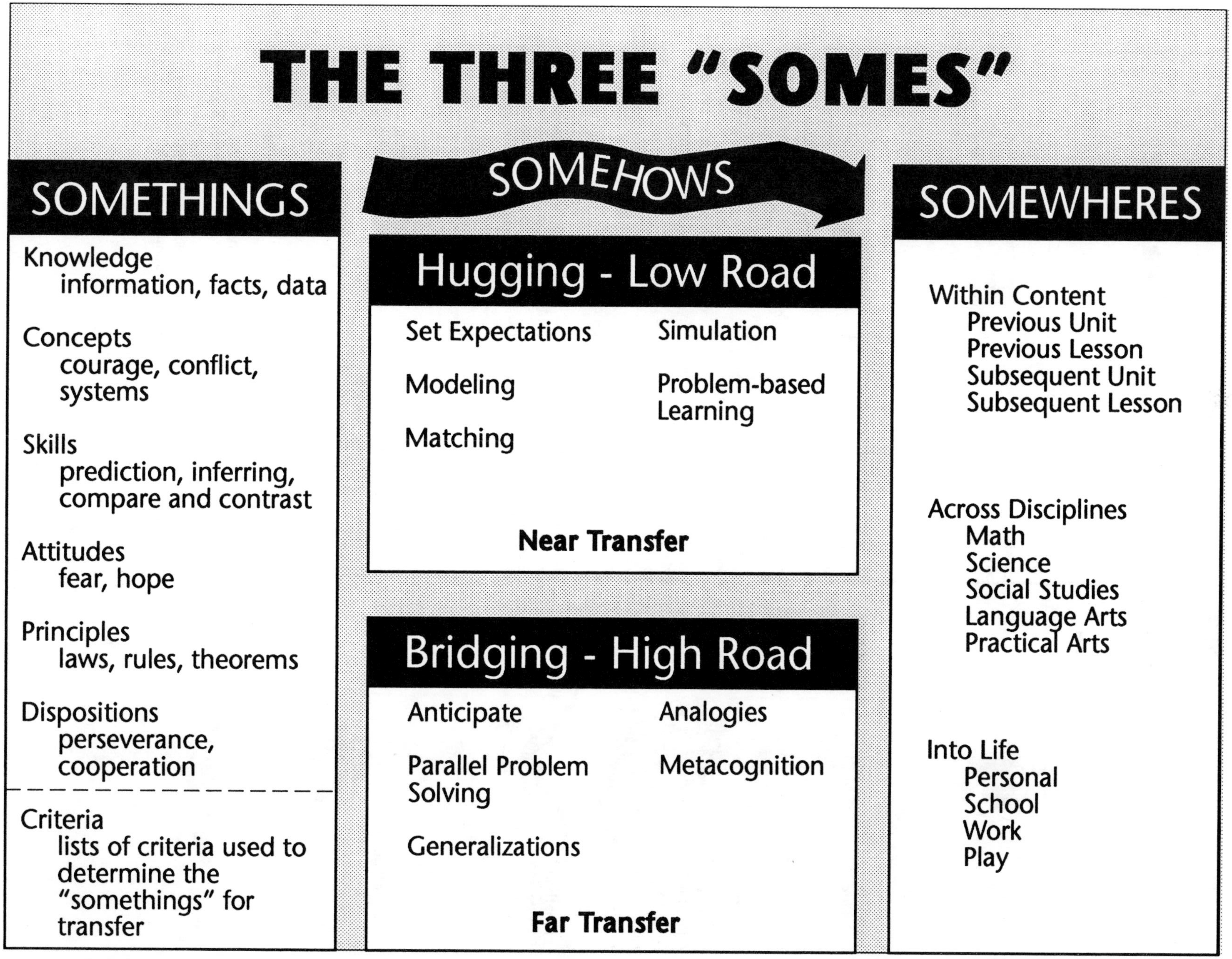

THE THREE "SOMES"

SOMETHINGS

Knowledge
information, facts, data

Concepts
courage, conflict, systems

Skills
prediction, inferring, compare and contrast

Attitudes
fear, hope

Principles
laws, rules, theorems

Dispositions
perseverance, cooperation

Criteria
lists of criteria used to determine the "somethings" for transfer

SOMEHOWS

Hugging - Low Road

Set Expectations

Modeling

Matching

Simulation

Problem-based Learning

Near Transfer

Bridging - High Road

Anticipate

Parallel Problem Solving

Generalizations

Analogies

Metacognition

Far Transfer

SOMEWHERES

Within Content
- Previous Unit
- Previous Lesson
- Subsequent Unit
- Subsequent Lesson

Across Disciplines
- Math
- Science
- Social Studies
- Language Arts
- Practical Arts

Into Life
- Personal
- School
- Work
- Play

Situational Dispositions for Transfer

Model	Illustration	Transfer Disposition	Looks Like	Sounds Like
Ollie the Head-in-the-sand Ostrich		**Overlooks**	Persists in writing in manuscript form rather than cursive. (New skill overlooked or avoided.)	*"I get it right on the dittos, but I forget to use punctuation When I write an essay."* (Not applying mechanical learning.)
Dan the Drilling Woodpecker		**Duplicates**	Plagiarism is the most obvious student artifact of duplication. (Unable to synthesize in own words.)	*"Mine is not to question why—just invert and multiply." (When dividing fractions.)* (No understanding of what she/he is doing.)
Laura the Look-alike Penguin		**Replicates**	"Bed to Bed" or narrative style. "He got up. He did this. He went to bed or He was born. He did this... He died." (Student portfolio of work never varies.)	*"Paragraphing means I must have three 'indents' per page."* (Tailors into own story or essay, but paragraphs inappropriately.)
Jonathan Livingston Seagull		**Integrates**	Student writing essay incorporates newly learned French words. (Applying: weaving old and new.)	*"I always try to guess (predict) what's gonna happen next on T.V. shows."* (Connects to prior knowledge and experience; relates what's learned to personal experience.
Cathy the Carrier Pigeon		**Maps**	Graphs information for a social studies report with the help of the math teacher to actually design the graphs. (Connecting to another.)	Parent-related story. *"Tina suggested we brain-storm our vacation ideas and rank them to help us decide."* (Carries new skills into life situations.)
Samantha the Soaring Eagle		**Innovates**	After studying flow charts for computer class student constructs a Rube Goldberg type invention. (Innovates: Invents; diverges; goes beyond and creates novel.)	*"I took the idea of the Mr. Potato Head and created a mix and match grid of ideas for our Earth Day project."* (Generalizes ideas from experience and and transfers creatively.)

SKILLS

Suggested Skills for Content Areas

Possible Thinking Skills Clusters For Subjects

SUBJECT	Thinking Skills	
READING	Visualizing Predicting Analyzing for Bias	Generalizing Inferring Sequencing
WRITING	Brainstorming Inventing Personifying	Making Analogies Analyzing for Assumption Problem Solving
MATH	Predicting Associating Relationships Inventing	Solving Analogies Problem Solving Evaluating
SOCIAL STUDIES	Determining Cause/Effect Dealing w/Ambiguity-Paradox Generalizing	Decision Making Comparing & Contrasting Prioritizing
SCIENCE	Hypothesizing Determining Cause/Effect Drawing Conclusions	Attributing Classifying Evaluating
PRACTICAL ARTS (PE/Music/Art Business/Home & Industrial)	Visualizing Brainstorming Sequencing	Inventing Problem Solving Decision Making

LEARNER STAGES: Skills

NOVICE	process pieces, not even in order.
ADVANCED BEGINNER	put together; practice in sequence; don't care about results; "Did I do it right?"
COMPETENT USER	cares about relationship of skill to content.
PROFICIENT PERFORMER	has forgotten how he/she does it; work is automatic; relates to classes or sets.
EXPERT	has forgotten everything; can't always explain; "let me show you"; skips steps; goes to "elegant" solution.

Assessing Student Proficiency in a Thinking Skill

PART I: **Content Area: Unit Test**

PART II:

1. DEFINE SKILL
(Which of the following best defines prioritizing? Multiple Choice)

Recognition
Recall

2. RECOGNIZE EXAMPLES
(Which of the following shows information that has been prioritized. Multiple choice of examples and non-examples)

Application

3. EXECUTE SKILL—SHOW ALL WORK
(Prioritize the following items based on ______________. List items and criteria.)

4. SAME AS #3
(list new items and criteria)

5. SAME AS #3
(list new items and criteria)

Metacognition

6. SAME AS #3
(list new items and criteria, but don't prioritize; write a set of directions explaining how to prioritize these items. Pretend you are explaining this process to a younger, inexperienced person.)

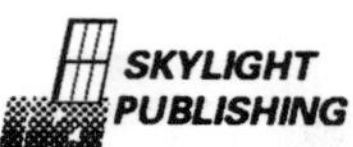

Assessing Student Proficiency In A Thinking Skill

A Sample Test

Recognition Recall

1. Which of the following best defines the skill of prioritizing?

(a) to invent a theory
(b) to put things together having common characteristics
(c) to arrange things in order by the value placed on the them

2. Which of the following shows information that has been prioritized?

(a)	A	(d)	B & C
(b)	A & B	(e)	C
(c)	B	(f)	A & C

A

The objects were placed carefully on the mantel. The candle was set to the right so its glow would light grandpa's picture. His pipe was laid carefully to the left next to his books. But the tinderbox with his gold coins was saved as the centerpiece to remind her of the best times with him.

B

bluff (bluf) n. A step headland or bank; cliff.

blunt (blunt) adj. Having a thick, dull edge or end.

blurb (blurb) n. A brief commendatory publicity notice, as on a book jacket.

boa (bo'a) n. 1. A large, nonvenomous, tropical snake that coils and crushes it prey.

boarder (bor'der) n. One who pays a homeowner for regular meals and lodging.

SKILLS

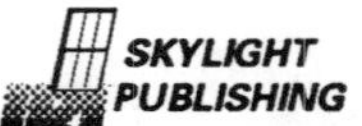

C

Urgent	Important	Pending
• Return phone calls	• Review listings	• Design new logo
• Meet with team	• Write proposal brochure.	• Sketch cover of brochure
• Finalize plan for conference	• Check expense record	
• Sign contract		

APPLICATION

3. Prioritize the following elements according to the importance of each component to a finished piece of writing. Show all your thinking. Then, write a brief paragraph justifying your priorities.

LISTING	RANKING
1. Grammar 2. Length 3. Originality 4. Spelling 5. First Sentence 6. Subject 7. Title 8. Style 9. Emotional Appeal	

METACOGNITION

Justification

Write about your thinking here:

SKILLS

4. DO NOT prioritize the following. Instead, write a set of directions explaining how to prioritize the items. Take time to explain your thinking fully, delineating the procedure you would follow if you were to rank these items according to their importance in school.

    1. math
    2. sports
    3. friends
    4. language
    5. teachers
    6. music
    7. social studies
    8. art
    9. science
    10. grades

Directions

SKILLS

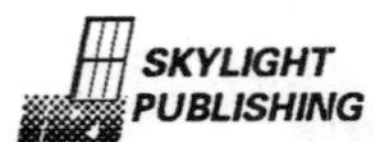

Sample Quiz

CONTENT: Physics—Periodic Chart

THINKING SKILL: Brainstorming

79
Au
197 (1)

Hey you! Tell me everything you know about Au!

1.______________________ 16.______________________
2.______________________ 17.______________________
3.______________________ 18.______________________
4.______________________ 19.______________________
5.______________________ 20.______________________
6.______________________ 21.______________________
7.______________________ 22.______________________
8.______________________ 23.______________________
9.______________________ 24.______________________
10.______________________ 25.______________________
11.______________________ 26.______________________
12.______________________ 27.______________________
13.______________________ 28.______________________
14.______________________ 29.______________________
15.______________________ 30.______________________

NAME______________________________ 3 pts. each 30 = C

SKILLS

Assessing Positive Thinking Behaviors

When you incorporate thinking skills into your teaching, you want to know if students are increasing their ability to think critically and creatively. One way to evaluate your students' thinking is to observe the degree to which students are exhibiting certain key behaviors. This checklist of positive-thinking behaviors will be useful.

☐ **Perseverance**—Do your students
- ❑ stick with it when trying to solve problems, answer questions, and complete assignments?
- ❑ try alternative strategies if they don't succeed?
- ❑ analyze problems systematically, following a logical sequence of steps?

☐ **Reflectiveness**—Do your students
- ❑ think before answering?
- ❑ take time to understand instructions thoroughly before beginning an assignment?
- ❑ plan their steps and rarely erase?

☐ **Flexibility**—Are your students
- ❑ comfortable with ambiguity?
- ❑ willing to consider alternative points of view?
- ❑ able to evaluate the consequences of different actions?

☐ **Metacognition**—
Are your students able to
- ❑ verbalize their thinking?
- ❑ list the steps involved in completing a task and describe where they are in that sequence?
- ❑ indicate at what point they ran into difficulty?
- ❑ describe their thinking at that point?
- ❑ indicate what steps they took to complete the task successfully?

☐ **Problem posing**—Do your students
- ❑ ask questions and identify problems on their own?
- ❑ ask their peers questions like, *How do you know that's true?* and *Why do you think that?*
- ❑ ask you *What do you think would happen if ...?* and, *Why does ...?*

☐ **Carefulness**—Are your students
- ❑ serious about their work?
- ❑ concerned about accuracy?
- ❑ taking pride in the quality of their work?
- ❑ regularly rechecking their answers?

☐ **Use of prior knowledge**—
Do your students
- ❑ recognize the importance of relating their prior knowledge to a new concept?
- ❑ say, *This reminds me of ...* or *This is like the time we ...?*
- ❑ use their previous knowledge and experience in the course of learning?

☐ **Precise language**—Do your students
- ❑ use descriptive words, correct names and analogies to describe objects, people and ideas?
- ❑ avoid vague terms such as "nice," "weird," "good" and "okay?"

☐ **Enjoyment of thinking**—
Do your students
- ❑ seek out situations which require them to think?
- ❑ exhibit an "I can" attitude?
- ❑ eagerly find answers on their own without help from you?
- ❑ say things like, *Don't tell me the answer, I want to figure it out for myself?*

☐ **Transference**—Do you find that
- ❑ students use their thinking skills both in and out of class?
- ❑ parents report that their children are becoming more interested in school?
- ❑ other teachers say that your students use higher level cognitive processes?

SECTION 5

INTERACTION

We are going to have to find ways of organizing ourselves cooperatively, sanely, scientifically, harmonically and in regenerative spontaneity with the rest of humanity around earth ....We are not going to be able to operate our spaceship earth successfully nor for much longer unless we see it as a whole spaceship and our fate as common. It has to be everybody or nobody.

—R. Buckminster Fuller

Student-to-Student Information Interaction

Research on cooperative learning is overwhelmingly positive, and the cooperative approaches are appropriate for all curriculum areas. The more complex the outcomes (higher order processing of information, problem solving, social skills, and attitudes), the greater are the effects.

—Bruce Joyce

Introduction

Let's look at cooperation,

(a) On A Planetary Scale: Buckminster Fuller coined the phrase "Spaceship Earth" when he envisioned his concept of a "global community"; cooperating and co-existing in a mutually beneficial way.

(b) On A Global Scale: Marilyn Ferguson writes about grass-root networks "conspiring" in interwoven cooperative efforts toward societal transformation.

(c) On An International Scale: The Japanese have skillfully adapted and refined the highly effective cooperative problem-solving model called Quality Circles.

(d) On A National Scale: Peters and Waterman look at examples of small-scale cooperative efforts within our nation's successful companies. They label these small-group undertakings "skunkworks" and they describe a method called "chunking" in which groups work on particular "chunks" of a project and ultimately bring the various "chunks" together in a cooperative culmination.

(e) On An Educational Scale: David & Roger Johnson elaborate on structured interaction in the classroom. Their research on "circles of learning" outlines a highly feasible classroom model that increases student interaction and involvement.

(f) On A Personally Relevant Scale: Throughout the lessons in *Patterns For Thinking—Patterns For Transfer*, structured interaction is fostered through small-group work. Roles are assigned, responsibilities are equally shared and routinely rotated. Students have ownership in their learning situations as their cooperative efforts determine group outcomes.

Specifically, one small-group structure that is utilized in the lessons is elaborated in this section: Johnson and Johnson's cooperative classroom groups.

Teaching with Thinking

Roger and David Johnson, two brothers who work cooperatively at the University of Minnesota, have researched the values of cooperative, competitive, and individualistic learning in the classroom. Their studies argue for the superiority of cooperative groups over competitively and individualistically organized classrooms. When properly implemented, cooperative groups are especially powerful in promoting thinking and problem solving in the classroom.

In the *Catch Them Thinking* lessons, we have adapted cooperative group methodology as the key to many of the structured activities. Classroom teachers who piloted many of these lessons preferred the cooperative group strategies for several reasons. First, the small group required more total involvement in the thinking tasks. It was very easy for even the more shy or the more resistant learner to get involved. The teacher could observe more student thinking. Secondly, the cooperative groups provided the less skilled thinkers with models and peer coaching. With the emphasis on cooperation rather than competition that produces winners and losers, a more positive classroom climate developed. Thirdly, as the groups became more skilled in their cooperation, the teacher was freed to concentrate less on management and more on helping individuals develop and apply the thinking skills. Fourth, the teachers felt more comfortable with the amount of cognitive processing that cooperative groups allowed.

Each of the lessons is designed for cooperative groups of 3-4 students. When organizing the groups we suggest that you follow these guidelines.

1. **Abandon The Bluebirds.** Do not use homogeneous groups for these activities. Instead, mix the groups so that there is a balance of high performers and low performers in each group. In the first few months, rotate groups so that there is a constant variation allowing most students to work with most other students. Don't allow student self selection, but work for constant mixes of male/female, task directed/socializers, majority/minority and so on.

2. **Balance The Time.** Some of the tasks have time limits. Other tasks you will have to judge for yourself. When you see one or two groups finish a task, announce "two more minutes" and stick to it. Some of the lessons will take 30 - 40 minutes; others several hours. For younger students, break the lessons into several parts and sequence the parts over several days. For the older students, you may want to do the lesson and the transfer lessons over two or three weeks. Keep groups intact through a lesson.

3. **Move Furniture Quietly.** Each lesson may call for two or three different arrangements of desks. All-class discussions are facilitated by a circle or half moon. Input requires students to face you and the board. Small groups will function with desks drawn close enough for low voice conversation, but removed from other small circles to avoid distractions. Model for students how to move the desks quietly and reinforce that behavior. Expect that desks are rearranged by the students for the next class.

4. **Prepare Materials Before.** Many of the lesson activities call for newsprint and markers. Have these ready for quick and easy distribution. Expect that all materials will be returned at the end of the task.

5. **Assign Task Roles.** Each student in the group should have a specific role and understand the responsibilities of that role. The most basic roles are the leader who keeps the group on task, the recorder who uses the newsprint or worksheet, and the timekeeper who watches the clock and checks task progress. Other roles, such as the observer who records and gives feedback to the group on how well members cooperate and the materials manager who makes sure that the group has all its materials, may also be needed. When assigning roles, try to ensure rotation so that all students learn all tasks. Selecting roles can be a creative endeavor. For instance, find the person who lives farthest from school, is tallest, is wearing the most of a color, has the most letters in the last name, etc. When that person is identified in each group, assign a role, then assign the other roles in an equally random way.

6. **Explain The Task.** Give clear, specific instructions. Especially in the beginning of the year, check for understanding by asking one or more students to explain your instructions in their own words. When necessary, ask other students to explain for you, especially when giving examples of key terms.

7. **Structure Positive Goal Interdependence.** Reinforce to each group that they have a team goal and must work cooperatively. They will sink or swim together. The final product is a group product.

8. **Structure Individual Accountability.** The group is responsible for making sure that every individual masters the thinking skill. Each individual will be expected to know key concepts, especially the mental menus and the skill definition.

9. **Specify and Observe Desired Behaviors.** Students should know which intelligent behaviors you are looking for. At the minimum, this will mean that they follow DOVE, participate actively in the discussion, and carry out individual roles. As the groups improve, carry a check sheet and record data that you can share later with the students. The check sheet will include such behaviors as contributing ideas, asking questions, actively listening, expressing support and acceptance, summarizing, giving positive direction to the group, encouraging others to participate, clarifying, affirming, and testing options.

10. **Set Clear Criteria For Success.** Provide examples to model high quality products which you expect from the group work. Make it possible for all to reach the criteria without penalizing others.

Initially students may find it difficult to maintain on-task behavior when in small groups. However if you approach the groupings with care and follow the guidelines, you will find that they soon become the most productive learning time in the day. The time you give to preparation and practice of group behavior in the beginning of the year, you will quickly make up within a few months. If breakdowns occur the best care is to stop the group, discuss the difficulty and encourage students to refine the classroom rules. You will find that they value the group learning so highly that they will police their own problems and return promptly to the challenge of thinking.

MRS. POTTER

Circles Of Learning

Adapted from *Circles of Learning*, (Johnson and Johnson, 1986)

A. Group Size:

- Three to four students make an ideal group.

B. Assigning Students:

- Intermix academically high, average and low students.
- Mix task-oriented with non-task-oriented students.
- Student selection is not recommended.
- Mix majority/minority; handicapped/nonhandicapped; male/female, etc.

C. Duration of Group Assignments:

- Consider the length of the instructional unit.
- Make them long enough for them to be successful.
- Consider their permanency for the year.
- Consider personal preferences.

D. Arranging the Room:

- Move circles close enough to each other for students to communicate effectively.
- Arrange circles far enough apart so as not to disrupt the other learning groups.
- Round tables, rug areas, or a circle of chairs is preferred.

E. Planning Instructional Methods:

- Materials interdependence: Give only one copy of a handout to each group so students in the group will have to work together.
- Information interdependence: Give members different resource books so that they will need to synthesize in order to be successful.
- Interdependence with other groups: Structure materials into a tournament format with intergroup competition to promote interdependence among group members.

F. Assigning Roles to Ensure Interdependence:

- Group roles and responsibilities are necessary ingredients in small-group work to "structure for success." The roles and corresponding responsibilities suggested throughout *Patterns For Thinking* lessons are:

  (1) ***The Discussion Leader:*** The leader is in charge of keeping the group "on task" and facilitating the discussion.

  (2) ***The Materials Manager:*** The manager assembles all the necessary materials for the group task, replenishes supplies as needed, and returns materials.

(3) ***The Recorder:*** The recorder writes, tallies, and charts the information generated by the group.

(4) ***The Observer/Timekeeper:*** The observer/timekeeper observes the group process and dynamics of the interaction, keeps track of time to ensure task completion and reports verbally for the group.

- Roles are rotated within the group each time the group meets so all students have an equal opportunity to learn all role responsibilities.

- Selecting roles can become an inventive procedure that enhances the activity. Some selection processes are:

  Person who: lives farthest away
  is the tallest
  has the largest last digit in phone number
  has the largest family
  has the biggest shoe size
  has the most freckles

- Each time the groups reconvene, the roles are shifted one person to the right. Groups can become permanent for any length of time—week, month or year.

G. Explaining the Academic Task:

- Give clear, specific instructions.
- Explain and post the lesson objective.
- Define relevant concepts.
- Check for understanding.

H. Structuring Positive Goal Interdependence:

- Communicate to students that they have a group goal and must work collaboratively.
- Reinforce the "sink or swim together" learning situation with
  - a single product, report or paper
  - group rewards

I. Structuring Individual Accountability:

- Assess level of individual member performance.

J. Structuring Intergroup Cooperation:

- Offer bonus points if all members of class reach the preset criterion of excellence.
- Encourage early finishing groups to help others.

K. Explaining Criteria for Success:
- Evaluation is based on criteria set for acceptable work.
- Students may reach criteria without penalizing others.
- Groups may reach criteria without penalizing other groups.

L. Specifying Desired Behaviors:
- DOVE Guidelines
- active participation
- metacognitive processing

M. Monitoring Students' Behaviors:
- Conduct observation with formal sheet for data.
- Reinforce positive behaviors such as:
  (1) contributing ideas
  (2) asking questions
  (3) expressing feelings
  (4) active listening
  (5) expressing support and acceptance
  (6) expressing warmth
  (7) summarizing
  (8) relieving tension
  (9) giving direction to the group
  (10) encouraging others to participate

N. Provide Task Assistance:
- clarify
- review
- answer questions
- teach task skills

O. Intervening to Teach Collaborative Skills:
- only when absolutely necessary
- to suggest procedures
- to consult with group

P. Provide Closure to Lesson:
- Students should be able to summarize.

Q. Evaluating Quality:
- Product is evaluated on criteria previously set.
- Group functioning is evaluated.
  - Was task accomplished?
  - Did group build constructive relationships?

Cooperative Groups: Some Suggested Member Roles

- **GENERAL:**
  Task leader: Encourages group in task
  Observer/Timekeeper: Observes group process
  Recorder: Writes and records
  Materials manager: Gets what is needed

- **FOR A MATH GROUP:**
  Calculator: Checks work on calculator
  Analyst: Analyzes strategies
  Bookkeeper: Checks answers and records time
  Inventory controller: Keeps inventories on materials and controls supplies

- **FOR A WRITER'S GROUP:**
  Editor In Chief: Tracks progress; sets deadlines
  Publisher: Sets guidelines
  Scribe: Keeps notes
  Author: Supplies the materials

- **FOR A NOVEL GROUP:**
  Discussion leader: Prepares and leads questions
  Vocabulary enricher: Selects enrichment questions
  Literary illuminary: Reads favored passages
  Agent: Gets materials

- **FOR A SOCIAL STUDIES GROUP:**
  Presiding officer: Presides over the group
  Parliamentarian: Observes group behavior
  Secretary: Records information
  Sargent at arms: Keeps the time; gets materials

- **FOR A SCIENCE GROUP:**
  Scientist: Observes progress and keeps times
  Researcher: Provides guidelines to follow
  Observer: Records information
  Lab technician: Sets up materials and equipment

- **FOR A PRIMARY GROUP:**
  Captain: Encourages group
  Umpire: Observes and reports
  Scorekeeper: Writes down information
  Runner: Gets what is needed

Sample Roles: Primary

	LEADER	1. Listen for rule following. 2. Keep group producing. 3. Think and tell.
	REPORTER	1. Observe what happens. 2. Think and tell. 3. Report what happens.
	COUNTER	1. Think and tell. 2. Count number of ideas. 3. Get the materials your group will need.
	RECORDER	1. Think and tell. 2. Write all ideas down. 3. Spelling doesn't count.

You will have a chance to be a Leader,  the Recorder ,

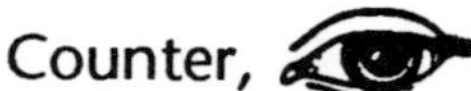
Counter, and Reporter 

Benefits and Barriers of Using Cooperative Groups

(...and other interactive strategies)

BENEFITS	BARRIERS
1.	1.
2.	2.
3.	3.
4.	4.
5.	5.
6.	6.
7.	7.
8.	8.
9.	9.
10.	10.

Paired Partners
(and Think Aloud Strategies)

"Paired partners" can be considered small cooperative groups, with similar structures applied. Often, in using groups with young children, dyads are viable beginnings.

Paired partners are also appropriate when groups of three or four are not working well. By restructuring more tightly in twosomes, students are lead into the roles and responsibilities required for group members.

However, paired partnerships have yet another strategy. As outlined by Arthur Whimbey, the "think aloud" strategy used to solve problems should be practiced in partnerships.

For example, in the "think aloud" strategy, one student verbalizes his thinking as he solves a math problem. He communicates his thoughts to his partner. The partner follows, listens and monitors the verbal thinking, asking clarifying questions when appropriate. For example, the listening partner may ask the problem solver, "Why did you subtract there?" or "Are you expecting a larger number or a smaller number in your answer?" However, the major benefit comes simply from the student articulating the problem-solving process.

After the paired partners have worked through the problem(s), they compare their strategies to "model" strategies used by "expert" problem solvers. With repeated practice and tracking, fallacies in problem-solving approaches emerge. Students also see their favored patterns. They can then begin to adjust these at a conscious level.

Students become more aware of gaps and inadequacies in the way they approach problems by mirroring their thinking with a partner. In addition, they are processing their approach to problems at a metacognitive level and they are learning to be thorough and methodical in solving problems.

Paired-Partner Teaching

"I'm not saying your answer is right or wrong, but tell me how you got it so I understand the information and steps you used."

"Read this (sentence, word, phrase, paragraph, mathematical symbol, graph) carefully again and tell me what it means."

"Have you solved a problem or answered a question like this one before?"

Five Elements of Cooperative Groups

Build in high-order thinking so students are challenged to think deeply and to transfer subject matter.

Unite the groups so students form bonds of trust, which enable team work.

Insure individual learning: Each student is accountable to master all skills and knowledge. The groups are a means to facilitate mastery before the teacher checks each individual through quizzes, tests, essays or more authentic assessment strategies.

Look back and debrief *what* and *how* students learned. Students are taught to "process" or "evaluate" their thinking, feelings and social skills. This emphasis on student self-evaluation shifts the responsibility for learning from the teacher to the student.

Develop students' social skills. By providing explicit training in the social skills, the teacher helps students master cooperative abilities during cooperative work.

Good Paired Partner Problem Solvers

Good problem solvers believe that they can solve just about any problem if they work at it long enough.

◆◆◆

Good problem solvers are persistent. They will work a long time on a problem before giving up.

◆◆◆

Good problem solvers read carefully. They often read the problem several times before beginning to solve it. They are certain that they know what has been said before they begin.

◆◆◆

Good problem solvers break down complex problems into smaller steps and solve each step at a time.

◆◆◆

Good problem solvers organize their work so that at any point they can back up and follow the steps they have taken. They often draw pictures to describe the problem.

◆◆◆

Good problem solvers habitually check what they have done, both at the end of the problem and at various steps along the way.

◆◆◆

Good problem solvers try many things when they solve problems. They sometimes draw pictures or try to visualize a concrete example. They jot down notes that translate what they have read into words or symbols that are easier to understand. If they cannot solve the problem that is given, they often try a simpler, related problem. For example, they might (a) substitute small numbers for large numbers, (b) substitute whole numbers for variables, or (c) restrict the conditions given in the problem.

◆◆◆

Good problem solvers guess and test. That is, they try something that may work and test it to see if it does work. If it does not, then they try something else.

Quick Reference to Cooperative Interactions

	Design	Symbol	Explanation
#1	Lecture/Rhetorical Questioning: Teacher Talk (Perhaps Professor Kingsfield)	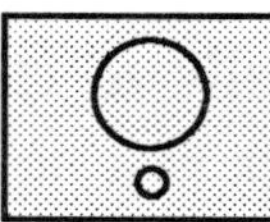	Stand-up teaching, lecturing to whole class.
#2	Signals/Direct Questioning: Surveying (Hunter)	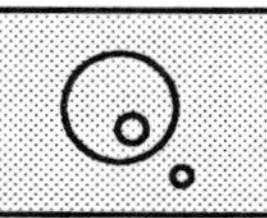	Lecturing to class, interrupting for signals by group or for answer by one student.
#3	Turn To Your Partner And. . . (TTYPA) (Weaver & Cotrell)		Informal sharing by partners in which interaction is brief and quick.
#4	Paired Partners: Think Aloud (Bloom; Whimbey)		One partner reflecting the thinking of the other partner who is talking aloud as he thinks through a problem.
#5	Dyads: Think/Pair/Share (Lyman & McTighe)	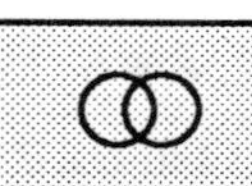	Partners first thinking alone and then sharing ideas—sometimes coming to one idea for their pair.
#6	Triads: Observer Feedback (Costa; Rowe)		Partner interaction enhanced by objective observer feedback.
#7	Tell/Retell: 2-4-8 (Fogarty & Bellanca)		Two people telling ideas; two sets of two retelling their partners' ideas, a group of eight retelling all ideas.
#8	Cooperative Learning: Groups (Johnson & Johnson; Kagan; Slavin)		Small groups of three students working interdependently, but all members accountable for all the work.
#9	Traveling Clusters: People Search (Workshop Leaders)	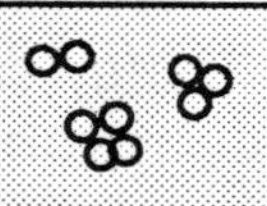	Students moving from group to group, forming informal clusters as they share information and gather signatures.
#10	Forced Response: Wraparound (Howe & Howe)	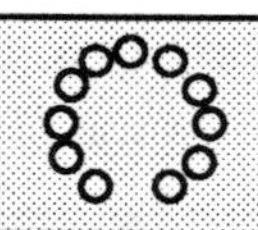	Round-robin style, students responding in turn to a lead-in statement cued by the teacher.
#11	Total Group Response: Human Graph (Fogarty)	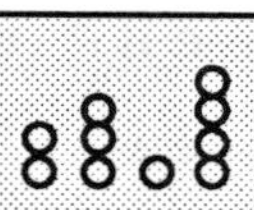	Students lining up on an imaginary graph to indicate their preferences.
#12	Group Investigation: Jigsaw (Aronson; Sharan & Sharan)	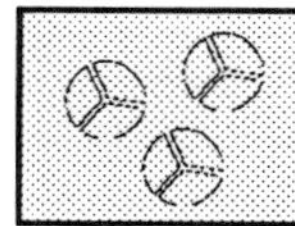	In groups of three, each member researching a third of the group work and then teaching it to the others in the threesome.

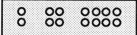

Notes

Notes

GRAPHIC ORGANIZERS: STUDENT-TO-INFORMATION INTERACTIONS

SKYLIGHT PUBLISHING

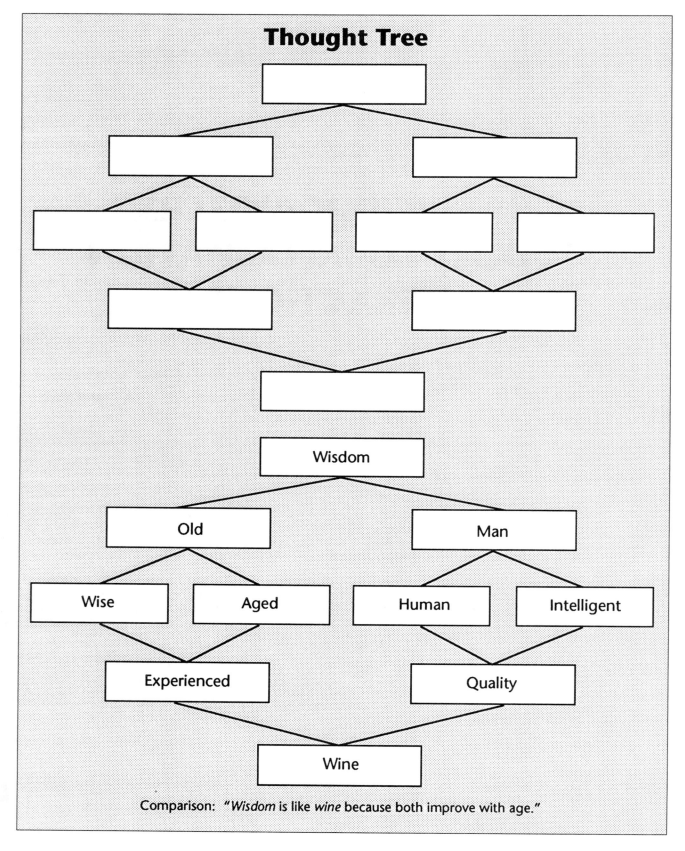

Thought Tree

Wisdom

Old

Man

Wise

Aged

Human

Intelligent

Experienced

Quality

Wine

Comparison: "*Wisdom* is like *wine* because both improve with age."

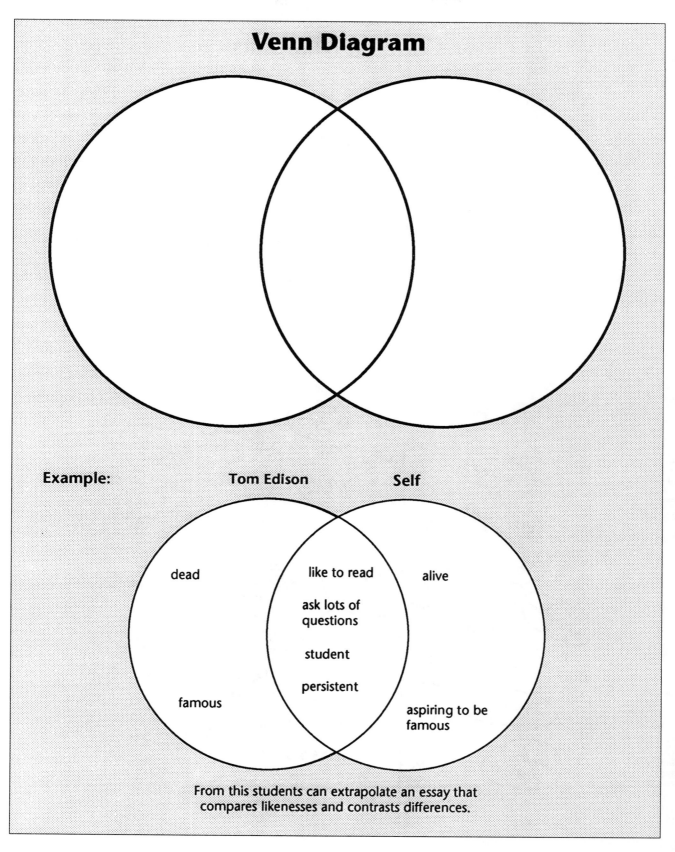

Venn Diagram

Example:

From this students can extrapolate an essay that compares likenesses and contrasts differences.

Concept Mapping

Work space:

Example:

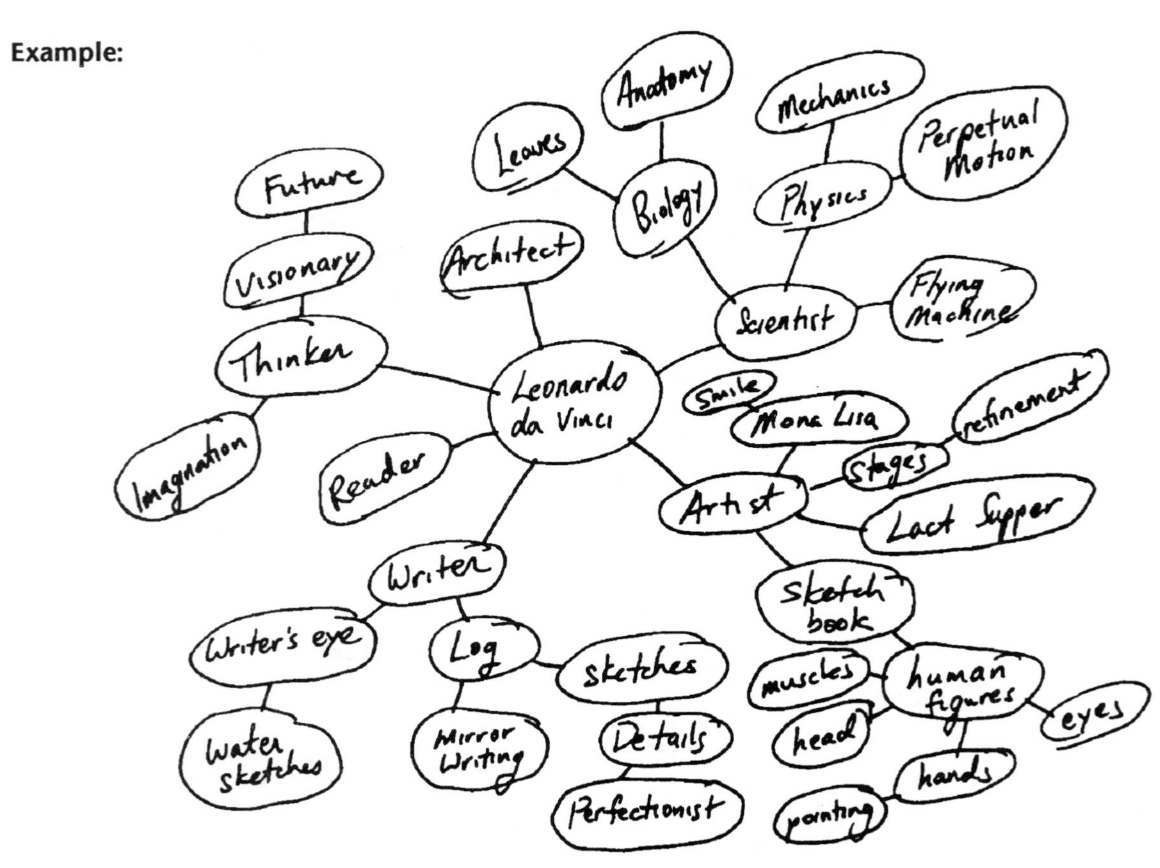

INTERACTION

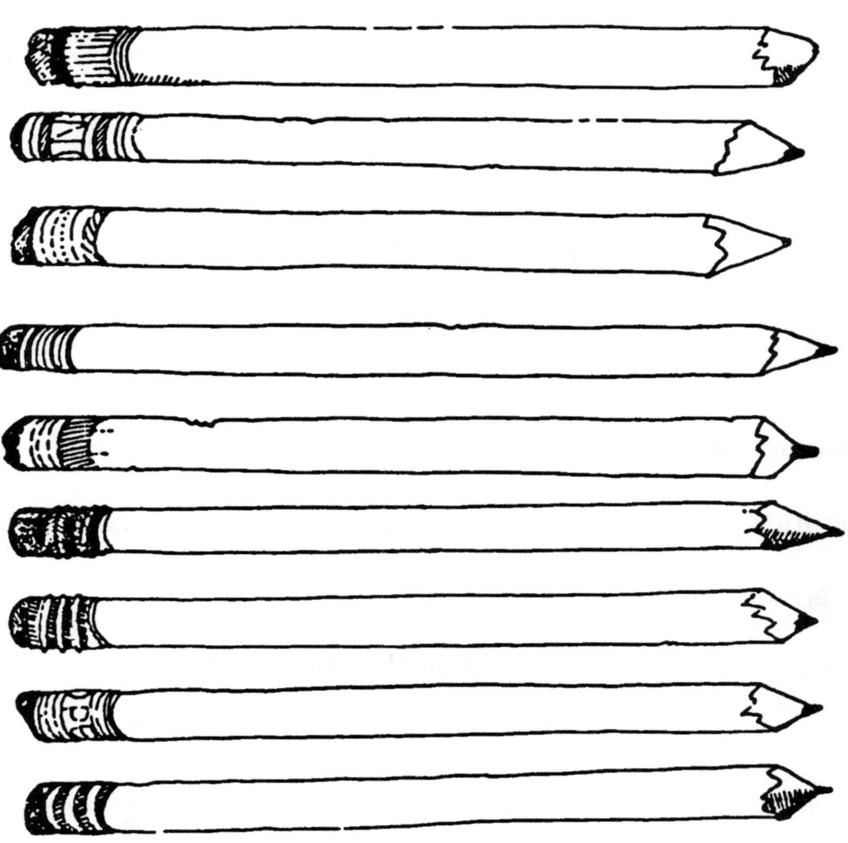

Rank these items according to your favorites:

spinach
squash
cauliflower
beans
peas
corn

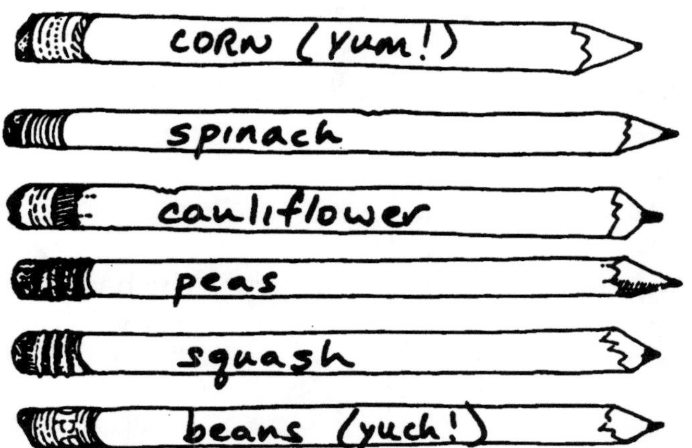

Metaphor Model

1. How is a ______________________ like a ______________________?
   Explain.

OR

2. ______________________ is like ______________________ because both

   ____.

3. Expanded Metaphor Model

   a. Focus on the concept: ______________________________________

   b. Choose an object: ____

   c. Compare the various parts of the object to the concept.

EXAMPLES

1. How is a coach like a clock? Both a coach and a clock signal.
2. Teaching is like a train because both connect things.
3. Concept: Fear
   Object: Suitcase

   We carry fear around with us like baggage. The handle represents the grip it has on us at times, while the latch signifies that fear which we keep locked away.

Agree/Disagree Statements

Input:

Statement	Before		After	
	Agree	Disagree	Agree	Disagree
1.				
2.				
3.				
4.				
5.				
6.				
7.				
8.				

Agree/Disagree Statements

Input: Charlottes Web

Statement	Before		After	
	Agree	Disagree	Agree	Disagree
1. Spiders are a nuisance.	X			X
2. Spiders are frightening.	X			X
3. Spiders have no feelings.	X		X	
4.				

INTERACTION

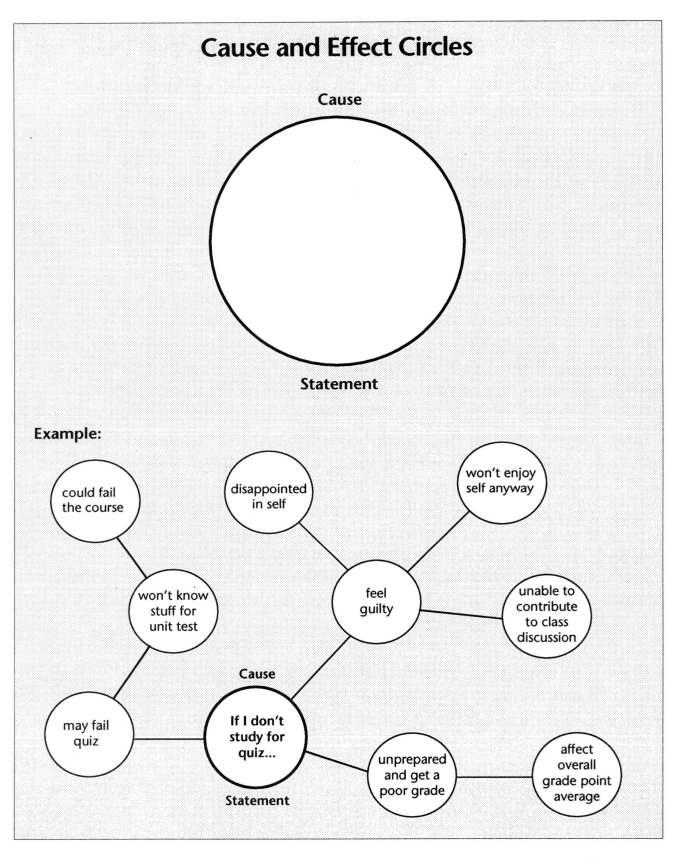

Cause and Effect Circles

Cause

Statement

Example:

Cause

If I don't study for quiz...

Statement

may fail quiz

won't know stuff for unit test

could fail the course

feel guilty

disappointed in self

won't enjoy self anyway

unable to contribute to class discussion

unprepared and get a poor grade

affect overall grade point average

Attribute Web

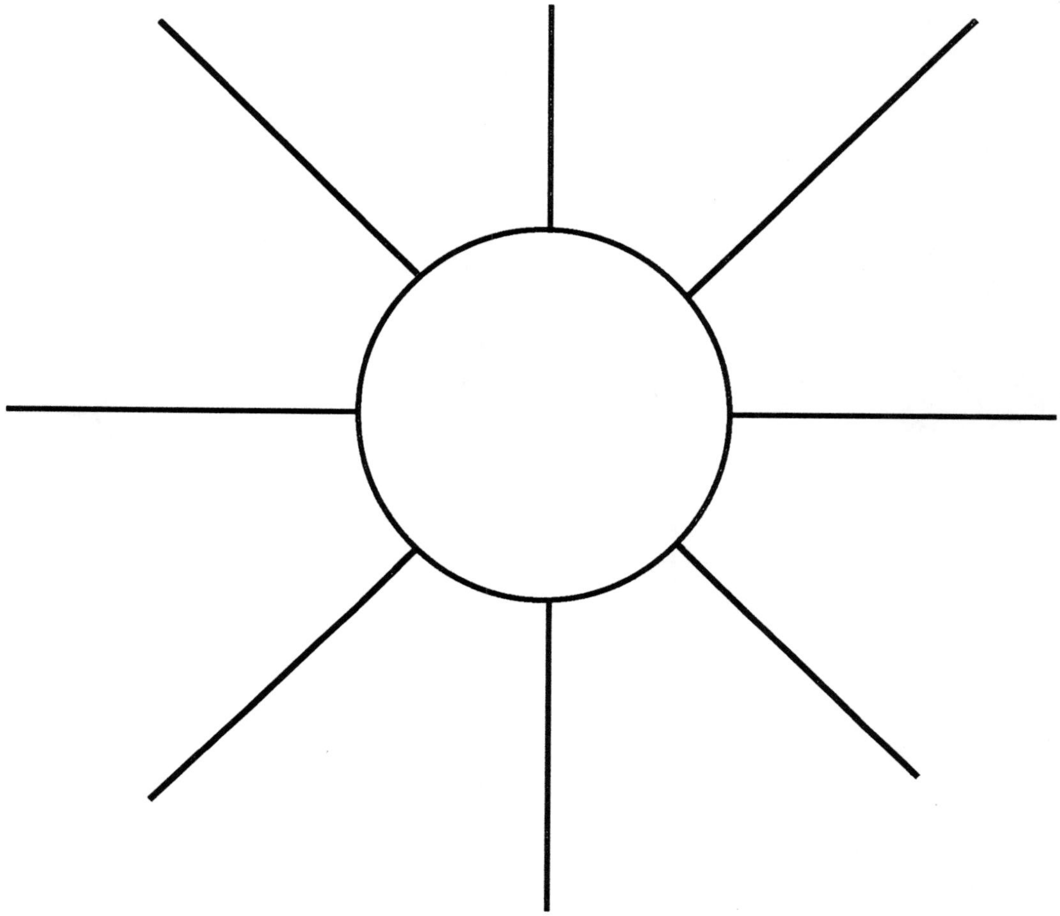

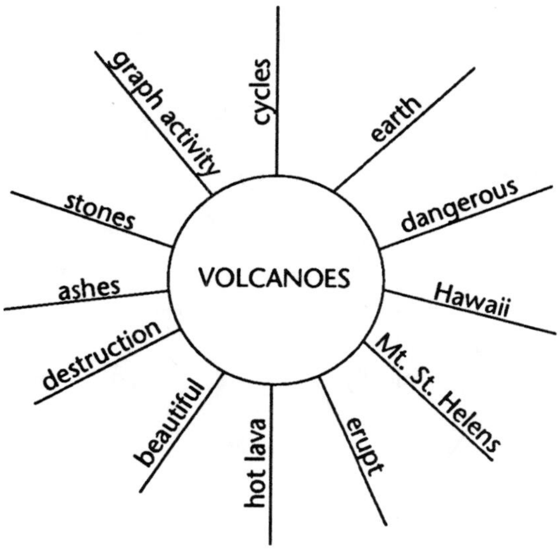

Hex Message

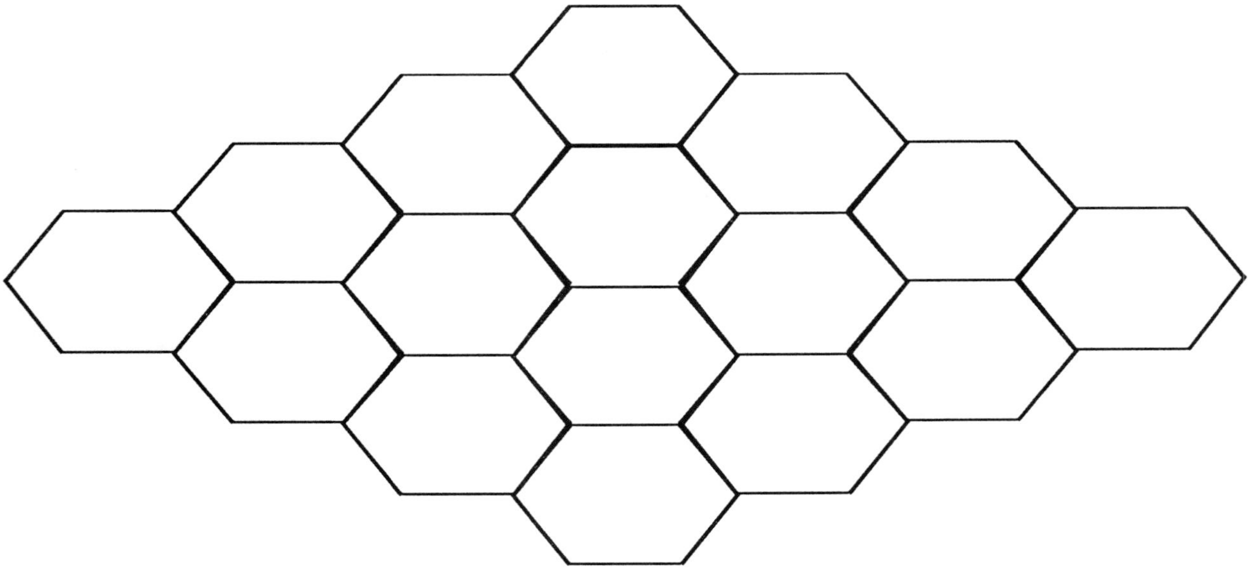

The
Message
Meaning
Sublty
Cleverly
Comically
Hidden
Evident
Exposed
Revealed
May
Will
Won't
Help
Hinder
Understanding

Sequential Thinking Model

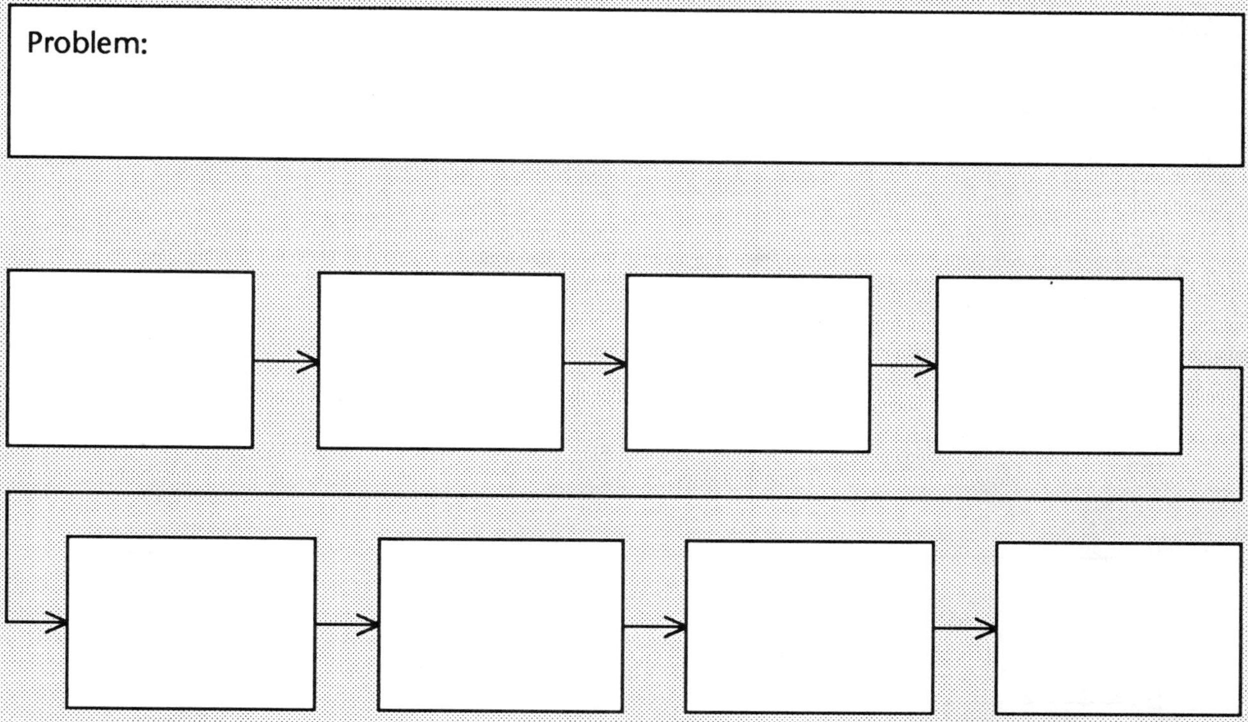

Problem:

[ ] → [ ] → [ ] → [ ] →

→ [ ] → [ ] → [ ] → [ ]

Example:

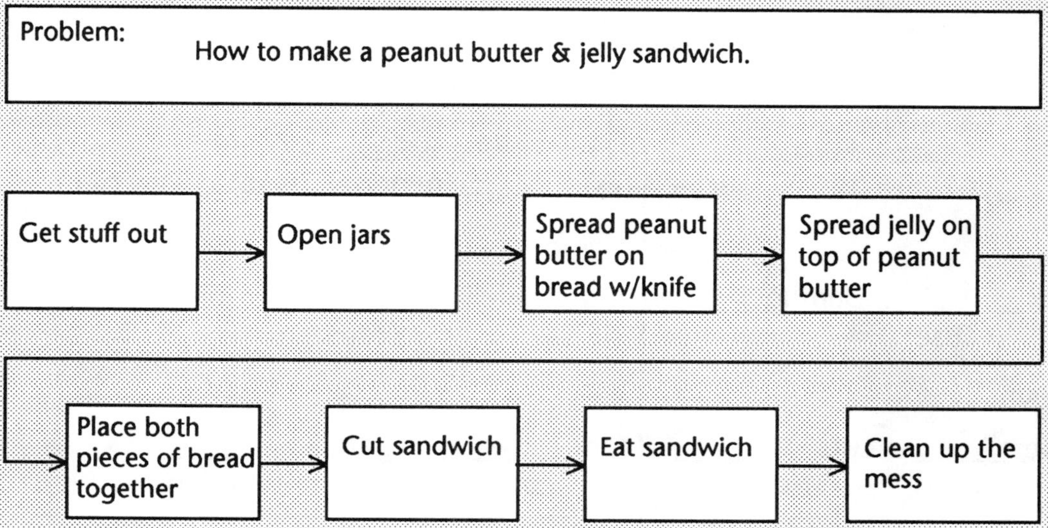

Problem: How to make a peanut butter & jelly sandwich.

Get stuff out → Open jars → Spread peanut butter on bread w/knife → Spread jelly on top of peanut butter →

→ Place both pieces of bread together → Cut sandwich → Eat sandwich → Clean up the mess

Analogy Model

1. ______________ : ______________ :: ______________ : ______________

2. ______________ : ______________ :: ______________ : ______________

3. ______________ : ______________ :: ______________ : ______________

4. ______________ : ______________ :: ______________ : ______________

5. ______________ : ______________ :: ______________ : ______________

Example:

1. auto________ : Ford________ :: Television________ : Zenith________
   (general) (is to) (specific) (as) (general) (is to) (specific)

2. crack________ : damage________ :: remodeling________ : improvement________
   (cause) (effect) (cause) (effect)

3. knife________ : cuts________ :: fork________ : gathers________
   (object) (function) (object) (function)

Newspaper Model—5W Model

Topic:

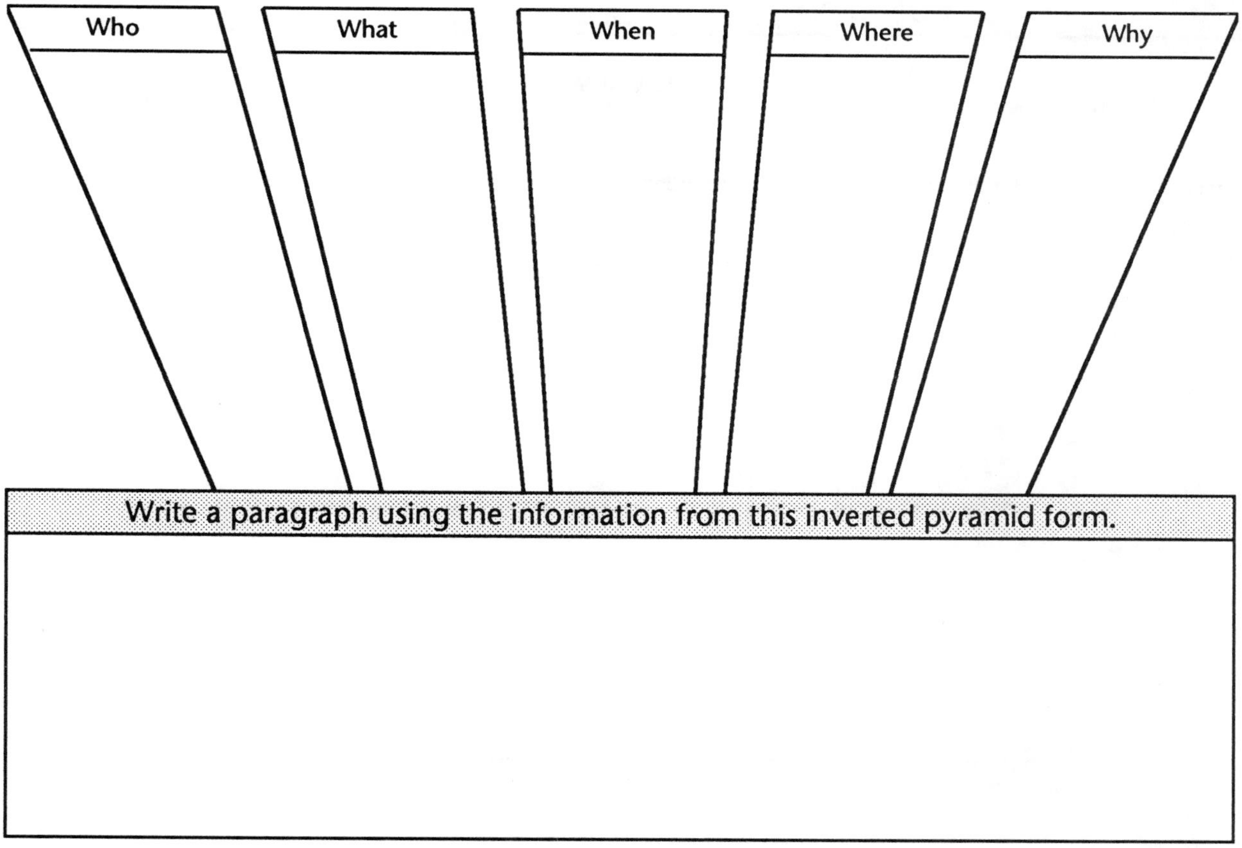

Who	What	When	Where	Why

Write a paragraph using the information from this inverted pyramid form.

Example: **Topic: The Boston Tea Party**

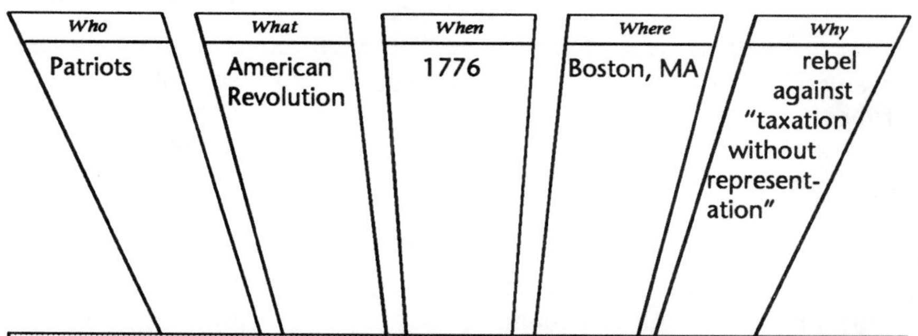

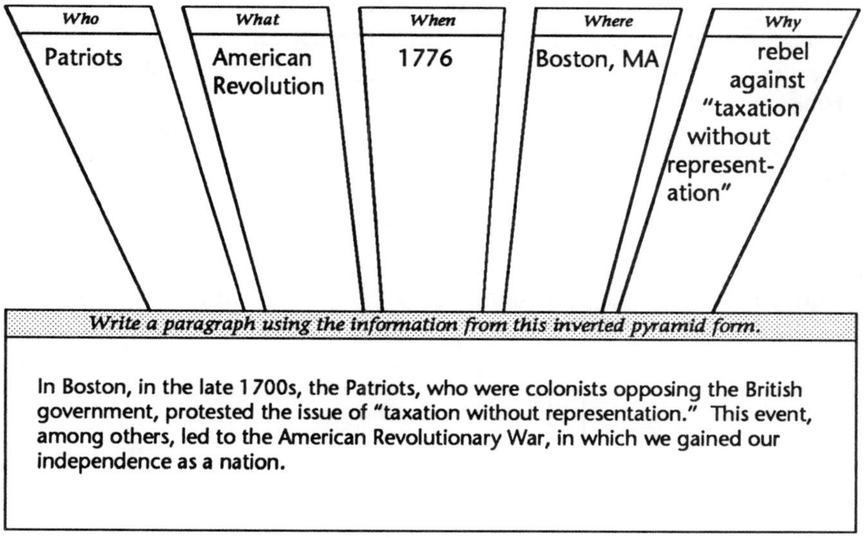

Who	*What*	*When*	*Where*	*Why*
Patriots	American Revolution	1776	Boston, MA	rebel against "taxation without represent-ation"

Write a paragraph using the information from this inverted pyramid form.

In Boston, in the late 1700s, the Patriots, who were colonists opposing the British government, protested the issue of "taxation without representation." This event, among others, led to the American Revolutionary War, in which we gained our independence as a nation.

Strategy Sheet

CONCEPT: ____________________

What we know	What we want to find out	What we learn

CONCEPT: Native Americans

What we know	What we want to find out	What we learn
1. Many different tribes.	1. How they lived.	1. Each tribe lived according to the demands of geographic location and tribal rituals.
2. They were moved from their homes.	2. What happened to them?	2. They live on reservations and have their own schools.
3.	3.	3.

Thinking-At-Right-Angles Model

A

B

Example:

Focus:
Reading about Leonardo daVinci to learn about creative genius.

A Leonardo was a scientist, inventor, philosopher & artist with keen observation and visualization skills.

RIGHT ANGLE THINKING:
Leonardo recorded his ideas in journals, sketch books, logs and diaries.

B RIGHT ANGLE IDEA:
Students could emulate the learning style and technique of Leonardo by keeping a thinking log. (Note: Right Angle idea is serendipitous thought that you want to capture for later scrutiny.)

Decision-Making Model

Decision

+	+	+	+
-	-	-	-

Consequences

Alternatives

What is the need for a decision?

Example:

People

Decision

↑

Opportunity to examine points of view not familiar with; study effective leader +	Chance to relate causes to modern times and study alternatives +	Will understand impact of Civil War on country today +	Will learn information I'm weak in +
- Need to choose rebel or yankee hero, etc.	- Complex issue	- Must choose long-term or short-term consequences	- Weak on information... need lots of research

Consequences

↑

People	Causes	Outcomes	Battles

Alternatives

↑

Need essay topic on Civil War

What is the need for a decision?

↑

START

Problem-Solving Model

Problem Statement: ________________	
1.	
2.	
3.	
4.	
5.	

Example:

Problem Statement: Privacy	
1. *Index the facts as you see them.*	*Lack of privacy affecting school work and "social" life (phone); one bedroom for 2 of you; some space available in basement; parents unsympathetic.*
2. *Define the problem*	*Want more privacy.*
3. *Expand on ideas or possible alternatives.*	*Find another space; divide room; schedule some private time for each for use of the room; live with it!*
4. *Adapt a criterion.*	*Expenses must be minimal; need parental approval.*
5. *Select and sell your idea to others involved.*	*Will convert part of basement to "study"; will do all work and pay for phone installation; will continue to sleep in bedroom with sibling.*

Suggested Skill and Graphic Organizer Patterns Guide

	SKILLS	GRAPHIC ORGANIZER
I.	Attributing	Web
	Classifying	Matrix/Chart
	Prioritizing	List
	Predicting	Agree/Disagree
	Visualizing	Story Grid
	Brainstorming	Clustering
II.	Inferring	Right Angles
	Personifying	Outline
	Inventing	Cluster Circles
	Sequencing	Sequence Model
	Comparing/Contrasting	Venn Diagram
	Analyzing for Bias	Web
III.	Generalizing	Newspaper Model—5Ws
	Drawing Conclusions	Sequence
	Cause/Effect	C/E Circles
	Hypothesizing	Fish Bone
	Problem-Solving	Problem-Solving Model
	Making Analogies	Thought Tree
IV.	Decision-Making	Decision-Making Model
	Solving Analogies	Analogy Model
	Analyzing for Assumptions	Sequence
	Associating Relationships	Hex Message
	Paradox/Ambiguity	Thought Tree
	Evaluating	Matrix (Grid)

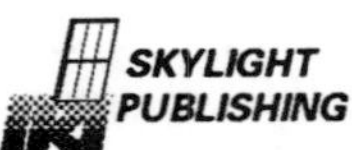

SECTION 6

METACOGNITION

An intellectual is someone whose mind watches itself.
—Albert Camus

Metacognition

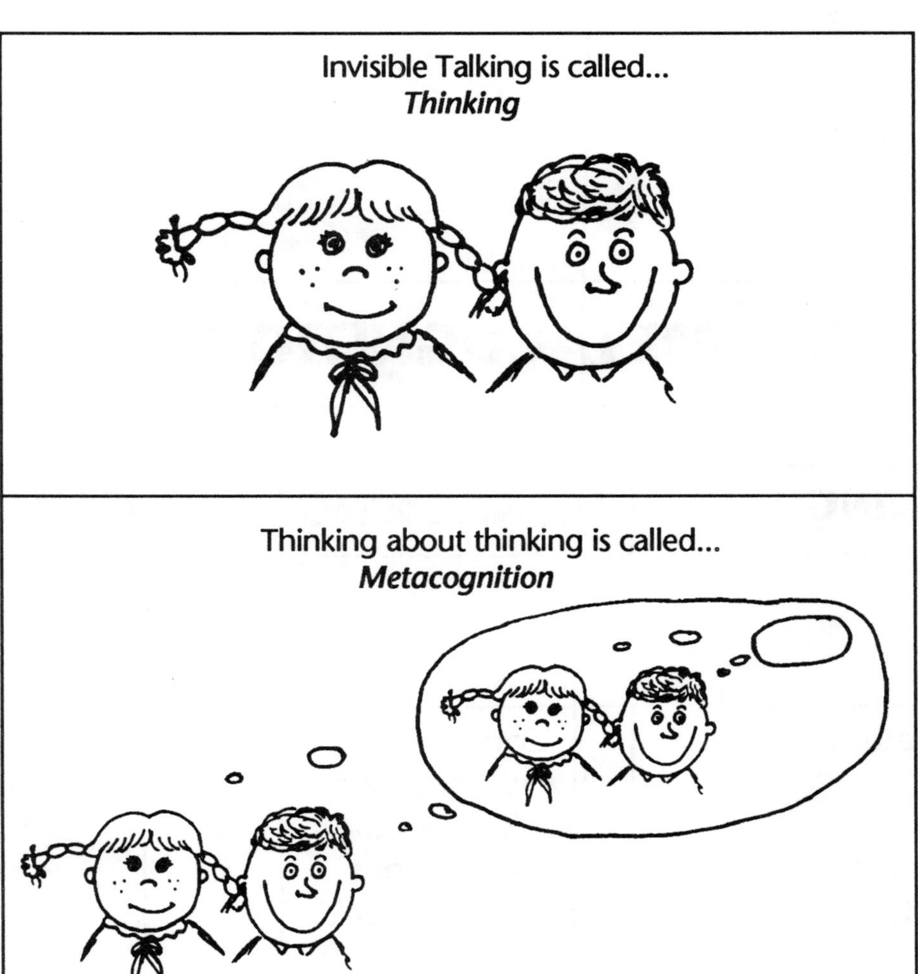

Invisible Talking is called...
Thinking
Thinking about thinking is called...
Metacognition

In a thinking classroom, the teacher helps make that thinking visible...

METACOGNITIVE BEHAVIORS

- Predicting...what next...why?
- Asking questions...reflecting
- Comparing
- Monitoring progress
- Evaluating

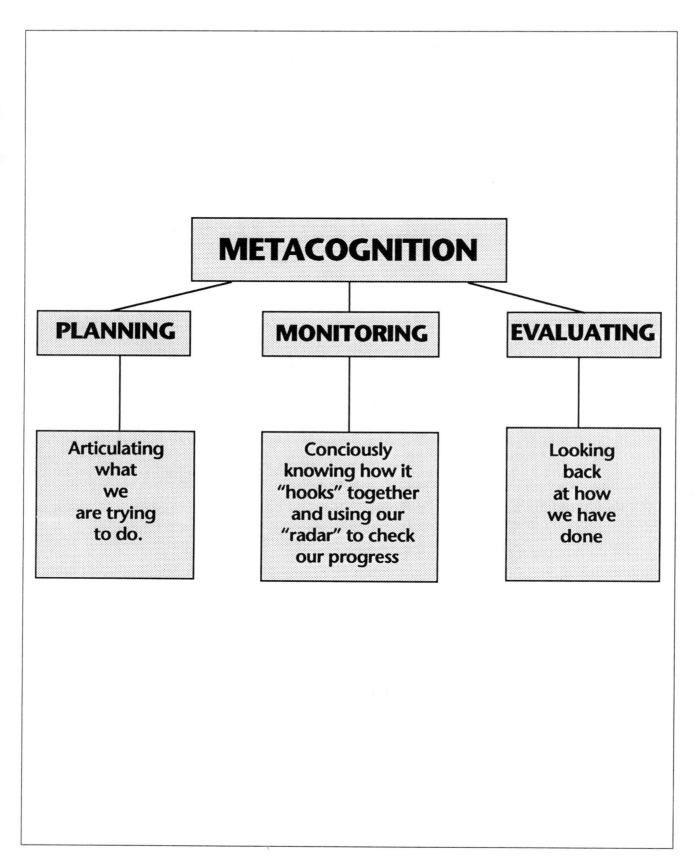

METACOGNITION

PLANNING	MONITORING	EVALUATING
Articulating what we are trying to do.	Conciously knowing how it "hooks" together and using our "radar" to check our progress	Looking back at how we have done

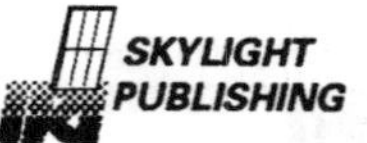

Introduction

Recent research in the area of reading comprehension has focused on the concept of metacognition—the ability to think about our thinking. Metacognitive processing allows the learner to step outside the situation and examine the process itself. For example, deliberately tracing the mental steps used in solving a problem propels the learner to a level of thinking that requires metacognitive behavior. She looks at the framework of problem solving versus the actual solution to the particular problem. Metacognition is the awareness of and control over your own thinking and behavior.

There appear to be four levels of metacognitive behavior: tacit use, aware use, strategic use and reflective use.

Level I	Level II	Level III	Level IV
Tacit Use	**Aware Use**	**Strategic Use**	**Reflective Use**
Uses problem solving but does not think **about** using any particular strategy.	Conscious of use and when using a particular strategy.	Organizes thinking by deliberately using a particular strategy.	Plans, monitors, and evaluates a particular strategy.

-Swartz & Perkins

This is best illustrated in the area of reading. While the good reader becomes abruptly aware when he has lost context with the text and shifts to a recovery strategy, the poor reader continues through the passage unaware—in essence he doesn't know what is going on.

In its fullest content, metacognitive processing envelopes planning, monitoring and evaluating thinking. The student exemplifies intelligent behavior as she deliberately plots a mental plan and tracks the progress of that plan, adjusting as necessary along the way and subsequently critiquing the final outcome.

A parallel example is the teaching process itself. The teacher plans the lesson. She monitors and adjusts during the lesson, often actually changing strategies midstream because of information recieved through "internal radar" systems. Finally, the teacher evaluates the success of the lessons for the next presentation based on the metacognitive feedback from that first try.

Teaching About Thinking

The Teaching About Thinking, what is properly called "metacognition" or "going beyond thinking," may be the most powerful and important of all the approaches. First, it is the glue that binds all the pieces. Isolated skills, no matter how well taught, have limited influence on the quality of thinking. Metacognitive activity encourages the skillful thinker to make the connections with conscious effort. Secondly, metacognition is a critical part of the process whereby the student masters any of the thinking skills.

After direct instruction of an explicit skill the student reviews the mental operations in the newly acquired skill before additional practice. After the practice, the student may examine the same operations and seek ways to refine their use. Thirdly, if the teacher is adept at asking metacognitive questions and if the peer climate is safe and secure, the teacher will extend student thinking beyond higher level questions with metacognitive questions.

As the research on cognition indicates, cognitive processing is one of the most important learning tools a student processes. It is not enough to absorb information. The student must take the time to make meaning from the facts and figures. In a hurry-up society full of mad hatters running around shouting "I'm late. I'm late for a very important date," students are more ready to adapt to the expectation for speed. How easy it is to get the message that a slow response is a dumb response!

To break the Mad Hatter Syndrome, the skilled teacher will use any and all the tools at her disposal to promote cognitive processing: wait time, higher order questioning, peer acceptance, cooperative problem solving, explicit lessons, active mental involvement and the high expectation that all students think about what they are thinking.

Cognitive processing is integral to every thinking classroom. It happens because the skilled teacher makes it happen. Each and every lesson, whether it is an explicit thinking skill or not, is enhanced when the lesson design incorporates processing time.

There are three teachable moments when cognitive processing can enhance a lesson: the set or focus activity, the metacognitive discussion or the checking for understanding, and the closure.

1. **THE ANTICIPATORY SET.** Rowe's early research called this "the advanced organizer." Madeline Hunter popularized the label "anticipatory set." The word "organizer" more accurately describes the cognitive behavior that occurs in the student's mind when the teacher focuses the student's attention on the lesson's aim. The organizer helps the student go to short term memory to review related material, fit it into the new context and make the needed connections. While many lessons will need only a short set to help the students with the needed mental organization, the skilled teacher will allow sufficient time and assistance for the students to acquire the needed focus. At no time

in the lesson is the adage "haste makes waste" more appropriate than during "the set" when students, each at an individual rate, are organizing for learning.

2. **CHECKING FOR UNDERSTANDING/DISCUSSION.** It is absurd to believe that simple signals can give clues to how well a student comprehends even the most simple instructions. Mass checking is the surest way to kill thinking in the classroom. Skilled checking will expect that all children take the time to think about their thinking and that the teacher will take the time to elicit sample responses. She will use all she knows about seeking multiple responses, attending to the perceived low performers and waiting after her thought-producing questions. And, as the occasion demands, she will check for application, analysis, and evaluation. When working with an explicit teaching skill, she will take enough time to guide the discussion into a complete cognitive processing of the skill itself, especially as the skill relates to other learned thinking skills and the application of the skill to real life situations.

3. **CLOSURE.** Cognitive processing is integral to successful learning. If we consider each lesson to have three parts, "what" and "so what" and "now what," we can examine the importance of closure. In the "what," students give evidence that they understand the critical pieces of the lesson. Can they put the objective in their own words, using information acquired during the lesson? If not, why go on?

   In the "so what," students must stop to make personal application. They link the new learning to past learnings, associated thoughts and feelings, and lock it into the larger contexts of the course and their own lives. In essence, this is the time that each discovers the meaning of what was taught.

   In the "now what," the student makes the information come alive as he investigates applications and projects the new learning into future situations. He is encouraged to make abstract ideas practical in a context that he can understand. This brings his thinking into final focus or closure.

   The "what," "so what," and "now what" parts challenge students to internalize what they are learning. Whether the teacher uses questions from Bloom, Gallagher, or Taba matters little. That the teacher takes the time with some set of higher order questions matters a great deal. Without this time, retention, motivation, and transfer will limp along, even disappear as the students read the mesage, "covering more material faster is more important than understanding any material well."

At whichever point you decide to process how students are thinking, there are several guidelines which can help:

1. When asking process questions, avoid question that students can answer with a "yes," or "no," or a one word answer. Note in the strategies, we have asked only open-ended questions. Even when we ask for a report on what students learned or did in coopera-

tive groups, we structure the questions for multiple responses.

2. All information questions are best followed by a series of higher order questions. The questions focus on the critical content or key concept of the lesson. If the lesson focuses on a thinking skill, the questions focus on that skill.

3. Ask only one question at a time. Tell students that you will only ask each question once and that you intend to wait for many responses. If a student does not understand you question, encourage the student to ask you to clarify the question. Don't fall into the repeater trap and please don't answer your own question.

4. Ask extending questions as often as you decide necessary. This is especially important when you feel unsure of a student's meaning or you feel that the response could be more specific.

5. Practice your wait-time. When you are using questions to structure metacognition, it is most important that you signal your respect for time to think.

6. To increase student involvement, especially the first time you ask metacognitive questions, have them write first and then share responses. The wraparound in the beginning is also helpful. Allow students to say "I pass" at any time. If passing becomes a problem, go back and examine what you can do to make the climate safer.

7. Vary the techniques you use to get students to process what they have learned. In th strategies, we have used the LOG, the wraparound, lead-ins, higher order questions on the Bloom model and creative activities (collages, essays, stories, etc.) in a variety of ways to focus on the skill of each lesson. You might want to change any of the suggestions such as using "what," "so what," "now what," "Mrs. Potter's Questions" or some other sequences of your choosing.

8. Always address processing questions to the entire class. This communicates that all must think about the question. Encourage the fast handwavers to take more time to think. After all have had the think time, call on your first choice.

9. Encourage active listening. We placed the "pre-skills" first among the strategies so that you can teach students how to listen to each other. If you find some students who are not listening to the processing done by their peers, you may want to ask those students to paraphrase what others are saying before they give their own answers.

10. Avoid the "why" questions such as "Why did Columbus sail to America?" Instead ask: "Why do you think...?" This avoids the one right answer syndrome and forces students to make personal connections. In addition, it leaves you ready to follow up with "What proof will you give?" when students are making wild assumptions.

11. Model acceptance. Overmodel it. As each student responds, keep strong eye contact, nod at key points and occasionally summarize key points. Don't interrupt and don't put the student down. If the logic is faulty, has incorrect information or false assump-

tions use your clarifying and extending skills to help the student discover the mistake. If you have asked the question so that the students must give an opinion (Why do you think...?), you will find that students will have little difficulty accepting a redirection for the sake of logic.

12. Acknowledge skillful thinking. Avoid praise for its own sake. This will keep you from sounding like a broken record to the students (good... good... good... wonderful... good...), but do indicate in very specific terms that a student has displayed skillful thinking. "I appreciate the detail you gave as your proof, Mary."
13. Encourage students to answer each other, not you. Tell them that you will be where you can hear, but that they should talk to the class. As discussions begin, encourage students to look at all responses from a variety of viewpoints. For instance, after a student has answered a question in the positive, ask who holds the opposite point of view. Or after one student completes a statement, ask for a show of hands. How many agree? How many disagree? Solicit responses from both sides.
14. Encourage students to focus, accept, and draw each other out. Demonstrate how they can use body language to show focus and discuss how it feels to have someone pay full attention to you. Teach them a few ways to draw out a response (clarifying questions, paraphrasing, etc.).
15. Label student thinking. When you hear a student analyzing, acknowledge that. When you notice that a student is classifying, note it to the student. If the student's classifying needs refinement, suggest changes.
16. Recognize that there are many chances to encourage metacognition. When students are reading, discuss the thinking skills they are applying. For instance, when they have to search out clues and "read between the lines," recall inferring.
17. Note that the main difference between the cognitive processing of content such as the "origin of the Civil War" and the metacognitive processing of one's thinking is the focus. The processing of one's thinking is doubly dependent on how well you set the safe climate, maintain the conditions, and hold the students to your high expectations for thinking about thinking. It helps students if you process concepts at least once a day. As they become used to processing concepts, you will find their readiness to metacognate will increase.
18. As students become more skilled in how they process both the concepts of your course and their own thinking, you will find that metacognition will "eat up" time. Once the students are comfortable with metacognition, you must plan more precisely when to cut off the discussions and when to move on. The LOG can help. Bring students to closure by inviting them to reflect in the LOG.
19. Grades. At some point, the question will arise. As soon as it does, you will find yourself a Catch 22 victim. If you must grade how well students think, try these suggestions.

a. Test for knowledge of a thinking skill (definition, uses, operations).

b. Give at least three application questions of the skill. Check for the student's ability to think through the operations.

c. Have students self-rate improvement in their intellectual behaviors and provide proof from their own experience (i.e., increased flexibility, fluency, creative problem solving, etc.)

The preference is that you not grade student thinking. Instead, look for improved intellectual behavior so you can reinforce skillful thinking and give positive feedback to the student.

In the lessons that follow, we have synthesized the best practices of effective teaching to produce more skillful thinkers. Classroom teachers piloted each lesson making adaptations for age, class size and background. Only those evaluated as most effective were included. We are sharing these with you so that you too can structure your classroom and "catch" your students thinking.

Mrs. Potter's Questions

In this strategy, Mrs. Potter's Questions, the evaluation stage of metacognition is the focus. A critical thinker is often described as a person who can evaluate the quality of thinking used to solve problems. The critical thinker makes sound, logical judgments about ideas she studies, reads, sees on TV or in the movies, and hears from friends, politicians, neighbors or peers. The thinking skills required for solid evaluation, however, are very difficult and complex. Before a student masters the complexities of evaluation, it is important that they develop a positive attitude about evaluation as a learning tool.

Mrs. Potter and her questions are viable tools with which the student can routinely "check" thinking, metacognitively. By introducing the student to Mrs. Potter and her four evaluation questions, teachers can "CATCH THEM THINKING."

Let me take a moment to introduce you to Mrs. Potter. Mrs. Potter is a "seasoned" teacher who has developed a repertoire of instructional strategies to "catch" kids thinking. She even distributes buttons for students to wear that issue this challenge:

"CATCH ME THINKING"

And she does just that. She catches them thinking and she catches them thinking about their thinking. Sometimes she even acknowledges that thinking with stickers that proclaim:

"I CAUGHT YOU THINKING"

These highly visible reinforcements suggest the high value Mrs. Potter (and the teacher) place on thinking in the classroom by all students.

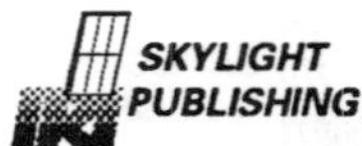

Mrs. Potter's Questions

- *What were you expected to do?*

- *In this assignment, what did you do well?*

- *If you had to do this task over, what would you do differently?*

- *What help do you need from me?*

Let's analyze the four questions more closely as a processing activity for a concept-webbing lesson in which students webbed the concept of a paragraph. Here is a sample student product:

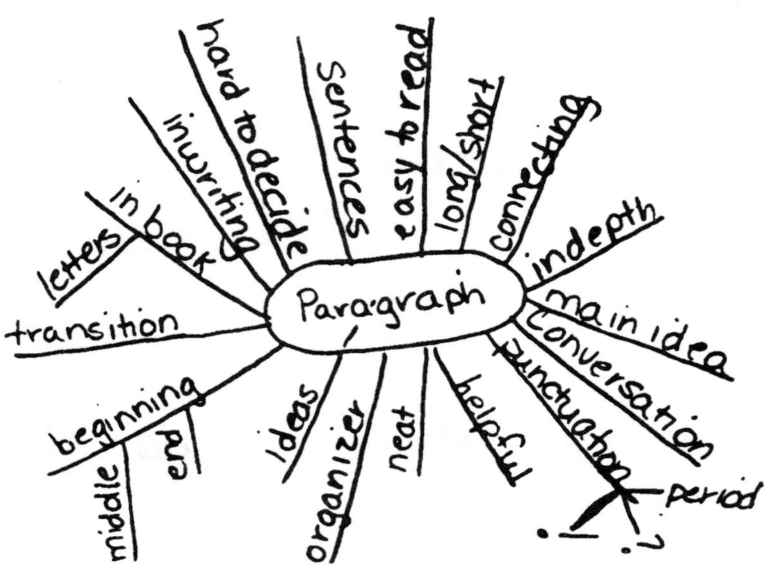

To evaluate the learning, the student asks:

1. WHAT WAS I EXPECTED TO DO?

Often the student does not complete a task successfully because the objective or instructions are unclear or misinterpreted. Mrs. Potter's first question is simply a restatement by students of the task expectations.

The student may articulate in this example, "The task was to brainstorm at least 15 ideas about paragraphs in three minutes."

2. IN THIS ASSIGNMENT, WHAT DID I DO WELL?

This second question leads the student to focus on the strengths and successes experienced in a task by identifying the things done well. In this example, the student might answer this self-query by thinking, "I was pretty fluent in the brainstorm. I know a lot about paragraphs."

Inherent in any task is some aspect that stands out as the most positive or rewarding part. By posing this question, the student deliberately and consciously targets the high points.

3. IF I HAD TO DO THIS TASK OVER, WHAT WOULD I DO DIFFERENTLY?

Conversely, Mrs. Potter's third question suggests that intelligent thinkers also are aware of what they would do differently, next time, to improve the performance or product. The student might reflect on the web in this illustration and think, "Perhaps if I had tried to associate or piggyback more, I might have generated even a greater number of ideas. For example, had I gone with the punctuation idea, I could have associated more specifics." By analyzing this area, the student receives a subtle message: Learning is a process and the process is ongoing.

4. WHAT HELP DO I NEED?

Finally, Mrs. Potter presents an opportunity for the student to indicate where he might need assistance. The student response in this case might be, "I need some help getting started. It took me quite a while to tune in and focus before I could really get rolling."

This last question invites the student to seek advice on specific areas of concern and helps the teacher focus on feedback that is relevant to student needs.

Mrs. Potter's Questions can be modeled initially with the whole class as a way to process group activities. Once familiar with the format, individual student applications are numerous. For instance, the student can evaluate the homework assignment, a lab experiment, a social studies project, a piece of writing or behavior on a field trip.

As the student becomes adept at using Mrs. Potter's Questions, he automatically applies the critiquing process and is practicing intelligent behaviors that easily transfer into life skills as well as to the academic situation mentioned here. As a result, the student is becoming a more skillful thinker—a problem solver—a decision maker!

☛NOTE: Further Applications

Peer Coaching Tool

Many schools are in various stages of implementing peer assistant coaching teams as part of extensive school improvement and staff development projects. "Mrs. Potter's Questions" is suggested as an initial observation/feedback instrument in those fragile first stages of peer coaching. In the post-observation conference, the coach simply poses Mrs. Potter's Questions to foster personal, reflective self-evaluation from the teacher who actually taught the lesson. It places the critiquing responsibility on the learner and avoids the "overload-feedback syndrome" that frequently inhibits the peer coaching relationship in its early stages.

Supervisory Conferencing Technique

Often in supervisory conferences with teachers, the supervisor does most of the talking. For supervisory personnel who prefer an interactive model in which teachers take a more active role, Mrs. Potter's Questions are ideal. The supervisor, much like the coach in the peer model, simply poses the four questions as the teacher processes the teaching situation observed. In this situation, however, the supervisor may take a more proactive stance and offer suggestions to the last two questions—but only after the teacher has had the opportunity to first reflect personally on these areas.

Mrs. Potter

BACKGROUND A critical thinker is often described as a person who can evaluate the quality of thinking used to solve problems. The critical thinker makes sound, logical judgments about ideas, he/she studies, reads, sees on TV or in the movies, and hears from friends, politicians, neighbors, or peers. The thinking skills required for solid evaluation, however, are very difficult and complex. Before a student masters the complexities of evaluation, it is important that they develop a positive attitude about evaluation as a learning tool.

THINKING SKILL: EVALUATING

FOCUS ACTIVITY Project Mrs. Potter's Questions on the overhead or hand a copy of the sheet to each student. Review the questions with the students in preparation for the task.

1. What were you expected to do?
2. In this assignment, what did you do well?
3. If you had to do this task over, what would you do differently?
4. What help do you need from me?

OBJECTIVE To identify four basic self-evaluation questions which will help you in judging the quality of your work and your thinking.

INPUT Indicate to the students that the word "evaluate" means to weigh, to judge, or to determine the value of something. One important evaluator is oneself. As we learn to evaluate, we set standards by which we judge the quality of our thinking and our work.

ACTIVITY Instructions:

A. Remind the students that after each group completes the task, the group will list responses to each of Mrs. Potter's Questions. Give each group a worksheet with the four questions.

B. Assign three students to each group.

C. Give each group a copy of these task instructions and review them.

Mrs. Potter

How Is...?

1. Assign an official group recorder. All will keep ideas and notes in their own LOGS, but the official recorder will turn in the worksheets.
2. Follow the DOVE Guidelines.
3. For each question, make a list of answers. You will have 10 minutes to get *as many* answers as possible for your group for the questions listed. Be sure you have at least two answers to each question.
   a. How is a TV like a snowflake?
   b. How is a table like a glove?
   c. How is a bird like a lightbulb?
   d. How is a house like a flower?
   e. How is a book like a shoe?

D. At the end of ten minutes, end the task.

E. Instruct each group to take ten minutes to respond to Mrs. Potter's questions *as a group*. They may list items about the *group* or about *individuals* in the group. Instruct them to be specific especially looking at how well they followed the given instruction, (i.e., DOVE, time, balance of questions) as well as the quality of the answers given. The recorder will write out the group responses for class sharing and to submit to you.

F. Sample responses to each question with the entire class.

METACOGNITIVE DISCUSSION

1. What are Mrs. Potter's four questions? (Write on board or overhead)
2. Put the four questions into your own words. (Select a variety of different answers for each.)
3. In your schoolwork, what/when would it help you to ask yourself these four questions? (List the various responses.)
4. What would be different about your homework (or substitute another opportunity) if you used Mrs. Potter's questions to evaluate how you did?

CLOSURE

Assign the students to use Mrs. Potter's questions with a homework assignment. Instruct them to hand in a Mrs. Potter's worksheet with the assignment.

That's A Good Idea

PURPOSE: To demonstrate the forced response behaviors.

INSTRUCTIONS:

1. Assign each participant to a group by handing out cards with group numbers. Each group should have one high, two average and one low.

2. Assign the recorder, leader, materials manager and timekeeper/observer. The recorder will use newsprint and marker. The leader will guide the group's task. The timekeeper/observer will keep time and the materials manager will get all the "stuff" needed.

3. Encourage the participants to listen carefully to instructions and also observe you. "After this activity is finished, you will identify how I modeled the forced response behaviors."

4. Begin the task instructions.

   (a) "As quickly as possible, brainstorm all the possible means of transportation you might have used to get here today—a horse and buggy, a space shuttle, a magic carpet. Be wild and creative; don't judge. Build on each other's ideas. Go as fast as the recorder can write."

   (b) Pause for three seconds.

   (c) "Thumbs up if you know what to do in the task." "Thumbs down if you are confused." Pause and select someone with thumbs up to repeat instructions. If he is 100 percent correct, give a hurrah! If not, dignify the response and have someone else add until the full answer is repeated. If you take a "thumb sideways" answer, ask the student to explain "what she does know" and then add on with other responses. Conclude with a reinforcement as appropriate.

   (d) Monitor the task by walking around.

   (e) When the lists are extensive, use your "hands up" signal to recall attention. Tell the recorder of each group to use the last digit in his/her phone to identify randomly an item from the group list and circle it.

(f) Ask recorders to report to the group the selected item.

(g) Begin your next instructions, "Listen carefully. First, rotate all roles one person to the right." Pause until this is done. "Next, the recorder will take one mode of transportation selected by the group, make one improvement and record it. For instance, an improvement for a bus might be a swimming pool. After the recorder marks that improvement, the person to his/her right will say "That's a good idea, because..." and tell the reason. The recorder will write down the reason. The person will then add another improvement. In turn, each will tell why the last idea was good and then add another improvement. Continue around until the stop signal is given. If you cannot answer either question, say "I pass."

(h) Pause and then ask for "thumbs up" to signal understanding of the instructions. Repeat (c).

(i) Monitor the task until the newsprint is full. Ask some observers to report.

5. After the task is over, instruct each group to use response in turn to identify the forced response methods you used in the activity. Just as they responded in turn with "That's a good idea because..." group members will do the same with the identified teacher behaviors. In this session, ask each member to record all responses on this chart.

Idea:	
Improvement	Reason

Plus/Minus/Intriguing	
P(+) *Plus*	
M(-) *Minus*	
I(?) *Intriguing* -Edward deBono	

Metacognition
What?
So What?
Now What?
What Else?

Strategy Sheet

Name ______________________________

What we know	What we want to find out	What we learned

Connecting With The Big Idea
THE ELEPHANT CONNECTION

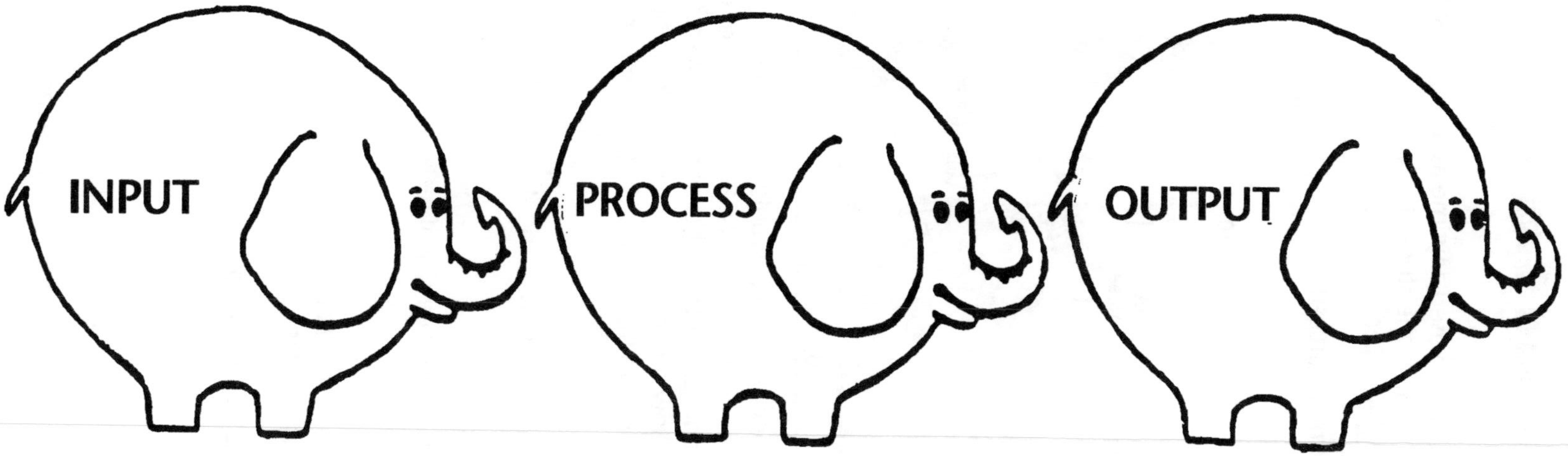

INPUT	PROCESS	OUTPUT
GATHERING	**PROCESSING**	**APPLYING**
What's the **BIG IDEA?**	How can **I CONNECT** this with what I already know?	How can **I USE** this?

The Human Graph

Strategy

The Human Graph is a generic strategy that can be used anytime as a choice or decision situation arises. Simply stand in the center of the room. Have the students cluster in front of you. Draw an imaginary line dividing the space. Assign degrees of agreement.

Pose the question as you indicate the side for each choice: would you rather _____ or _____? Watch as they move to one side or the other. Then, ask WHY? LISTEN! Permit time for one to explain his decision. WAIT! Let him fully develop the depth of his thoughts as he discovers the connection between his decision and his experiences. Allow movement caused by changing of minds, but also encourage advocating opinions. Move on through the "graph" in this manner.

Metacognitive Processing

As the human graph evolves, be aware of and discuss with the students the metacognitive levels of evaluative processing. Note the following:

- How quickly one reaches a decision
- How far to the side one moves signifying intensity of feelings
- How often one changes his mind
- How one comes to his decision
- How one reacts in a minority/majority position
- How one reflects his attitudes in his choices

Through the interactive nature of critical analysis and creative synthesis:

... Decisions are made
... Convictions are crystallized
... Beliefs are solidified
... Actions are taken

Decisions are made moment by moment—let's examine and exercise the processes with students.

The Thinking Log

The Inking of Our Thinking

Journal + Notebook = Thinking Log

A thinking log is much like a footprint. Both are uniquely personal impressions that mark one moment in time. Yet, whereas the footprint may disappear with the wind, the thinking log cements the thought-filled page for all of time.

The log is a hybrid created from the personal journal and the traditional class notebook. A journal is usually a daily barometer of events and feelings that are evoked by day-to-day happenings, while a notebook typically is a collection of classroom notes and doodles, permanently etched on paper in a personalized shorthand that is all too soon indecipherable. Neither the journal nor the notebook offers the scope of the thinking log because the log records immediate, gut reactions to learning that just occurred.

FIGURE 1
Entries on Various Concepts

LOGGING

NOTHING IN LIFE IS TO BE FEARED. IT IS ONLY TO BE UNDERSTOOD.
MARIE CURIE

Oct 5, 1988: A theory I have about this thing called fear is that only I can control my fears. And the first step is to face them.

January 15, 1989: My own thinking on this idea of freedom is that the more we have, the more responsibility we have also. I think this is good. It forces us to become our own keepers.

February 10, 1989: My hypothesis on conflict is simple. If we reach out, look at the other person's point of view (which isn't easy), we can usually find a middle ground.

Teachable Moments

Inking Our Thinking

By planning for youngsters to process their thinking in written form, teachers ultimately have at their disposal a versatile and valuable teaching tool.

Taking advantage of the teachable moment, students process reflectively by logging their thinking. They catch the freshness of first impressions; jot down the milieu of ideas swarming about their heads; explore for understanding; analyze for clarity; synthesize into personal mean ing; apply functionally; judge worth; and make the critical connections between new data and past experience.

FIGURE 2
A Series of Entries
On A Single Concept: Bias

To piggyback on an idea...

LOG

A way I could use what I learned today is:

I could think deeper into a problem and come up with the best solution.

I could judge decisions more fairly.

I could understand other people's views better.

About bias, I wonder:

Why do I have them?
Who has the same as mine?
What decisions have been affected?
Who is against me?

In the future:

I will think more broader and deeper and not let the bias affect my decisions so much that I do not see the other side.

The Look of the Log

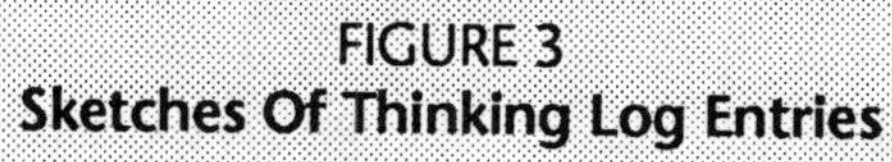

Verbal

Date_____
One point of view is_____

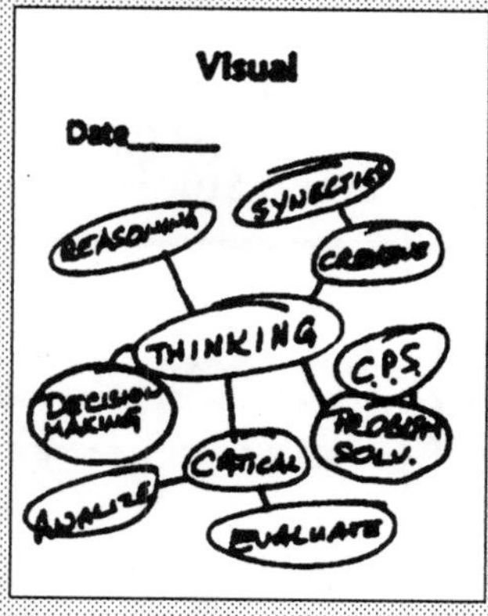

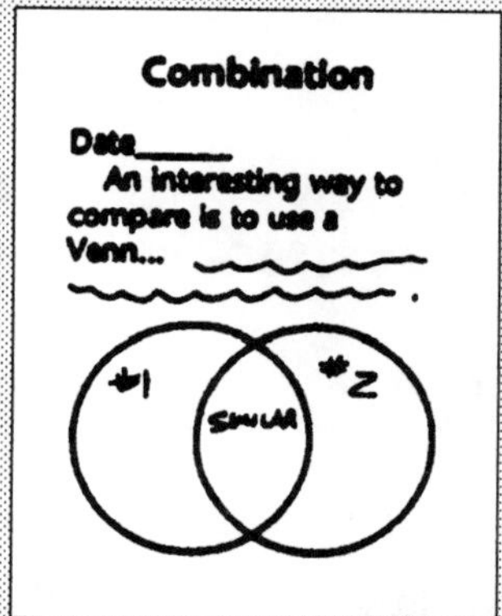

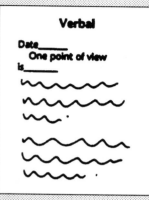

The writing in the thinking log may take many forms. It may be a narrative, a quote, an essay, jottings, a drawing, a cartoon, a diagram, webs or clusters, a soliloquy, a riddle, a joke, doodles, an opinion, a rebuttal, a dialogue, a letter, a flow chart, or just an assortment of phrases and ideas.

FIGURE 4
Visual & Verbal Thinking Log Entries

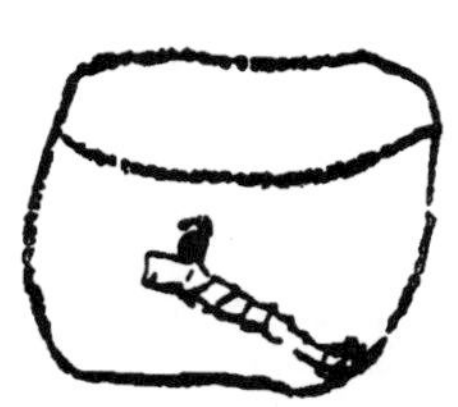

Did you know brine shrimp have gills?
They have very small gills!
Their gills help them breath.

by Katie, Joe, Eric, Hari, Rodney, Angelo, Josh

Transparent

Did you know you can see through brine shrimp? Brine shrimp are transparent which that means you can see through them.
We think it is neat.

by Nicole, Raymond, Judy, Rob, and Geof

Did you know brine shrimp eat bacteria? Brine shrimp like bacteria. Mrs. Clark said If you put dirt on your finger and put it in the tank they will eat right off your finger!

by Timmy, Roger, Zach, Becky, Mark

The entries may be reflective, evaluative, questioning, personal, abstract, introspective, cynical, incomplete, revealing, humorous, communicative, thoughtful, poetic, ramlbing, formative, philosophical, or none of the above. There are no right or wrong ways to do the log. It's just a log of one's thinking—whatever that thinking may be. It's a personal record of the connections being made within the framework of the students' cognitive capacities and their experiences.

FIGURE 5
Entries Sampled From Several Students

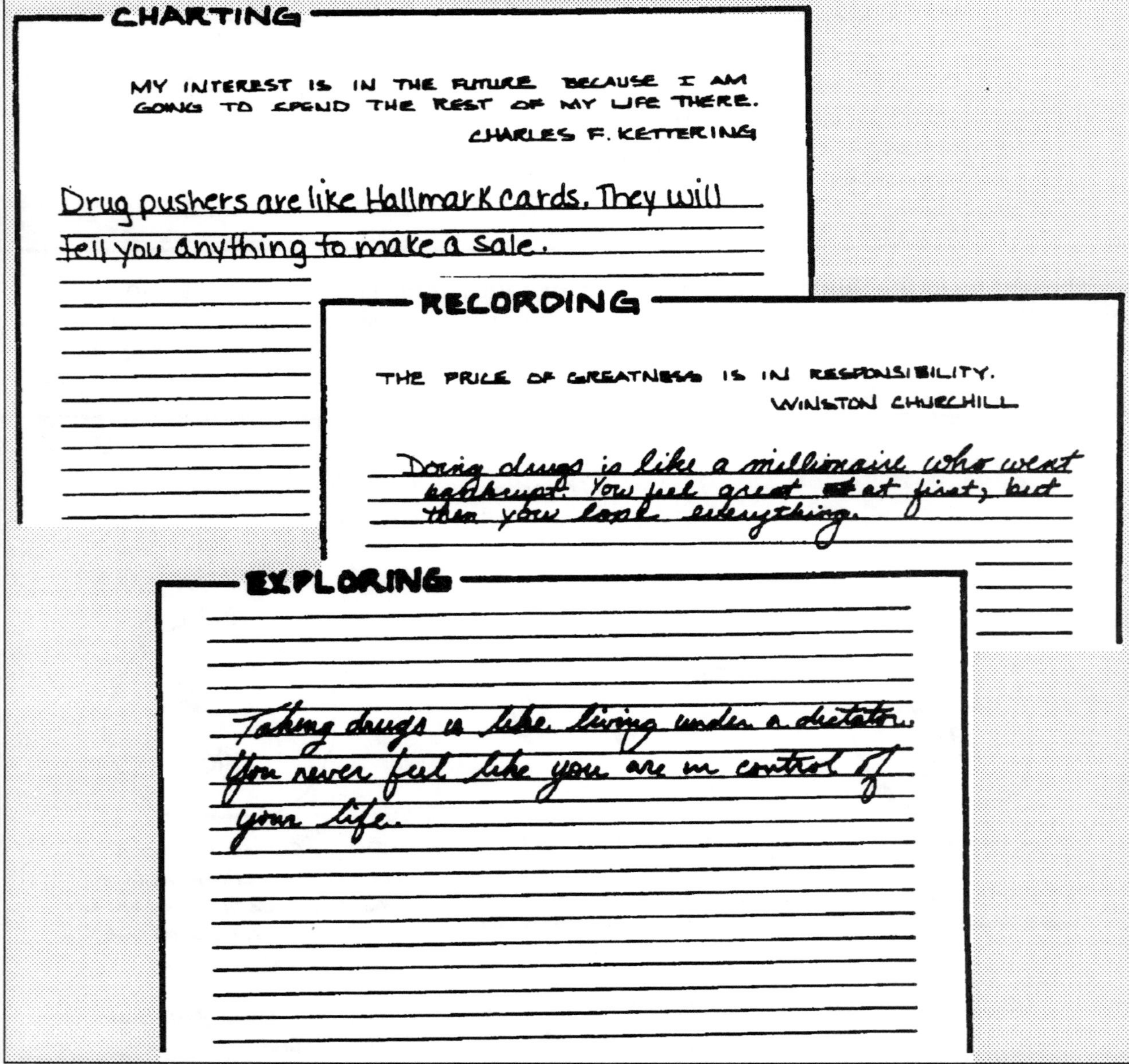

CHARTING

MY INTEREST IS IN THE FUTURE BECAUSE I AM GOING TO SPEND THE REST OF MY LIFE THERE.
CHARLES F. KETTERING

Drug pushers are like Hallmark cards. They will tell you anything to make a sale.

RECORDING

THE PRICE OF GREATNESS IS IN RESPONSIBILITY.
WINSTON CHURCHILL

Doing drugs is like a millionaire who went bankrupt. You feel great at first, but then you lose everything.

EXPLORING

Taking drugs is like living under a dictator. You never feel like you are in control of your life.

A Time to Think

The few minutes immediately following a lesson are ideal for using the thinking log. This transitional time allows flexiblity for the "fast finishers" and for the students who need a minute or two more to finish up.

The log may be used solely in one subject area or as a focused follow-up at randomly selected spots of the lessons presented throughout the day. It can be structured formally with designated sections for information or it can be informally structured through student preference and use.

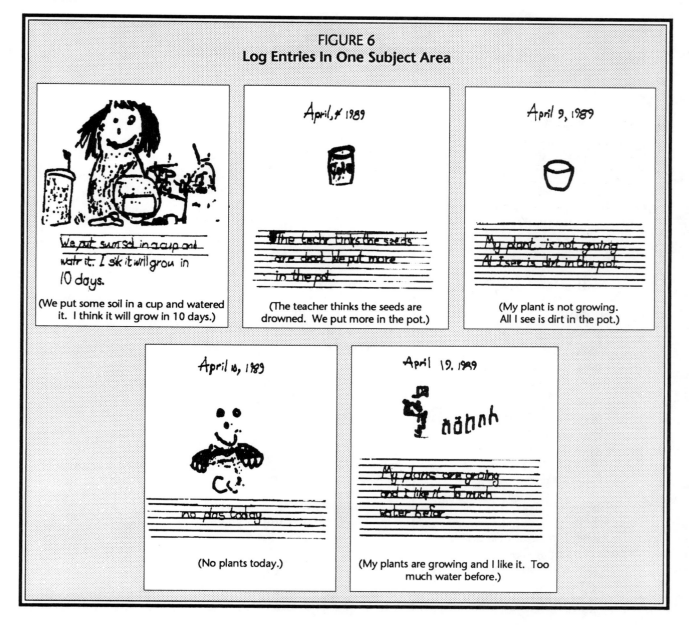

FIGURE 6
Log Entries In One Subject Area

We put sum sd in a cup and watr it. I sik it wrll grou in 10 days.

(We put some soil in a cup and watered it. I think it will grow in 10 days.)

April 4 1989

The techr tinks the seeds are drond. We put more in the pot.

(The teacher thinks the seeds are drowned. We put more in the pot.)

April 9, 1989

My plant is not groing. Al I see is dirt in the pot.

(My plant is not growing. All I see is dirt in the pot.)

April 16, 1989

no plas today

(No plants today.)

April 19, 1989

My plans are groing and I like it. To much water befor.

(My plants are growing and I like it. Too much water before.)

Lead-Ins for Logging

Thinking log "lead-ins" can "lead" students into higher level thinking processes and provide the needed versatility to develop alternative patterns for thinking. The lead-in dictates to some degree the mode of thought. For example, lead-ins can encourage responses that are analytic, synthetic, or evaluative. They also can be used to promote problem solving and decision making, or to foster a particular style of learning. The chart suggests some possibilities to illustrate the focus flexiblity of lead-ins.

Lead-Ins That Promote Thinking At Higher Levels

Analysis

Compared to...
The best part...
On the positive scale...
An interesting part is...
Take a small part like...
A logical sequence seems to be...
On the negative side...
Similarly...
By contrast...

Synthesis

Suppose...
Combine...
Possibly...
Imagine...
Reversed...
What if...
I predict...
How about...
I wonder...

Evaluation

How...
Why...
It seems irrelevant that...
One point of view is...
It seems important to note...
The best...
The worst...
If ___ then...

Application

Backtracking for a minute...
A way to...
I want to...
A connecting idea is...
A movie this reminds me of is _____ because...
If this were a book, I'd title it _____
I think this applies to...
Does this mean...

Problem Solving

I'm stuck on...
The best way to think about this...
I conclude...
I'm lost with...
I understand, but...
I'm concerned about...
My problem is...
A question I have is...

Decision Making

I disagree with ___ because...
I prefer___ because...
If I had to choose...
I believe...
My goal is...
I hate...
One criticism is...
I can't decide if...

Lead-Ins That Promote Different Styles of Thinking

Visual Representations

Try to visualize...
My picture of this...
A diagram of this idea looks like...
I feel like...
A chart...
I'm ___ like ___ because...

Verbal Presentations

Another way of saying this is...
I learned...
I discovered...
A quote that seems to fit is...
I want to read___ because...
I want to talk to ___ because...

FIGURE 7
Log Entry Of Lead-in

a ROOT is to
a PLANT as a
ball and chain is to
a prisoner.

As students grapple with new material and struggle with fleeting, diconnected thoughts, the thinking log impacts in yet another way. The students begin to become aware of the thought process itself. Again, the sensitive teacher captures the moment by prodding the youngsters to think about their thinking in deliberate and intentional metacognitive discussions. Kids start to see that they do have patterns for thinking as they find the words to articulate their thought processes. They assign labels to these processes, labels that identify strategies like reasoning by analogy, classification, logical thought and intuitive leaps. They begin to choose HOW they want to process new ideas. They begin to build a repertoire of thinking patterns as they express their ideas in writing...they begin "inking their thinking."

The log also becomes an indicator for instructional assessment, as teachers note the inner language of the thinking mind, for the students have deliberately and consciously been given the most precious commodity of modern man—TIME!...TIME TO THINK!...TIME to wrestle, even, if momentarily, with new ideas...TIME to absorb strange bits of information and attempt to fit the pieces into the tapestry of personal experiences.

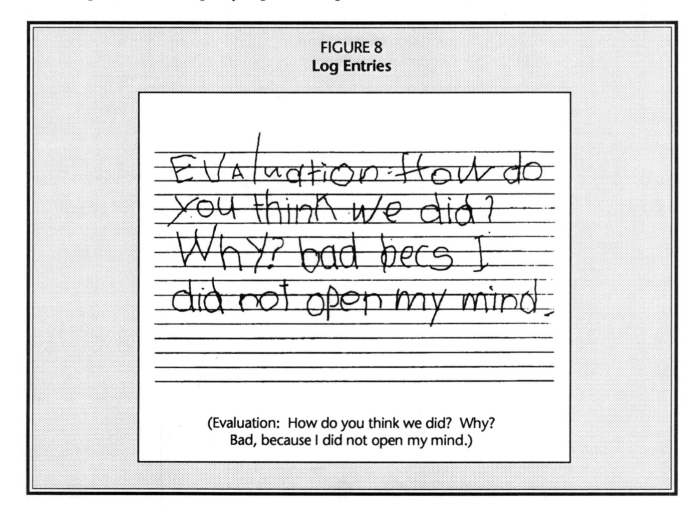

FIGURE 8
Log Entries

EvAluation: How do
you think we did?
Why? bad becs I
did not open my mind.

(Evaluation: How do you think we did? Why? Bad, because I did not open my mind.)

Tracking the Inking of our Thinking

In the initial act, students log their thinking and record an immediate reaction to an experience. With a later reading they have a chance to ponder the initial interpretation and to modify or enhance it with a seasoned second look. And, in the final analysis, with their writing providing the "track sheet," they have "logged" evidence to learn about HOW THEY THINK. Their favored patterns for thinking are revealed within the pages as they leaf through their logs. And that, perhaps, is the most significant outcome of all, kids that can articulate not only WHAT they are thinking, but HOW they arrive at that thinking...for they have a log of their thinking.

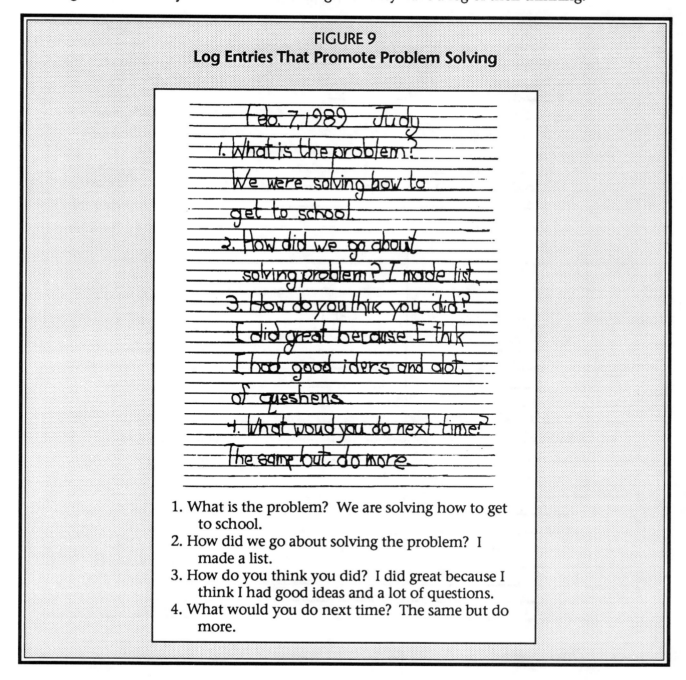

FIGURE 9
Log Entries That Promote Problem Solving

Feb. 7, 1989 Judy
1. What is the problem?
We were solving how to get to school.
2. How did we go about solving problem? I made list.
3. How do you thik you did? I did great because I thik I had good iders and alot of queshens.
4. What woud you do next time? The same but do more.

1. What is the problem? We are solving how to get to school.
2. How did we go about solving the problem? I made a list.
3. How do you think you did? I did great because I think I had good ideas and a lot of questions.
4. What would you do next time? The same but do more.

Logs for Adult Learning

One last note about thinking logs concerns the value of this reflective tool for both youngsters and adults. Using the thinking log concept as a means of processing ideas is becoming a common practice in staff development. Both individual reflection and peer-partner dialogues are viable models.

FIGURE 10
Reflective Log Entries

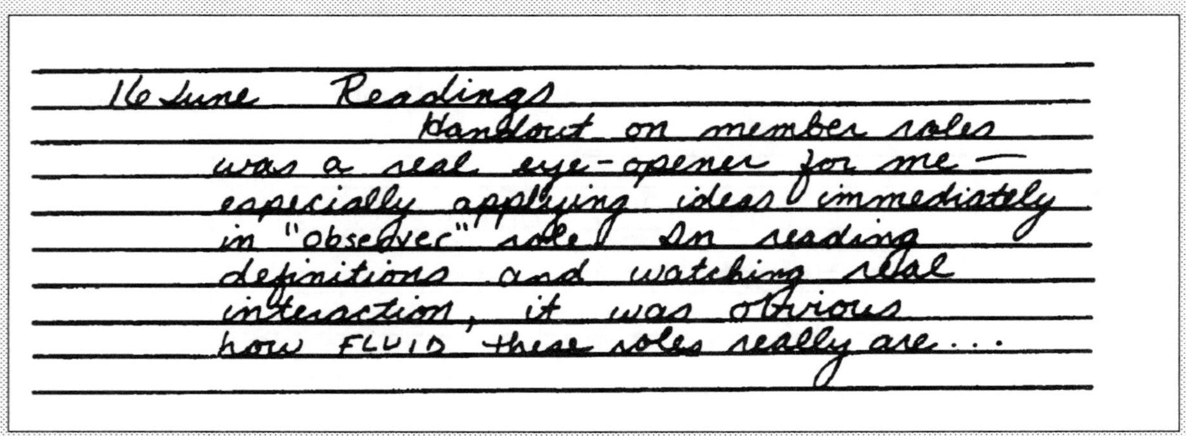

16 June Readings
Handout on member roles was a real eye-opener for me—especially applying ideas immediately in "observer" role! In reading definitions and watching real interaction, it was obvious how FLUID these roles really are...

FIGURE 11
Log Entry Dialogue

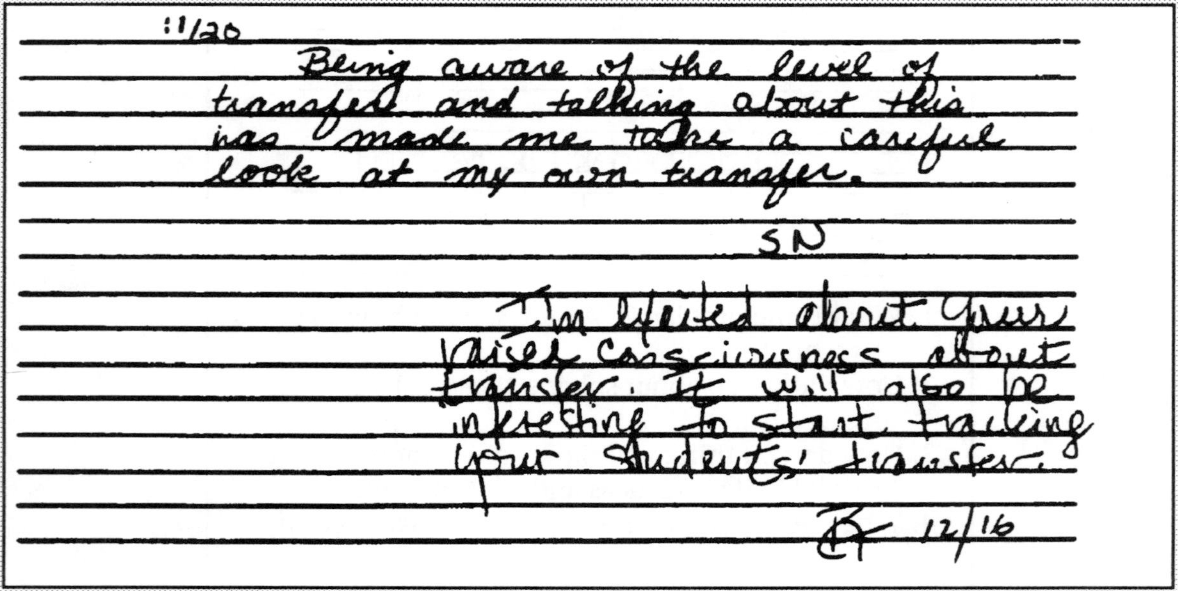

11/20
Being aware of the level of transfer and talking about this has made me take a careful look at my own transfer.
SN

I'm excited about your raised consciousness about transfer. It will also be interesting to start tracking your students' transfer.
RF 12/16

SECTION 7

STRATEGIES

Education is what survives when what has been learned has been forgotten.

—B.F. Skinner

PART 1

CATCH THEM THINKING CREATIVELY

STRATEGIES

The Story Grid

BACKGROUND

How items are arranged will vary on the purpose of the arrangements. A grocery store will arrange objects for shoppers' convenience: all the soups in one section, the noodles in another. A salesman will arrange his calendar by sales priorities. Stories also have a sequence or arranged pattern which is basically a combination of time and cause-effect. The characters, events, or setting may vary, but the plot will dictate the arrangement of what takes place. In all cases, a pattern emerges with "variations on a theme." The creative artist often has the most freedom and the most difficulty in composing these variations. The story grid or morphological grid is a tool that professional script writers use to change the content of stories when they have a set plot. It allows them to maintain interest and novelty without using up their creative genius.

THINKING SKILL: ARRANGING A PATTERN

FOCUS ACTIVITY

Ask the students to describe their favorite cartoon serial or soap opera. IF they were the story writers, what would they do to write 100 or more stories week after week? What would be some difficulties/challenges in their job?

OBJECTIVE

To identify a tool for creating a variety of story sequences.

INPUT

Ask students to guess about the difficulties of creating a TV show week after week with the same characters and story line.

After someone has described how hard it would be to keep interest and variety week after week with the same cast of characters, describe how Fran Stryker, writer of the Lone Ranger story, invented a method to help him keep the creativity alive with different variations in the basic story by creating the morphological or story grid.

ACTIVITY

Instructions:

1. On the overhead or blackboard, show this grid.

	HERO	HEROINE	VILLAIN	CONFLICT	SETTING	THE ENDING
1						
2						
3						
4						
5						
6						
7						
8						
9						
10						

The Story Grid

2. Ask the students to give names of anyone in history, literature, their lives, films, TV, etc. whom they would call the hero. Write the first ten in the hero column. Repeat for the heroine and the villain. (They should not try for a horizontal match up.)
3. List possible conflicts (i.e., fist fight, argument, etc.) and setting (OK corral, NY City, backyard.)
4. Finally, list possible endings to a story (rode into the sunset, lived happily ever after, etc.)
5. Ask one student provide the last six digits in his/her phone number.
6. Select one word for each column that corresponds to each number given and circle the items.
7. Assign students to groups of four. Instruct each group to take the items circled and create a story line for a TV show. Allow five to ten minutes and ask sample groups to share their stories.

METACOGNITIVE DISCUSSION

Conduct a classroom discussion by asking students the following:

1. Describe the steps you took in deciding how to make the story from the six elements. (You may want to describe how you would do it.) Encourage half of the class to listen for the differences used in deciding. Encourage the second half to listen for the similarities. Paraphrase responses to check out and extend the reports.
2. Ask for the differences that were noted. Make list on the board. Make sure that the differences are clarified.
3. Ask for the similarities. List and clarify the responses as needed.
4. Ask the students to speculate on the reasons for the differences in thinking that went into making each story line.

CLOSURE

Ask each student to use the last six digits of his/her phone number and create a new story line.

OR

Ask the small groups to construct some rules for creating many story sequences even though they are limited to a set number of factors. Share the rules with the class.

OR

Ask students to share when a word grid would be helpful in (a) this class or (b) another class.

Do You Want to Bet?

BACKGROUND

One of the conclusions that we have reached about skillful thinkers is that they are risk-takers who use data to make sound predictions. The better they are as thoughtful students of data, the more successful they are as predictors. In essence, they do not need to take wild guesses; they take calculated risks based on a careful study. Their bets are safe bets that usually "bring home the bacon." Studies are also showing us that there is a strong correlation between the skill to make predictions in reading and the skill to make predictions in critical thinking.

THINKING SKILL: PREDICTING

FOCUS ACTIVITY

Invite one student to the front of the classroom. Show a coin and predict whether it will fall heads or tails. Have the student flip the coin and tell you whether you won or lost. Ask the class to guess how many times out of a hundred flips, it will turn up heads? out of a thousand?

OBJECTIVE

To improve the skill of predicting.

INPUT

Using the board or overhead, provide the students with this information:

A definition of *Prediction:* anticipating what will occur with a high degree of success. (80%) An example: X number of coin flips will turn up tails. When it's important: in reading fiction, in scientific experiments, in detective work, in an operation, and in math problem solving.

The menu of operations:

Base on facts.
Examine clues for probability and possibility.
Tender your bet and make a guess.

If you run into difficulty: infer from feelings, tone, attitudes, and keep studying the facts.

ACTIVITY

Instructions:

1. Distribute copies of the shortened story, "The Dinner Party." Pre-fold the sheets on the lines.
2. Invite the students to silently read the first segment. When they are ready, tell them to use BET to predict what will happen next. Elicit responses by identifying the facts, discussing the clues and making solid guesses.
3. Continue through each segment.

Do You Want to Bet?

The Dinner Party

By Mona Gardner

The country is India. A colonial official and his wife are giving a large dinner party. They are seated with their guests—army officers and government attaches and their wives, and a visiting American naturalist—in their spacious dining room, which has a bare marble floor, open rafters, and wide glass doors opening onto a veranda.

("BET" what will happen next? Why do you think so, find data to support. Read to verify.)

A spirited discussion springs up between a young girl who insists that women have outgrown the jumping-on-a-chair-at-the-sight-of-a-mouse era and a colonel who says that they haven't.

"A woman's unfailing reaction in any crisis," the colonel says, "is to scream. And while a man may feel like it, he has that ounce more of nerve control than a woman has. And that last ounce is what counts."

("BET...")______________________________

The American does not join in the argument but watches the other guests. As he looks, he sees a strange expression come over the face of the hostess. She is staring straight ahead, her muscles contracting slightly. With a slight gesture she summons the native boy standing behind her chair and whispers to him. The boy's eyes widen, and he quickly leaves the room.

Of the guests, none except the American notices this or sees the boy place a bowl of milk on the veranda just outside the open doors.

("BET...")______________________________

The American comes to with a start. In India, milk in a bowl means only one thing—bait for a snake. He realizes there must be a cobra in the room. He looks up at the rafters—the likeliest place—but they are bare. Three corners of the room are empty, and in the fourth the servants are waiting to serve the next course. There is only one place left—under the table.

His first impulse is to jump back and warn the others, but he knows the commotion would frighten the cobra into striking. He speaks quickly, the tone of his voice so arresting that it sobers everyone."

"I want to know just what control everyone at this table has. I will count three hundred—that's five minutes—and not one of you is to move a muscle. Those who move will forfeit fifty rupees. Ready!"

("BET...")______________________________

The twenty people sit like stone images while he counts. He is saying" ...two hundred and eighty..." when, out of the corner of his eye, he sees the cobra emerge and make for the bowl of milk. Screams ring out as he jumps to slam the veranda doors safely shut.

"You were right, Colonel" the host exclaims. "A man has just shown us an example of perfect control."

"Just a minute," the American says, turning to his hostess. "Mrs. Wynnes, how did you know that cobra was in the room?"

A faint smile lights up the woman's face as she replies: "Because it was crawling across my foot."

STRATEGIES

Do You Want to Bet?

METACOGNITIVE DISCUSSION Invite students to answer the following:

1. Explain BET in your own words.
2. What are some things that you might use BET? (school and non-school). Explain and clarify how.
3. How is this method of reading different from what you ordinarily have done?
4. What would happen if you were to use BET in preparing for your next major test?
5. What are the strategies and disadvantages to using BET? (Make a chart.)

CLOSURE Instruct the students to write a short letter to the President or a Congressman. In the telegram, make a prediction, based on facts you know, what will happen if a specific policy is followed.

OR

Write a short letter to the students government and make a prediction what will happen if... Collect the letters and read samples.

Notes

The Planet Creon

BACKGROUND

In order to be a skillful creative and critical thinker, one of the skills that has multiple uses is the skill of imaging or visualizing. A thinker wh can see "with the mind's eye" is able to reduce issues and problems to a concrete picture. By recreating the concrete, the thinker is able to study the problem from multiple views, analyze the parts and evaluate which thinking skills to use. Metacognitive studies of famous scientists, artists and mathematicians have revealed how and why they are successful thinkers. They have developed the ability to see problems in the concrete, even when the seeing is restricted to creating a visual picture, better than those who remain average thinkers. Recent studies of world class and olympic athletes has corroborated the effectiveness of imaging. Currently, research is focusing on how the athlete can use images to picture a goal, such as a record performance or a gold medal, visualize movement based on memorized motion studies, and retrace one's own movements to reflect these mental pictures.

THINKING SKILL: IMAGING

FOCUS ACTIVITY

Ask the students to close their eyes and relax in their seats. Talk them slowly into relaxing. Ask them to use the inside of their eyelids as a movie screen. On the screen, they are to imagine that they are in the gym and that there is no gravity. They should create a movie picture of the gym filled with students and no gravity. What do they see? What are some of the possibilities of things that they could do? What would the wall and floor surfaces look like? What is the gym teacher doing? The students? After a few minutes, call the students to attention. Ask them to share what they imagined in as much detail as possible.

OBJECTIVE

To improve imaging as a thinking skill.

INPUT

Select a description passage from Joseph Conrad's *Lord Jim*. Read it to the class and ask them to listen and list samples of the following.

COLOR	SHAPES	SOUNDS	SMELLS

Ask the students to speculate how Conrad could come up with such a lush, specific description without ever having directly experienced what he described so well. Ask them to identify some instances that they have experienced in which they imagined in great detail something that they had not directly experienced. Present the word "imaging: to visualize or make a mental image of a new experience based on similar past experiences."

The Planet Creon

ACTIVITY Instructions:

1. Divide the class into groups of three. Give each group newsprint, crayons and tape. One student will draw while the other two close eyes and visualize the imaginary planet Creon. These are the conditions: "The two have just beamed down to the planet from their spaceship. The planet has no gravity, but does have oxygen and a temperate climate. Because it faces two stars, it has no night and no water."
2. The two seers are to take turns creating a picture of the planet: its inhabitants, life forms, landscape, etc. The only conditions that apply are the ones described already. The artist will sketch, as well as possible, what they describe in their five minute vision. After the seers are done, the artist may add any two touches he or she chooses as long as they fit the vision. Tape the finished images around the room and allow the class a few minutes to view them.

METACOGNITIVE DISCUSSION Ask the students to describe the origins of the details in their images. How did they transform what they had experienced in the past to the new picture? What was difficult about the task? How might they use imaging in tasks that they have to do?

CLOSURE Tell the students that one helpful place to use imaging is in goal setting. Have them record this mental menu in their LOGS.

a. Imagine a goal
b. Mentally pick a starting point.
c. Add each step from start to finish.
d. Graph your steps on an imaginary map.
e. Eliminate barriers.
f. Sense the feeling of triumph.

Give an example from your own experience, retracing your steps on the blackboard or overhead transparency. Describe any barriers and how you overcame them. Finally, describe your feelings when you attained your goal.

Invite each student to close his/her eyes and picture a goal (school, family, work etc.). Talk them through each of the six steps of IMAGES. After you have completed all steps, do a class wraparound with a stem selection from "I learned..." "I noticed..." "I wonder..." or "I pass."

STRATEGIES

PART 2

CATCH THEM THINKING CRITICALLY

The Attribute Web

BACKGROUND No thinking skill is more basic to critical thinking than attribute determination. Being able to determine those essential characteristics of a person, place, thing or idea that make it similar or different to others, helps us define and classify objects. Without the skill students mix up ideas, become confused and have no way to sort out or group objects.

THINKING SKILL: ATTRUBUTING

FOCUS ACTIVITY Invite three students who have three similar characteristics (i.e., hair or eye color, shoes, height) to stand in the front of the class. Ask the remaining students to tell why you selected this group.

OBJECTIVE To identify critical attributes by which one can group or classify like objects.

INPUT On the overhead, write the words:

5 **S** = **S**ense
Sound
Smell
Size
Specialty

Using a cow; a flower, and a bar of soap, show how we use sense (taste and touch), sound (noise and voice), smell (odor), size (height, weight, width, depth) and specialty (use) to define or describe an object via our 5 senses (smell, taste, touch, hearing, sight). The information we gather through our senses gives us the characteristics of objects. The unique arrangement of characteristics allows us to determine what an object is. When we group or classify all objects with similar characteristics, this unique arrangement of traits allows us to be more accurate. Those unique characteristics which are true only of a special group are called critical attributes.

One the board or overhead, draw this demonstration attribute web.

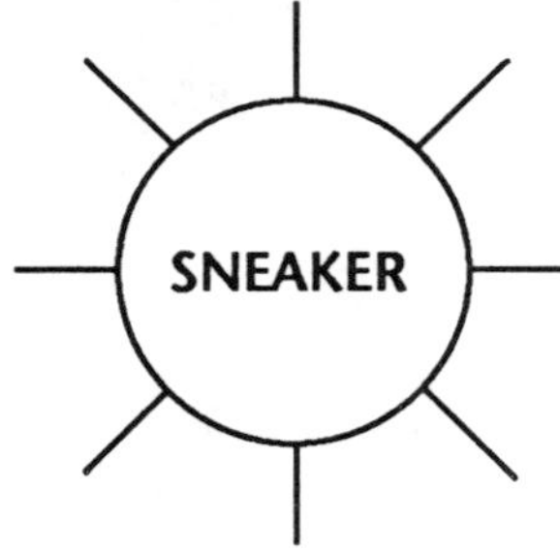

Ask the students to give you characteristics or attributes which will describe a sneaker. Put up all ideas given on the rays. After you have filled 10 to 20 rays, ask the class to identify only those characteristics which are true of all sneakers. Star (*) those and indicate that these are the critical attributes.

STRATEGIES

The Attribute Web

ACTIVITY

Instructions:

1. Put 5-7 students in a huddle. Instruct each student to select three other students with at least one characteristic (non-critical attributes) in common with themselves and sit down in a group of four.

2. Assign by height a leader, a timekeeper, a recorder, and materials manager in each group.

3. Have the recorder pick up newsprint, marker and tape for the group.

4. Prepare timekeeper for a 10 minute task. Observers will have to note what each person did to help in addition to his/her special job.

5. Instruct the recorder to draw a large attribute web on the newsprint. From a hat or box, have each leader pick out one of these titles or others of your choice to place in the center of the web.

   - paragraph
   - peace
   - family
   - light bulb
   - addition
   - dentist

6. With each person contributing in turn or saying, "I pass," allow 10 minutes for web work.

7. At the end of the time, instruct the group to select the critical attributes from its web. Post and discuss the webs.

METACOGNITIVE DISCUSSION

1. Ask several groups to identify the critical attributes selected. Ask them to describe how they made the selection decision.

2. How did the 5 "S's" help them select the critical attributes?

3. How might the web help them in social studies? English or reading? math? science? Ask individuals to describe a specific example in each academic area.

4. What did each member add to the discussion? Give examples.

CLOSURE

In the LOGS, instruct students to respond to the following:

1. In your own words, explain the term "critical attribute."

2. Make a web for a reading assignment. Identify the critical attributes of the material read. You may wish to discuss these in class the next day.

CLUES

BACKGROUND Drawing inferences is much like filling in a missing clue. Students must discover the hidden, or at least, less obvious connections between words, phrases and sentences, and draw conclusions that are valid. Readers become like detectives as they search for the missing clues.

THINKING SKILL: CLASSIFYING

FOCUS ACTIVITY Ask students to identify the names of several detectives they know from reading, TV, or movies. Ask what a detective might conclude from these words: knife, blood, corpse. Indicate that the detective fills in the missing blanks by clustering words and drawing inferences.

OBJECTIVE To cluster or classify common words in order to draw inferences from limited data.

INPUT On overhead or handout introduce the acronym CLUES and explain what each letter represents.

C = Cluster like words
L = Label clusters
U = Untangle sub-clusters
E = Examine clusters and sub-clusters
S = Set Patterns

Explain how they can use the word CLUES to remind them how to group or *classify* words or concepts in order to identify the *inferences* suggested. Highlight the importance of *inferential* reading and show how it is much like the *clue* finding that detectives do.

Use the following collection of words to demonstrate how to use each letter in the acronym, CLUES. [Radar, jet, flames, base, news, cost, fog] Go letter by letter and check for understanding.

Example: **C** *Cluster*.........1. (radar, radio, TV, news)— 2. (cloud, fog)— 3. (airport, base, jet)— 4. (flames, cost)

L *Label*........... **communications** (radio, radar, TV,news), **weather** (cloud, fog), **planes** (airport, jet, base), **accident** (flames, cost)

U *Untangle*....**warning device:** (radar), **news announcement** (TV, news, radio)

E *Examine*...

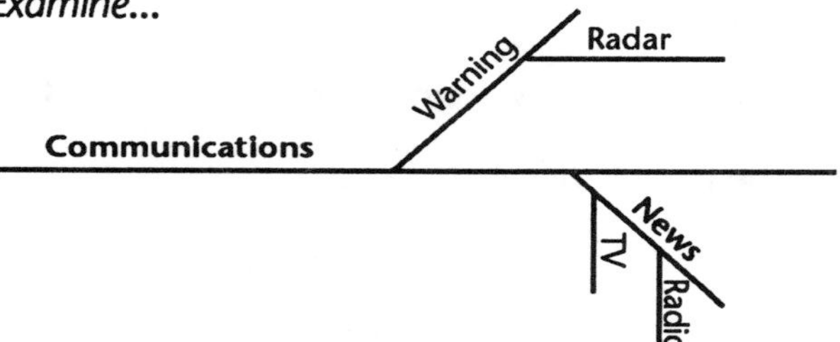

S *Set Pattern*..bad weather ➪ jet plane crash ➪ news ➪ cost

CLUES

ACTIVITY Instructions:

1. Ask students to explain CLUES in their own words.
2. Use the overhead or handout worksheets with the words listed below in the attribute web.

Students may work along or in small groups. Provide newsprint or blank overheads for each group to work a web. They may add as many branches or sub-branches as they desire. The core concept will go in the middle. There is no one right answer, but groups will have to explain how and why they formed their clusters.

The words: astronaut, star seeker, laser beam, shuttle, booster rocket, gravity, lead books, light years, solid fuel, capsule, heat shield, moon walker, launch pad.

You may substitute any group of 20-40 words. Take an article from a newspaper or magazine or a chapter from the textbook. In your list include the title, sub-topic nouns, and a random selection of words from each sub-topic; mix the list.

3. Allow 5 to 10 minutes for the completion of the webs.
4. Select one or more groups to explain their clusters. Encourage questions about "how" and "why" from the class about the sample webs. Be sure that the sample webs are visible (overhead or newsprint) to the class. Encourage acceptance of different classifications as long as they author group can explain its clusters.

METACOGNITIVE DISCUSSION

1. Review CLUES.
2. Ask another sample group or two to trace the clustering they did with the webs in relation to the CLUES guidelines.
3. Identify which items students had difficulty in clustering. What did they do to solve the problem(s)?
4. What general rules can one make about "classifying" when clustering problems occur?
5. When might you use CLUES in your studies? When else might CLUES help your thinking?

CLOSURE In the thinking LOG have students:

A. Summarize CLUES in their own words.

B. Record "What to do if" guidelines for their future use.

C. List "good times to use" CLUES.

D. Practice with a new webbing from the class textbook or newspaper.

STRATEGIES

The Priority Ladder

BACKGROUND Whenever we feel overwhelmed, rushed, harried, or hurried, we find it difficult to focus on what tasks are most important to do, what comes first, or what is our priority focus. Sometimes we are confused by too many choices. To help select our first choice, second choice, etc., we need a guideline. The guidelines are priorities which give us the focus to make a thoughtful selection.

THINKING SKILL: SETTING PRIORITIES

FOCUS ACTIVITY Present the students with these *forced* choices. For each sample, they must select one or the other and explain *why*. For each sample,listen to several different responses/reasons. A choice and a reason are required even though many will protest "I can't."

1. Which do you prefer: peanut butter and jelly or ham and cheese?
2. Which do you like better: fruit or vegetables?
3. Which is more important for you: a good night's sleep or a good test grade?

OBJECTIVE To identify priorities needed to make choices or decisions.

INPUT Explain to the class that *priorities* are those values, beliefs, interests that guide us in making selections or choices. A priority in selecting one food over another may be a health belief or a test preference. In some cases, both the belief and the like may be priorities which support each other. I both like applies and believe they are healthier. In other cases, they may conflict. "I know the apple is more healthy, but I have the taste and want to spend my money on candy, which is less healthy." Which will come out as the #1 priority? The challenge comes when one must act on priorities. The more clearly one thinks through their beliefs, values, preferences, and interests and separates the priorities, the more easily one can evaluate situations.

ACTIVITY Instruction:

1. On the board overhead, sketch a priority ladder or give each student a pre-sketched worksheet.

The Priority Ladder

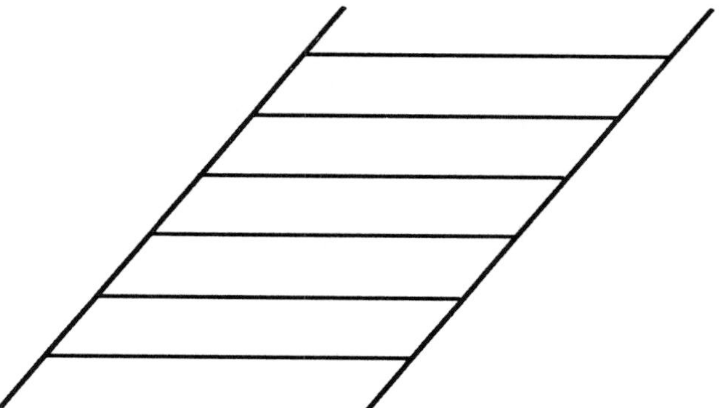

2. Project these words on the overhead: money, car, food, house, TV, job, friends.

3. Instruct each student to place the words on the ladder. In the bottom rung, place the word that is most important to you. Work up the ladder until you write in the least important on the top rung.

METACOGNITIVE DISCUSSION

1. Assign students to threes. Assign a rotation number (1,2,3). Number 1 will be our focus for three minutes. You are the class timekeeper. In the three minutes, #1 will explain his/her ranks. The partners will follow DOVE as active listeners.
2. Rotate the focus persons each three minutes.
3. After all are completed, invite #2 from several different trios to report on the top priorities.
4. Discuss the important considerations one must make when setting a priority.

CLOSURE

In the LOG, each student will take his/her top priority and sketch a 4-step ladder. On the ladder, the student will identify and rank the top benefits for the selected priority. (i.e., Car = (1) get to job; (2) emergencies; (3) family trips; and (4) going to store).

STRATEGIES

Notes

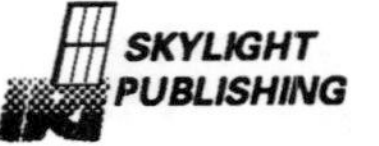

SECTION 8

SOURCES

Intellect ... is the critical, creative, and contemplative side of mind ... intelligence seeks to grasp, manipulate, re-order, adjust; intellect examines, ponders, wonders, theorizes, criticizes, imagines.

—*Richard Hofstadter*

Models For Thinking

A. Published Programs

To provide background and information for further research, this is an alphabetical listing of existing thinking skills programs.

	PROGRAM & FOUNDER(S)	CONTENT AND LEVELS
1.	British Primary Schools. Science and Mathematics: Nuffield Mathematics, John Wiley, New York.	Science and Mathematics Materials for instruction in British primary schools. Grades K - 7
2.	Building Thinking Skills I, II, III: Howard and Sandra Black, Midwest Publications, Pacific Grove, California.	Verbal and figural forms of micro-skills include similarities and differences, sequencing, classification and analogy. Grades 2 - 9
3.	(CATS) Critical Analysis and Thinking Skills: Dr. Jerry Applegate, Salt Lake City, Utah.	Integrated instruction in social studies as separate courses; rational decision making, constructive criticism, identifying and solving problems. Grades 10 - 12
4.	Creative Problem-Solving Models Sidney Parnes, Creative Education Foundation Buffalo, New York.	Students use a creative process to solve personal, organizational and hypothetical problems. Grades 1 -12
5.	Critical Thinking I and II: Anita Harnadek, Midwest Publications, Pacific Grove, California.	Integrated into English or social studies, micro-skills include formal and informal logic, language in reasoning, propaganda, persuasion, debate, and decision making. Grades 7 - 12
6.	Critical Thinking in History Project: Kevin O'Reilly S. Hamilton, Massachusetts.	U.S. History supplemental logic course with micro-skill lessons in evaluation of evidence and value statements, logical thinking, types of reasoning, and analysing arguments. Grades 10 -12
7.	(CCYC) Cognitive Curriculum For Young Children H. Carl Haywood, Penelope Brooks, and Susan Burns, Charlesbridge Publishing Watertown, Massachusetts.	Teaching and classroom activities stimulate children's thinking about their own thinking process and about generating, applying and evaluating appropriate learning and problem-solving strategies.

	PROGRAM & FOUNDER(S)	CONTENT AND LEVELS
8.	Cognitive Level Matching Project: Martin Brooks, Shoreham, New York.	Piagetian instructional methods applied to academic subjects. Grades K - 12
9.	Comprehensive School Mathematics Program: Claire Heideman, St. Louis, Missouri.	Experiential approach to teaching mathematics including classification, elementary logic and number theory. Grades K - 6
10.	(CoRT) Cognitive Research Trust: Edward deBono, Elmsford, New York.	Problem-solving strategies focus on breadth, organization, interaction, creativity, information, feeling and action. Grades 1 - 12
11.	Creative Learning and Problem Solving Scott G. Isaksen and Donald J. Treffinger (based on the work of Osborn, Parnes, Noller, and others), Buffalo State College, Elmwood, Buffalo.	Students are taught guidelines and thinking "tools" for generating and analysing ideas. These tools are then applied as part of a systematic process for dealing with challenges, which is then applied to dealing with many structured situations.
12.	Early Prevention of School Failure: Lucille Warner Peotone, Illinois.	Modality training for gross and fine motor development, visual and auditory discrimination, and language skills. Grades 3 - 6
13.	Expand Your thinking David Hyerle (based on the work of Albert Upton) Innovative Sciences, Inc. Stamford, Connecticut.	Students working in cooperative pairs are introduced to an integrated model of six fundemental thinking processes and corresponding graphic organizers for applying each of them. Grades 5-7
14.	Future Problem Solving E. Paul Torrance (based on work by Alex Osborn and Sidney Parnes) Laurinburg, North Carolina.	Student teams of four follow multiple-step problem solving process.
15.	Guided Design Charles Wales Morgantown, West Virginia.	Content area of problem solving, finding causes of problems, anticipating potential problems, identifying, and prioritizing problems. Grades 10 - College
16.	Higher Order Thinking Skills (HOTS) Stanley Pogrow University of Arizona, College of Education Tuscon, Arizona.	Program combines computers, curricular materials and Socratic teaching strategies. Teachers are trained to probe student answers and act as coaches who guide students to construct and test their own understanding in solving problems posed by the teacher.

17.	(ICE) Institute for Creative Education: E. Paul Torrance.	Micro-skills include fluency, flexibility, originality and influence, and elaboration related to content objectives. Grades 1 - 12
18.	Instrumental Enrichment: Reuven Feuerstein, University Park Press, Baltimore, Maryland.	Analysis of figural and and verbal problems using discussion to describe the process, not integrated into content areas. Grades 4 - 12
19.	Intelligence Applied Robert J. Sternberg Harcourt Brace Jovanovich San Diego, California.	Combines class discussion, written excercises, papers, projects, quizzes and group work.
20.	Learning to Learn: Marcia Herman Massachusetts.	Content learning strategies that engage students in hypothesizing and analyzing with feedback and correction. Grades 1 - 12
21.	Odyssey A team of Harvard University educators, Bolt Beranek and Newman, Inc., and the Venezuelan Ministry of Education. Charlesbridge Publishing Watertown, Massachusetts.	The emphasis is on discussion and student engagement in problem solving, reasoning, decision making, and creative activities.
22.	Patterns For Thinking—Patterns For Transfer: Creative and Critical Thinking In The Classroom Robin Fogarty and James Bellanca, Skylight Publishing, Inc., Palatine, Illinois.	Teaching For, Of, With and About Thinking. Explicit skill lesson and transfer lessons in creative and critical thinking for problem solving and decision making. Grades K - 12
23.	Philosophy for Children: Mathew Lipman, Montclaire, New Jersey.	Through discussion triggered by stories about children, students learn the rules to logical reasoning. Grades 3 - 12
24.	Project Impact: Lee Winocur, Director, Costa Mesa, California.	Direct instruction in micro-skills arranged in hierarchial sequence and presented in concrete and abstract learning units. Grades 7 - 12
25.	S.O.I.: Mary and Robert Meeker (based on J.P. Guilford's Structure of Intellect Model), El Segundo, California.	Diagnostic/prescriptive remediation and enrichment in areas of cognition memory, divergent and convergent production, and evaluation. Grades K - 12

	PROGRAM & FOUNDER(S)	CONTENT AND LEVELS
26.	Strategic Reasoning: Innovative Sciences, Inc. Think Program (based on Albert Upton's Model), Stamford, Connecticut.	Micro-skills include thing making, qualification, classification, operation, analysis, and analogy. THINK II is content related. Grades 5 - 9
27.	Talents Unlimited: Florence Replogle: (Based on Calvin Taylor's multiple talent theory.) Mobile, Alabama.	Micro-skill lessons in productive thinking, planning, communication, forecasting, and decision making. Grades 1 - 6
28.	Tactics for Thinking: Robert J. Marzano and Daisy E. Arredondo, Alexandria, Virginia.	ASCD endorsed model with 3 skill categories—learning to learn, content skills, reasoning skills—complete with manual and video tape.
29.	Thinking to Learn Educational Testing Service Diane Wah, Project Director Princeton, New Jersey.	Strategies staff development program is a two-phase "training for trainers" model to help teachers of grades 7-12 integrate thinking skills with subject area instruction. The Inside Story instructional unit is computerized and teacher-led classroom activities designed to help grade 6 and 7 students integrate thinking skills with language arts instruction.
30.	Thinking to Write Frances R. Link President Curriculum Development, Inc. Washington, D.C.	Includes documentary evidence in the form of student and teacher work journals, classroom videotapes, and pre- and post- profiles of changes in student's cognitive behavior, as well as test essays to asses transfer of learning.
31.	The Touchstones Project G. Comber, H. Zeiderman and N. Maistrellis, Annapolis, Maryland.	Text from a Touchstones volume is read aloud. Students work in groups to devise questions and approaches to the reading. The groups are later brought together for a larger discussion.
32.	Young Think, Just Think and Stretch Think Programs Sydney Billing Tyler Thomas Gaele Publications, Inc. Montara, California.	Curriculum to teach thinking. Each program is a reusable, year-long curriculum which includes everything the teacher needs for implementation. Teachers and Parents.

Models For Thinking

B. Cognitive Models

Critical Thinking

Definition: The correct assessment of statements.

12 Aspects of Critical Thinking

1. Grasp the meaning of a statement.
2. Judge whether ambiguity exists.
3. Judge if contradictions exist.
4. Judge if a conclusion necessarily follows.
5. Judge the specificity of a statement.
6. Judge if a statement relates to a certain principle.
7. Judge the reliability of observation.
8. Judge if an inductive conclusion is warranted.
9. Judge if a problem has been identified.
10. Judge if a definition is adequate.
11. Judge if a statement is credible.
12. Judge if something is an assumption.

Reference: Ennis, R. H., (1962, Winter). "A critical concept of critical thinking." *Harvard Review, 32*(1).

Bloom's Taxonomy of Educational Objectives

KNOWLEDGE
1. Knowledge of Specifics
   - knowledge of terminology
   - knowledge of specific facts
2. Knowledge of Ways and Means of Dealing with Specifics
   - knowledge of conventions
   - knowledge of trends and sequences
   - knowledge of classifications and catagories
   - knowledge of criteria
   - knowledge of methodology
3. Knowledge of Universals and Abstractions in a Field
   - knowledge of principles and generalizations
   - knowledge of theories and structures

SKILLS
define
recognize
recall
identify
label
understand
examine
show
collect

COMPREHENSION
1. Translation
2. Interpretation
3. Extrapolation

translate
interpret
explain
describe
summarize
demonstrate

APPLICATION
1. Use of Abstractions in Specific and Concrete Situations

apply
solve
experiment
show

ANALYSIS
1. Analysis of Elements
2. Analysis of Relationships
3. Analysis of Organizational Principles

connect
relate
differentiate
classify
arrange
group
interpret
organize
categorize
take apart
compare

SYNTHESIS
1. Production of a Unique Communication
2. Production of a Plan of Operation
3. Derivation of a Set of Abstract Relations

design
redesign
combine
add to
compose
hypothesize
construct
translate
imagine

EVALUATION
1. Judgments in Terms of Internal Evidence
2. Judgments in Terms of External Evidence

interpret
judge
criticize
decide

Reference: Bloom, B. S., Engelhart, M. D., Furst, E. J., Hill, W. H., Kratwohl, D. R., (1956). *Taxonomy of educational objectives, Handbook I.* New York: David McKay Co.

Creative Problem Solving

The Creative Process applied to problem solving:

1. **Fact Finding:** gathering data in preparation for defining the problem.
   - Identify the problem by asking questions: *Who? What? Where? Why?*

2. **Problem Finding:** analyzing problematic areas in order to pick out and point up the problem to be attacked.
   - Question: "In what ways might I . . .?"
   - Gather data

3. **Idea Finding:** producing ideas—thinking up, processing and developing numerous possible leads to solutions.
   - Put to other uses
   - Modify
   - Magnify
   - Rearrange
   - Combine
   - Adapt
   - Minimize
   - Substitute
   - Reverse

4. **Solution Finding:** evaluating potential solutions against defined criteria.
   - Establish criteria
   - Evaluate
   - Verify
   - Test

5. **Acceptance Finding:** adopting—developing a plan of action and implementing the chosen solution.
   - Implement
   - Prepare for acceptance

The following diagram suggests the way in which this process alternates within each step between "imaginative" (divergent) thinking and "judicial" (convergent) thinking.

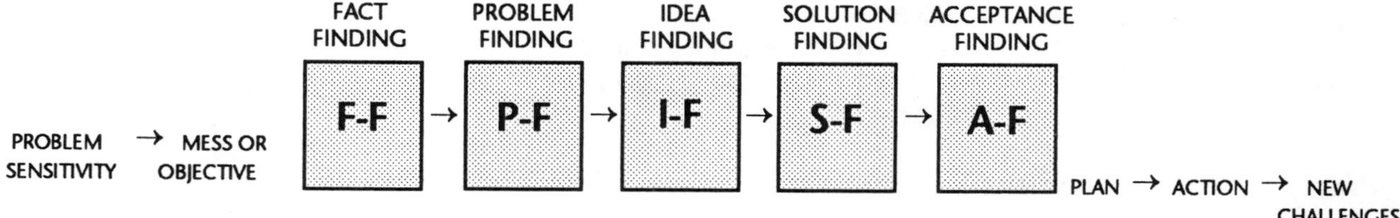

References: Parnes, S. J., Noller, B., & Biondi, A. (1976). *Creative action book.* New York: Charles Scribner & Sons.
Osborn, A. F. (1963). *Applied imagination.* New York: Charles Scribner & Sons.

SOURCES

SOURCES

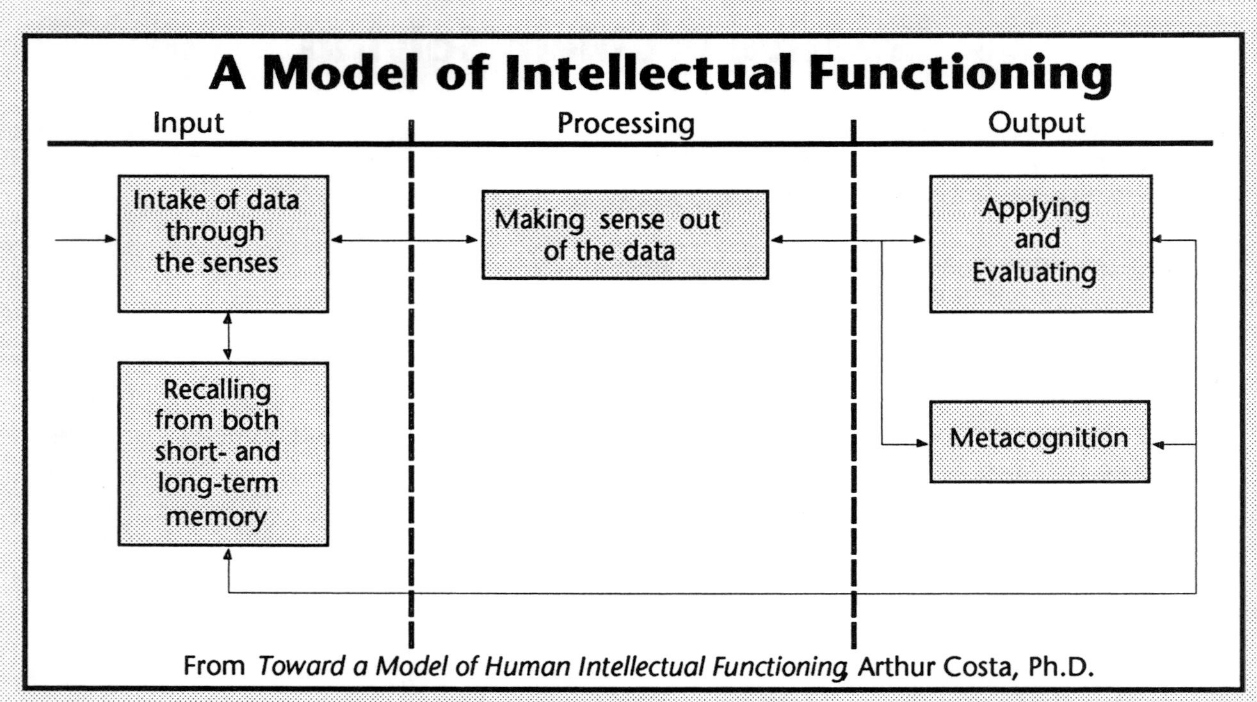

INQUIRY TRAINING

The inquiry training model based on the work of R. Suchman identifies these processes:

Confrontation with the Problem—

- encountering the environment
- students are presented with something to explain or assimilate

Period of Inquiry—processing the data found

- students question and probe the thing under question to collect data about it
- students analyze the acquired data and formulate
- principles about the causal relationship found among the data's variables

Analysis of Inquiry Strategy

- students and teachers evaluate the inquiry process and develop more effective strategies of investigation
- students assimilate the explanation into their conceptual system

Reference: Joyce, Bruce, and Weil, Marsha. (1972). Inquiry training model. *Models of Teaching*. New York: Prentice-Hall.

Guilford's Structure of the Intellect

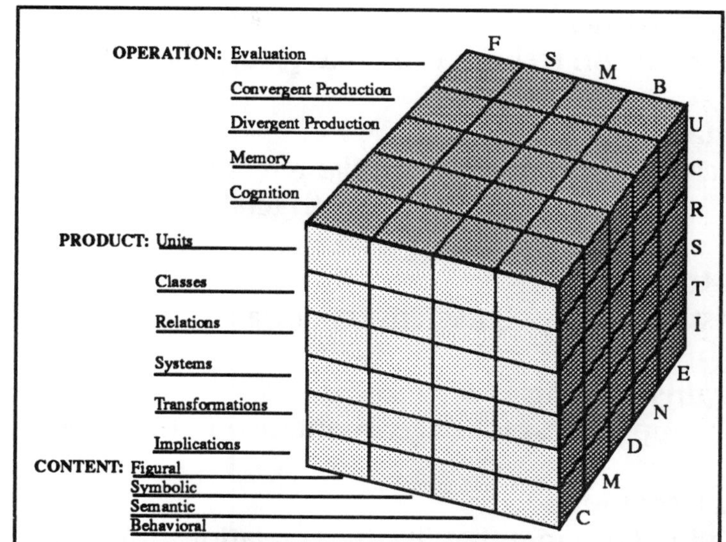

Operations: Intellectual Process

Cognition—discovery, rediscover, or recognition of information
Memory—retention or storage of information
Evaluation—decision making or rendering judgments
Convergent Production—generation of information from acquired information with emphasis on accepted best outcome
Divergent Production—generation of information from acquired information with emphasis on variety and quality of outcome

Content: Classes or Types of Information

Figural—visual or kinesthetic forms
Symbolic—numeral or letter
Semantic—words and ideas
Behavioral—manifestations of a response to a stimulus

Products: Organization that Information Takes

Units—single word or idea
Classes—group of information
Relations—connection between information
Systems—structure of information
Transformations—redefining or modifying existing information
Implications—foreseeing consequences

Interactions: Combining Operations, Contents and Products

Example:
CSR—convergent production, production of symbolic relations
DFT—divergent production of figural transformations

Reference: Guilford, J.P., (1967) The nature of human intelligence. (McGraw-Hill Psychology Series), New York: McGraw-Hill
Meeker, Mary N., (1969) The Structure of Intellect. Columbus, OH: Merrill Publishing Co.

Synectics

Developed by Gordon, Synectics is a process for developing creativity based on the use of metaphorical forms.

1. **Personal Analogy**—This procedure involves getting students to identify with a person, plant, animal, or non-living thing. It emphasizes empathetic involvement.

Example: How would I feel as a cloud?

2. **Direct Analogy**—This procedure involves analogizing the conditions of problems in new settings and using the analogy as the basis of generating a solution to a problem. It is a comparison of two objects.

Example: Person grows like a plant.

3. **Compressed Conflict**—This procedure requires description of an object from two frames of reference.

Example: Poor little rich person.

References: Gordon, W. J. (1970). *The metaphorical way of learning and knowing.* Cambridge, MA: Synectics Education Press.

Glossary

User's Guide to Definitions of Terms

Agree/Disagree
A prediction technique used to focus, diagnose and forecast.

Analogy
A comparison showing similar relationships (e.g., apple: fruit; squash: vegetable; or a book is like a person because both relate feelings).

Attributes
Distinguishing characteristics or traits.

Brainstorming
A group process to trigger spontaneous, fluent production of ideas.

Concept Map
A visual diagram that illustrates relationships in free-flow of thoughts.

Cooperative Groups
Structured small groups with designated role responsibilities for each member.

Cause/Effect
One factor (or set of factors) determining the outcome; a chain of events.

Clustering
Free-flowing technique to plot spontaneous verbal associations used in writing to initiate, focus, or elaborate.

Creative Thinking
Using skills of application and synthesis to generate ideas; producing.

Creative Problem Solving
A somewhat hierarchial model to generate alternatives and evaluate choices. The process includes fact, problem, idea, solution, and acceptance finding.

Critical Thinking
Using skills of analysis and evaluation to determine the work of idea; critiquing.

Deductive Reasoning
Reasoning from a general rule to a specific case—i.e., does it fit the rule or generalization?

SOURCES

Decision Making
Judging choices and basing final selection on evaluation of criteria.

Explicit Skill
Teaching a thinking skill as the content of the lesson (e.g., teaching classification as a skill of organization).

Fishbone
A diagram used in analytic problem solving to show relationship.

Flow Chart
A sequential diagram to show possibilities or choices.

Forced Responses
Strategies to structure responses from all students such as whip, wraparounds, signals and systematic sampling.

Guided Imagery
An imagination exercise directed orally by a leader.

Hex Message
A cluster of hexagons used to structure writing.

Human Graph
A simulation of a graph with participants selecting a position along a continuum to indicate choices in a hypothetical decision.

Inductive Reasoning
Reasoning from specific examples to a general rule—i.e., given the facts, what generalization can be made?

Macro-skills
Critical and creative processes comprised of several micro-skills (e.g., synthesis requires skills of analytic evaluation and divergent thinking).

Metacognitive Processing
Thinking about thinking; tracking how one thinks, using structured discussion or written records.

Metaphor Model
An elaboration of a metaphor by using more than one part in the comparison (e.g., an argument is like a fire; the insult is the spark; the reaction is the kindling).

Micro-skill
The skill taught in isolation (e.g., classification, sequencing, compare and contrast).

Problem Solving
Specific strategies that use creative synthesis and critical analysis to generate viable alternatives to perplexing situations.

Ranking
A rating system that forces prioritization of choices.

Reinforcers
Verbal and nonverbal teacher behaviors that positively support developing student behaviors.

Target Analysis
A visual to help identify priorities.

Thinking Log
A student log of visual or verbal entries reflecting a person's reactions to learning.

Transfer
Bridging the micro-skills (e.g., classification) into content areas in the classroom and in real-life situations; application.

Venn Diagram
Overlapped circles used to compare and contrast.

Wait Time
A strategy to promote thinking that uses three to ten seconds of silence following a teacher-initiated question or a student response.

Whip
Students responding in turn around the room; they may pass. (Same as wraparound)

Word Trees
Stream of consciousness, word by association diagram used to generate creative thinking.

Wraparound
Students responding in turn; they may pass. (Same as whip)

SECTION 9

BIBLIOGRAPHY

A book is the only place in which you can examine a fragile thought without breaking it, or explore an explosive idea without fear it will go off in your face....

—Edward P. Morgan

Bibliography

Adler, M. J., & Van Doren, C. (1972). *How to read a book*. New York: Simon & Schuster.

Ainsworth-Land, V., & Fletcher, N. (1979). *Making waves with creative problem solving*. Buffalo, NY: D.O.K.

Becoming a nation of readers. (1984). The report of the commission on reading: NIE.

Bellanca, J., & Fogarty, R. (1990). *Catch them thinking: A handbook of classroom strategies*. Palatine, IL: Skylight.

Bellanca, J., & Fogarty, R. (1986). *Teach them thinking*. Palatine, IL: Skylight.

Bellanca, J. (1984). *Quality circles for educators*. Palatine, IL: IRI Group.

Beyer, B. K. (1983, November). Common sense about teaching thinking skills. *Educational Leadership*, p. 57-62.

Beyer, B. K. (1985, January). Teaching thinking skills: How the principal can know they are being taught. *NASSP Bulletin*.

Beyer, B. K. (1984, March). Improving thinking skills—defining the problem. *Phi Delta Kappan*, p. 486-490.

Beyer, B. K. (1987). *Practical strategies for the teaching of thinking*. Boston, MA: Allyn & Bacon.

Biondi, A. (ed.). (1972). *The creative process*. Buffalo, NY: D.O.K.

Black, H., & Black, S. (1981). *Figural analogies*. Pacific Grove, CA: Midwest Publications.

Bloom, B. S. (1981). *All our children learning. A primer for parents, teachers, and educators*. New York: McGraw-Hill.

Bloom, B. S., Engelhart, M. D., Furst, E. J., Hill, W. H., & Kratwohl, D. R. (1956). *Taxonomy of educational objectives: Cognitive domain, Handbook I*. New York: David McKay Co.

Brandt, R. (1988, April). On teaching thinking: A conversation with Arthur Costa. *Educational Leadership*, p. 11.

Burns, M. (1975). *I hate mathematics*. Boston, MA: Little, Brown & Co.

Burns, M. (1976). *The book of think or how to solve a problem twice your size*. Boston, MA: Little, Brown & Co.

Buscaglia, L. F. (1972). *Love*. Thoroughfare, NJ: Slack.

Campbell, T. C., Fuller, R. G., Thornton, M. C., Peter, J. L., Patterson, M. Q., Carpenter, E. T., & Narveson, R. D. (1980). A teacher's guide to the learning cycle. A Piagetian-based approach to college instruction. In R. G. Fuller, et al. (Eds.), *Piagetian programs in higher education*. Lincoln, NE: ADAPT, University of Nebraska-Lincoln, p. 27-46.

Carpenter, E. T. (1980). Piagetian interviews of college students. R. G. Fuller, et al. (Eds.), *Piagetian programs in higher education*. Lincoln, NE: ADAPT, University of Nebraska-Lincoln, p. 15-21.

Carpenter, T. P., Corbitt, M. K., Kepner, H., Lindquist, M. M., & Reys, R. W. (1980, Ocrober). Student's affective responses to mathematics: National assessment results. *Educational Leadership*, p. 34-37, 52, 531-539.

Chase, L. (1975). *The other side of the report card*. Glenview, IL: Scott Foresman.

Clark, B. (1988). *Growing up gifted*. Columbus, OH: Merrill Publishing.

Clement, J. (1982). Algebra word problem solutions: Thought processes underlying a common misconception. *Journal of Research in Mathematics Education*, p. 13, 16-30.

Clement, J. (1982). Students' preconceptions in introductory mechanics. *American Journal of Physics*, p. 50, 66-71.

Convigtona, M. V., Crutchfield, R. S., Davies, L., & Olton, R. M. (1974). *The productive thinking program: A course in learning to think*. Columbus, OH: Merrill Publishing.

Costa, A. L. (Ed.) (1985). *Developing minds*, Alexandria, VA: ASCD.

Costa, A. L. (1984, November). Mediating the metacognitive. *Educational Leadership*, p. 57-62.

Costa, A. L. (1981, October). Teaching for intelligent behavior. *Educational Leadership*, p. 29-32.

Costa, A. L. (1985). The behaviors of intelligence. In *Developing Minds*. (p. 66-68). Alexandria, VA: ASCD.

Costa, A. L., & Garmston, R. (1985, March). *The art of cognitive coaching: Supervision for intelligent teaching*. Paper presented at the Annual Conference of the Association for Supervision and Curriculum Development, Chicago.

deBono, E. (1973). *Lateral thinking: Creative step by step*. New York: Harper and Row.

deBono, E. (1976). *Teaching thinking*. New York: Penguin Books.

Easterling, J., & Pasanen, J. (1979). *Confront, construct, complete*. Rochell Park, NJ: Hayden Publishing.

Eberle, B., & Stanish, B. (1980). *CPS For Kids*. Buffalo, NY: D.O.K.

Eberle, B. (1982). *Visual thinking*. Buffalo, NY: D.O.K.

Edwards, B. (1979). *Drawing on the right side of the brain*. Los Angeles: J. P. Tarcher.

Eggen, Kauchak, & Harder. (1979). *Strategies for teachers*. New York: Prentice-Hall.

Eisner, E. W. (1983, October). The kind of schools we need. *Educational Leadership*, p. 48-55.

Elbow, P. (1981). *Writing with power*. New York: Oxford University Press.

Elbow, P. (1973). *Writing without teachers*. New York: Oxford University Press.

Ferguson, M. (1980). *The aquarian conspiracy*. Los Angeles: J. P. Tarcher.

Feuerstein, R. (1980). *Instrumental enrichment*. Baltimore, MD: University Park Press.

Fogarty, R. (1989). *From training to transfer: The role of creativity in the adult learner*. Doctoral dissertation, Loyola University of Chicago.

Frostic, G. (1967). *Wing-Borne*. Benzonia, MI: Benzonia Press.

Fullan, M. (1982). *The meaning of educational change*. New York: Teachers College Press.

Gallagher, J. (1985). *Teaching the gifted child*. Boston, MA: Allyn & Bacon.

Gallelli, G. (1977). *Activity mindset guide*. Buffalo, NY: D.O.K.

Gardner, H. (1983). *Frames of mind: The theory of multiple intelligence*. New York: Basic Books.

Gardner, et al. National Commission on Excellence in Education. (1983). *A nation at risk: The imperative for educational reform*. Washington, DC: Department of Education.

Gardner, M. (1942, January 31). The Dinner Party. *Saturday Review*.

Glatthorn, A. (1984). *Differentiated supervision*. Alexandria, VA: ASCD.

Good, T. L. (1981, February). Teacher expectations and student perception: A decade of research. *Educational Leadership*, p. 415-422.

Goodlad, J. I. (1984). *A place called school, prospects for the future*. New York: McGraw-Hill.

Gordon, W. J. J., & Pose, T. *Activities in metaphor*. Cambridge, MA: Porpoise Books.

Gordon, W. J. J., & Pose, T. *Teaching is listening*. Cambridge, MA: Porpoise Books.

Gordon, W. J. J. (1961). *Synectics: The development of creative capacity*. New York: Harper and Row.

Guilford, J. P. (1975). *Way beyond the IQ*. Buffalo, NY: Creative Education Foundation.

Hall, G., & Loucks, S. (1979). *Implementing innovations in schools, a concerns-based approach*. Austin, Texas: University of Texas at Austin, CBFM Project—Research and Development Center for Teacher Education, The University of Texas at Austin.

Harnadek, A. (1977). *Basic thinking skills, Analogies-D*. Pacific Grove, CA: Midwest Publications.

Harnadek, A. (1980). *Critical thinking*. Pacific Grove, CA: Midwest Publications.

Harnadek, A. (1977). *Basic thinking skills, Patterns*. Pacific Grove, CA: Midwest Publications.

Hunter, M. (1971). *Transfer*. El Segundo, CA: TIP Publications.

Johnson, R., & Johnson, D. (1987). *Learning together and alone: Cooperative, competitive and individualistic learning*. New York: Prentice-Hall.

Johnson, R., & Johnson, D. (1986). *Circles of learning: Cooperation in the classroom*. Alexandria, VA: ASCD.

Johnson, R., & Johnson, D. (1982, October). Cooperation in learning: Ignored but powerful. *Lyceum*.

Joyce, B. R. (1986). *Improving America's schools*. New York: Longman.

Joyce, B. R., & Showers, B. (1980, February). Improving inservice training: The message of research. *Educational Leadership*, p. 380.

Joyce, B. R., & Showers, B. (1983). *Power in staff development through research and training*. Alexandria, VA: ASCD.

Karplus, R. (1974). *Science curriculum improvement study teachers handbook*. Berkeley, CA: University of California.

Krupp, J. A. (1982). Adult development. *Adult learning and development*. Connecticut.

Krupp, J. A. (1981). The adult learner. *Adult learning and development*. Connecticut.

Larkin, J. H., McDermott, J., Simon, D. P., & Simon, H. A. (1980, June 20). Expert and novice performance in solving physics problems. *Science*, p. 1335-1342.

Machado, L. A. (1980). *The right to be intelligent*. New York: Pergamon Press.

Maraviglia, C. (1978). *Creative problem-solving think book*. Buffalo, NY: D.O.K.

Marzano, R. J., & Arredondo, D. E. (1986, May). Restructuring schools through the teaching of thinking skills. *Educational Leadership*, p. 23.

McCloskey, M., Carmazza, A., & Green, B. (1980, December 5). Curvilinear motion in the absence of external forces: Naive beliefs about the motion of objects. *Science*, p. 1139-1141.

Nickerson, R. S. (1982). *Understanding understanding*, (BBN Report No. 5087).

Nickerson, R. S. (1983). Computer programming as a vehicle for teaching thinking skills. *Journal of Philosophy for Children, 4*(3&4).

Nickerson, R. S., Perkins, D. N., & Smith, E. E. (1984). *Teaching thinking*, (BBN Report No. 5575).

Nickerson, R. S., Salter, W., Shepard, & Hernstein, J. (1984). *The teaching of learning strategies*, (BBN Report No. 5578).

Nisbett, R., & Ross, L. (1980). *Human inference: Strategies and shortcomings of social judgment*. Englewood Cliffs, NJ: Prentice-Hall.

Noller, R., Parnes, S., & Biondi, A. (1976). *Creative action book.* New York: Charles Scribner & Sons.

Noller, R., Treffinger, D., & Housemann, E. (1979). *It's a gas to be gifted or CPS for the gifted and talented.* Buffalo, NY: D.O.K.

Noller, R. (1977). *Scratching the surface of creative problem solving: A bird's-eye view of CPS.* Buffalo, NY: D.O.K.

Osborn, A. F. (1963). *Applied imagination.* New York: Charles Scribner & Sons.

Parnes, S. (1975). *Aha! Insights into creative behavior.* Buffalo, NY: D.O.K.

Parnes, S. (1972). *Creativity: Unlocking human potential.* Buffalo, NY: D.O.K.

Pearson, C. (1980, February). Can you keep quiet for three minutes. *Learning.*

Perkins, D. N. (1988, August 6) *Thinking frames.* Alexandria, VA: Paper delivered at ASCD conference on Approaches to Thinking, p. 14-15.

Perkins, D. N. (1986). *Knowledge as design.* Hillsdale, NJ: Lawrence Erlbaum Associates, p. 5, 222-231.

Perkins, D. N. , & Salomon, G. (1989, January-February). Are cognitive skills context bound? *Educational Researcher,* p. 16-25.

Perkins, D. N., & Salomon, G. (1988, September). Teaching for transfer. *Educational Leadership,* p. 22-32.

Peters, T., & Austin, N. (1985). *Passion for excellence.* New York: Random House.

Peters, T., & Waterman, R., Jr. (1982). *In search of excellence.* New York: Warner Communications.

Polette, N. (1981). *Exploring books for gifted programs.* Metuchen, NJ: Scarecrow Press.

Posner, M. I., & Keele, S. W. (1973). Skill learning. In Robert M. W. Travers, (Ed.) *Second handbook of research on teaching* (p. 805-831). Chicago, IL: Rand McNally College Publishing Co.

Problem cards: Attribute games and problems. (1966). New York: Webster Division of McGraw-Hill (ESS Science Series).

Raths, L. (1967). *Teaching for thinking.* Columbus, OH: Merrill Publishing.

Rico, G. L. (1983). *Writing the natural way.* Los Angeles: J. P. Tarcher.

Scardamalia, M., Bereiter, C., & Fillion, B. (1979). *The little red writing book: A source book of consequential writing activities.* Ontario, Canada: Pedagogy of Writing Project, O.I.S.E.

Schoenfeld, A. H. (1980). Teaching problem-solving skills. *American Mathematical Monthly, 87*(10), p. 794-805.

Sergiovanni, T. (1987, May). Will we ever have a true profession? Supervision in context. *Educational Leadership,* p. 44-49.

Smith, F. (1986). *Insult to intelligence: The bureaucratic invasion of our classrooms*. New York: Arbor House.

Sternberg, R. J. (1984, September). How can we teach intelligence? *Educational Leadership*, p. 38-48.

Sternberg, R. J. (1981, October). Intelligence is thinking and learning skills. *Educational Leadership*, p. 18-21.

Sternberg, R. J. (1986). *Intelligence applied: Understanding and increasing your intellectual skill*. New York: Harcourt Brace Javanovich.

Tolkien, J. R. R. (1937). *The Hobbit*. New York: Ballantine Books.

The College Board. (1983). *Academic preparation for college*. New York.

Torrance, E. P. (1979). *The search for satori and creativity*. Buffalo, NY: Creative Education Foundation, & Great Neck, NY: Creative Synergetics Associates.

Trowbridge, D. E., & McDermott, L. C. (1980). Investigation of student understanding of the concept of velocity in one dimension. *American Journal of Physics, 48*(12), 1010-1028.

Tversky, A., Kahneman, D. (1974, September 27). Judgment under uncertainty: Heuristics and biases. *Science*, p. 1124-1131.

Tyler, R. W. (1986, December-1987, January). The five most significant curriculum events in the twentieth century. *Educational Leadership*, p. 36-37.

Underwood, V. L. (1982). *Self-management skills for college students: A program in how to learn*. Unpublished doctoral dissertation, University of Texas.

Von Oech, R. (1986). *A kick in the seat of the pants*. New York: Harper and Row.

Von Oech, R. (1983). *A whack on the side of the head*. New York: Warner Books.

Wallace, R., & Editors of Time-Life Books. (1966). *The world of Leonardo* (p. 1452-1519).

Warner, S. A. (1972). *Teacher*. New York: Vintage Books.

Wason, P. C. (1974). The psychology of deceptive problems. *New Scientist, 63*, 382-385.

Wayman, J. (1981). *The other side of reading*. Carthage, IL: Good Apple.

Weber, P. (1978). *Promote...Discovering ways to learn and research*. Buffalo, NY: D.O.K.

Weber, P. (1978). *Question Quest: Discovering Ways to Ask Worthwhile Questions*. Buffalo, NY: D.O.K.

Weinstein, C. E. & Underwood, V. L. (1983). Learning strategies: The how of learning. In J. Segal, S. Chipman, & R. Glaser (Eds.). *Relating instruction to basic research*. Hillsdale, NJ: Lawrence Erlbaum Associates.

What works: Research about teaching and learning. (1986). U.S. Department of Education. Washington, DC.

Whimbey, A. (1975). *Intelligence can be taught.* New York: Innovative Science.

Williams, F. E. (1970). *Classroom ideas for encouraging thinking and feeling.* Buffalo, NY: D.O.K.

Wittrock, M. C. (1967). Replacement and nonreplacement strategies in children's problem solving. *Journal of Educational Psychology*, p. 69-74.

SECTION 10

TRAINING LOG

A word is not a crystal, transparent and unchanged; it is the skin of a living thought and may vary greatly in color and content according to the circumstances and time in which it is used.

—Oliver Wendell Holmes, Jr.

Thinking About Transfer

Making Creative Connections

_______________'s Log

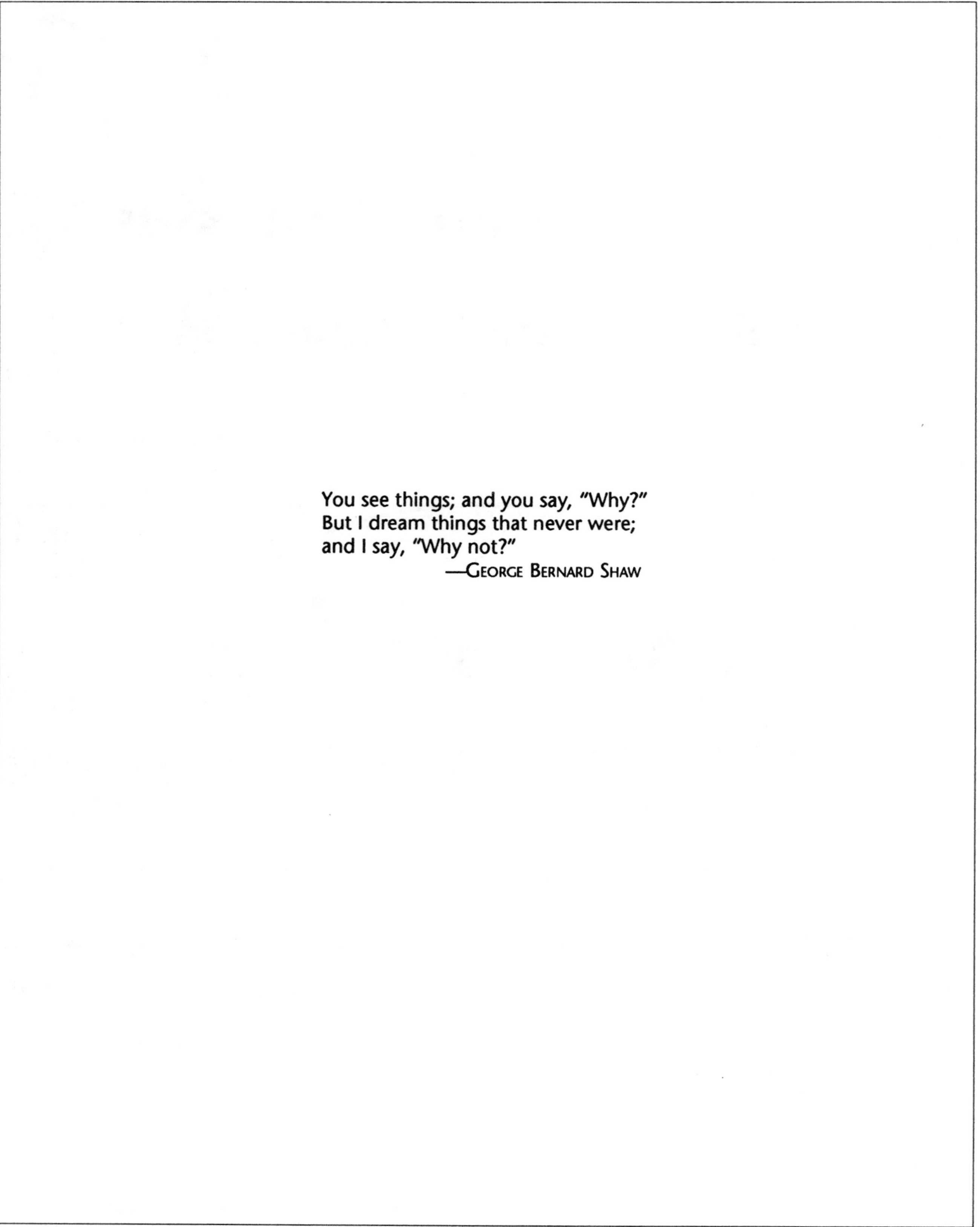

You see things; and you say, "Why?"
But I dream things that never were;
and I say, "Why not?"

—George Bernard Shaw

SKYLIGHT PUBLISHING

Log Table of Contents

A Word About Transfer

All teaching is for transfer; all learning is for transfer. To extend learning; to bridge the old and the new; and to lead students toward relevant transfer and use across academic content and into life situations, is the mission of the thinking classroom.

In some cases, the transfer of learning is obvious because the learned skills seem close to the skill situation in which they are used or transferred. For example, when teaching "supermarket math"—price comparisons, making change etc.—the learning situation "hugs" the life situation. The transfer is clear. This transfer is called simple transfer.

However, in other instances, the learning in the school situation seems far removed or remote from the transfer across content or into life. For example, a high school student spends a great deal of time and energy staring at, memorizing and using the Periodic Table of Elements. However, unless the student is destined for a scientific career in which frequent reference and deep understanding of the table is essential, it is difficult for the student to feel that the learning is really useful. Does one really need to know that Au is gold?

Most students do not "see" how this learning is useful. The transfer is complex. They miss the connection between the rigors of learning the elements and the similar rigors of visualizing, practicing and memorizing other material. Few students note that the analytical skills used in "reading" the table of elements are similar to the critical thinking used in analyzing other charts or graphs. Seldom are students aware that the patterns evident in the table of elements set a model for searching for patterns in other phenomena or constructing similar matrices or grids. The transfer here is remote; it is obscure. The student needs explicit instruction in making these and other connections. In these situations, teachers can help kids make relevant transfer through mediation or "bridging" strategies.

The six transfer strategies illustrated below require explicit instruction with students to help them make application, in other words, to help them transfer.

Transfer: The Creative Connection

Mediation Strategies That Bridge Learning

Transfer Strategy #1: Setting Expectations

SET EXPECTATIONS for transfer. Elicit examples of when the information, skill or concept is used in other content or life situations. Ask students how they might use this new learning; how it connects to past experiences; how it might be useful in particular subject areas or life situations.

Transfer Strategy #2: Reflecting Metacognitively

REFLECT ON YOUR TRANSFER LEVEL by asking: Am I...

Ollie		**Head-in-the-sand Ostrich**	Missing appropriate opportunities; overlooking; persisting in former ways?
Dan		**Drilling Woodpecker**	Performing the drill exactly as practiced; duplicating with no change; copying?
Laura		**The Look-alike Penguin**	Tailoring, but applying in similar situations; all looking alike; replicating?
Jonathan		**Livingston Seagull**	More aware; integrating; sublty combining with other ideas and situations; using with raised consciousness?
Cathy		**The Carrier Pigeon**	Carrying strategy to other content and into life situations; associating and mapping?
Samantha		**The Soaring Eagle**	Innovating; taking ideas beyond the initial conception; risking; diverging?

Transfer Strategy #3: Making Connections With Questions

USE BRIDGING QUESTIONS such as:

OVERLOOKING

Think of an instance when the skill or strategy would be inappropriate.

"I would not use__________when__________________________."

DUPLICATING

Think of an "opportunity passed" when you could have used the skill or strategy.

"I wish I'd known about _____________ when _______________ because I could've____."

REPLICATING

Think of an adjustment that will make your application of ____ more relevant.

"Next time I'm gonna ___________________________________ ____."

INTEGRATING

Think of an analogy for the skill or strategy.

"____________________ is like _____________________ because both ____."

MAPPING

Think of an upcoming opportunity in classes to use the new idea.

"In ____________, I'm gonna use _________________________ to help ____."

INNOVATING

Think of an application for a "real-life" setting.

"Outside of school, I could use __________________________ when ____."

LOG

Transfer Strategy #4: Modeling

MODEL EXAMPLES of how the skill or strategy has been used by showing or referring to explicit models. Share specific examples through "artifacts" collected from students and/or teachers—people using the ideas.

Transfer Strategy #5: Promote Risk Taking

CREATE CONNECTIONS by promoting risk taking that stretches learning across content and into life. Foster "safe risks" by encouraging students to play with ideas.

Teacher Transfer—Student Transfer

Knowledge and Understanding of Transfer

Setting Expectations for Teacher Use

Giving Relevant Examples

Teacher Self-reflecting on Levels of Transfer

Peer Coaching on Levels of Transfer

Hugging/Bridging Questions for Transfer

Begin Same Transfer Cycle with Students

Teacher Transfer

My Log

Student Transfer

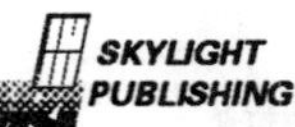

Ollie
Head-in-the-sand Ostrich

Overlooking opportunities, persisting in former ways.

Overlooking opportunities, persisting in former ways.

I will never. . .

SKYLIGHT PUBLISHING

Overlooking opportunities, persisting in former ways.

A strategy I choose not to use. . .

Overlooking opportunities, persisting in former ways.

Something that seems unrelated to anything I do is. . .

LOG

Overlooking opportunities, persisting in former ways.

Something I've overlooked but am thinking about is. . .

Flashes of Genius. . .

You may find yourself about to have an idea.
It may be a small idea; it may be a big idea.
Here is a place to put it.

Dan

The Drilling Woodpecker

Duplicating, copying an activity and practicing as learned

Duplicating, copying an activity and practicing as learned

I'd like a copy of. . .

Duplicating, copying an activity and practicing as learned

An activity I will "steal" as a thinking thief is. . .

Duplicating, copying an activity and practicing as learned

I wish I'd known about_______. I could've used it when. . .

Duplicating, copying an activity and practicing as learned

I want to borrow. . .

Flashes of Genius. . .

You may find yourself about to have an idea.
It may be a small idea; it may be a big idea.
Here is a place to put it.

Laura
The Look-alike Penguin

Replicating, tailoring to needs, and using often in similar content or situation

Replicating, tailoring to needs, and using often in similar content or situation

By changing. . .

Replicating, tailoring to needs, and using often in similar content or situation

When I use _____, this time I'm gonna. . .

Replicating, tailoring to needs, and using often in similar content or situation

Next time, I'll. . .

Replicating, tailoring to needs, and using often in similar content or situation

To use in *my* class. . .

Flashes of Genius. . .

You may find yourself about to have an idea.
It may be a small idea; it may be a big idea.
Here is a place to put it.

Jonathan
Livingston Seagull

Integrating, combining old and new with the raised consciousness and awareness of what one is doing

Integrating, combining old and new with raised consciousness and awareness of what one is doing

An old idea this brings to mind is. . .

Integrating, combining old and new with raised consciousness and awareness of what one is doing

This seems to fit with. . .

Integrating, combining old and new with raised consciousness and awareness of what one is doing

I could combine with. . .

Integrating, combining old and new with raised consciousness and awareness of what one is doing

_____ is like _____ because both. . .

Flashes of Genius. . .

You may find yourself about to have an idea.
It may be a small idea; it may be a big idea.
Here is a place to put it.

Cathy
The Carrier Pigeon

Mapping, strategically carrying across various content and into life situations

Mapping, strategically carrying across various content and into life situations

An idea I can apply in several ways is. . .

Mapping, strategically carrying across various content and into life situations

A strategy to carry across. . .

Mapping, strategically carrying across various content and into life situations

_____ can bridge into ______________________ . . .
(life situation)

Mapping, strategically carrying across various content and into life situations

I plan to use. . .

Flashes of Genius. . .

You may find yourself about to have an idea.
It may be a small idea; it may be a big idea.
Here is a place to put it.

Samantha
The Soaring Eagle

Innovating, diverging, creating with novelty, originality and insight

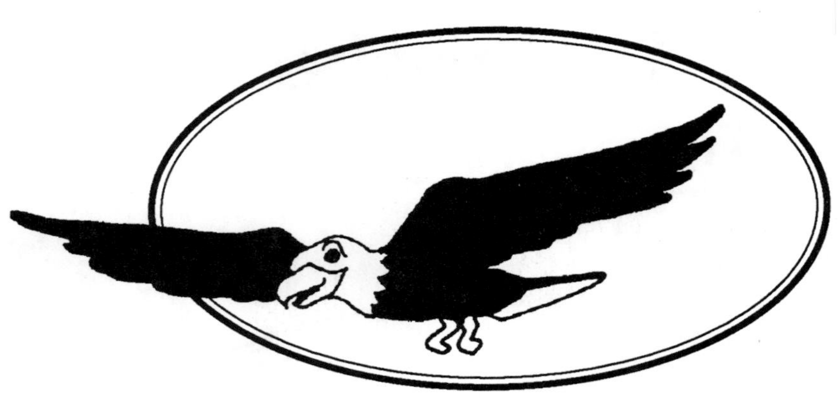

Innovating, diverging, creating with novelty, originality and insight

A new idea incubating is. . .

Innovating, diverging, creating with novelty, originality and insight

What if. . .

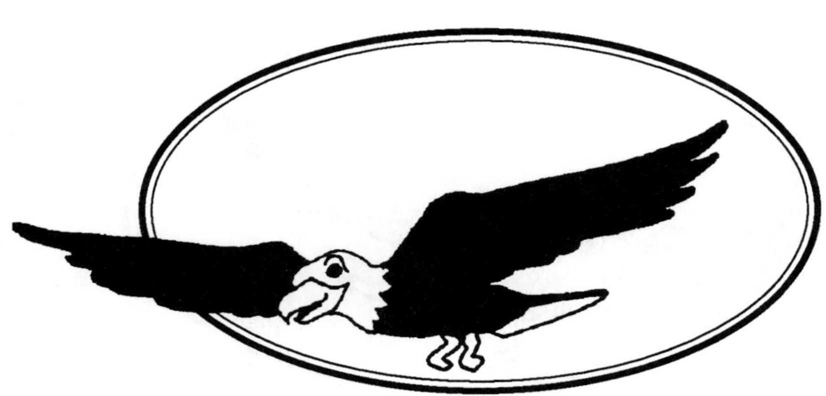

Innovating, diverging, creating with novelty, originality and insight

I see a million ways to use. . .

Innovating, diverging, creating with novelty, originality and insight

I've totally redesigned. . .

Flashes of Genius. . .

You may find yourself about to have an idea.
It may be a small idea; it may be a big idea.
Here is a place to put it.

What about transfer for kids?

What is it that you are teaching that transfers?

What skills/strategies/behaviors are you seeing students transfer?

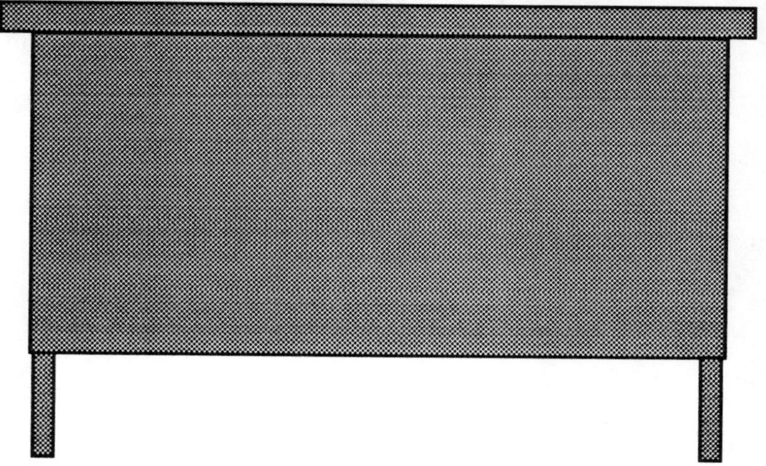

Some Student Behaviors I'm Seeing Are

- ☐ Persistence
- ☐ Decreasing impulsivity
- ☐ Listening with empathy
- ☐ Flexibility in thinking
- ☐ Checking for accuracy & precision
- ☐ Question and problem posing
- ☐ Precision in language and thought
- ☐ Ingenuity/Originality/Insight
- ☐ Wonderment
- ☐ Efficacy as thinkers
- ☐ Metacognition
- ☐ Using all senses
- ☐ Making connections (prior knowledge → new information)

Ways To Help Students Carry Ideas Across Content

1. Set expectations

2. Talk about transfer levels

3. Bridge with questions

4. Model transfer and application

5. Promote risk taking and "playing with ideas"

Evidence Of Student Transfer Across Subject Areas and Into Life Situations

(Evidence of transfer beyond the classroom will be found embedded in the stories and vignettes of students, parents, and colleagues. Listen for it.)

SECTION 11

APPENDIX

Patterns In Review: Day 1

Climate

Active Listening

Focus Interview

Overview

Three-Story Intellect Questioning Model
- Input—getting information
- Process—connecting new
- Output—using synthesis
- Teacher Questions
- Textbook Questions
- Student Questions

DOVE Guidlines

Hurrahs & Energizers

Skills

Target Skill
- Analysis of Attributes

Subskills
- Brainstorming
- Prioritizing
- Analogies

Interaction

People
- People Search
  - Focus
  - Sponge
  - Review
- Turn To Your Partner and...
- Cooperative Groups
  - Roles
  - Tasks
  - Social Skills
  - Processing

Graphic
- Attribute web
- T Chart

Metacognition

- P. N. I.
- Thinking Log
- Wraparound

Peer Partner
- Identify Partner
- Commit To Planning Conference: That's A Good Idea
- Share With Artifacts
- Keep a Log

Patterns In Review: Day 2

Climate

Room Arrangement

Teacher Mobility
- Climate Video

Response Strategies
- Wait time pause
- Multiple answers
- Wraparound Forced Response
- Physical Response (hands)
- Student repeats directions
- Student-to-student piggybacking

Skills

Thinking Skills
- Prediction (BET)
- Classification

Subskills
- Synthesizing
- Evaluating

Interaction

People
- 2-4-8 Sharing
- Triads

Graphic
- BET Chart
- Agree/Disagree
- Venn Diagrams
- Matrix

Metacognition

- Mrs. Potter's Questions
- What? So What? Now What?

Peer Partner
- Plan with That's A Good Idea
- Observe via:
  visit
  audio
  video
  artifact
- Dialog using Mrs. Potter's Questions
- Keep a log

PACTS—Peer Assisted Coaching Team
- 2-4-8 Sharing of Artifacts

Patterns In Review: Day 3

Climate

That's A Good Idea

Skills

Thinking Skill
- Brainstorming

Interaction

Cooperative Groups
- Quads
- Cooperative Learning Video

Chart

Story Grid

Metacognition

Transfer: Bird's-eye View
- Teacher Cues

Plan

Monitor

Evaluate

Peer Partners
- Plan w/That's A Good Idea
- Observe via
  visit
  audio
  video
  artifacts
- Dialog using Mrs. Potter's Questions
- Keep a log

PACTS: 2-4-8 Sharing of artifacts

Patterns In Review: Day 4

Climate

Skills

Prioritizing
- Concepts
- Seatwork/homework

Visualizing

Interaction

Think/Pair/Share

Human Graph

Venn

Hex

Thought Tree

Clustering

Metacognition

Transfer: Bird's-eye View
- Student Cues

Assessing Thinking

Peer Partners
- Continue cycle

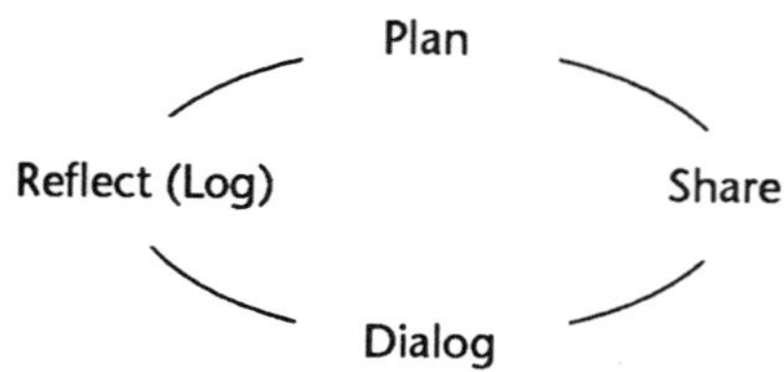

PACTS: 2-4-8 Sharing

Index

SKYLIGHT
PUBLISHING

T

V

W

Notes

Notes

Notes

Notes

Notes

There are
one-story intellects,
two-story intellects, and three-story
intellects with skylights. All fact collectors, who have
no aim beyond their facts, are one-story men. Two-story men compare,
reason, generalize, using the labors of the fact collectors as well
as their own. Three-story men idealize, imagine, predict—
their best illumination comes from above,
through the skylight.

—Oliver Wendell
Holmes